HANDBOOK OF
WILD FLOWER
CULTIVATION

HANDBOOK OF
WILD FLOWER
CULTIVATION

by *Kathryn S. Taylor*
and *Stephen F. Hamblin*

with illustrations by Catherine R. Hammond

COLLIER BOOKS
A Division of Macmillan Publishing Co., Inc.
New York

COLLIER MACMILLAN PUBLISHERS
London

Macmillan Publishing Co., Inc.
866 Third Avenue, New York, N.Y. 10022
Collier Macmillan Canada, Ltd.

Library of Congress Catalog Card Number: 62-8915

Handbook of Wild Flower Cultivation is also published in a hardcover edition
by Macmillan Publishing Co., Inc.

First Collier Books Edition 1976

Printed in the United States of America

DEDICATION

This handbook, compiled by her friends and associates
of the New England Wild Flower Preservation Society,
is lovingly dedicated to the memory of Henrietta M. Crosby,
a founder of the Society, and its president
from 1922 to 1948.

Contents

Flowering Trees and Shrubs   229

Appendix A

Appendix B

Appendix C

Appendix D

Index of Illustrations

General Index

Preface

This handbook has evolved as a result of many requests received by the New England Wild Flower Preservation Society for more specific information on the culture of native plants.

The Society carries on an active program of classes in wild flower culture and identification with field trips and wild flower conferences. It maintains a Nature Trail with the Weston (Massachusetts) Forest and Trail Association and has started a Wild Flower Area Fund to help in purchasing land where choice native plants, still found in abundance, would otherwise be destroyed. The royalties from the sale of this book will be used entirely to help carry on this work.

All true nature lovers understand the pleasure and satisfaction to be derived from walks in the woods and fields to enjoy wild life in its various aspects, particularly the wild flowers. Many wild flower enthusiasts are content to visit such areas periodically and, if the plants are still there in abundance, to leave them untouched to give renewed pleasure another year. This policy was once considered to be the only proper approach to true conservation, and might still be approved if it were possible to ensure that any given habitat could remain undisturbed over a considerable period of time. However, between the construction of new roadways and the unparalleled exodus of city families to the country, no stand of wild flowers can now be judged safe from intrusion, no matter how remote the colony may seem.

Man is not the sole agent responsible for the disappearance of choice wild flowers. Deer consume whole stands of trillium, orchids, and other succulent plants quickly and completely. Rabbits and woodchucks also eat the blossoms and the new growth of many plants; ants love the seeds of arbutus, and slugs eat many seedlings and blossoms as well. Forest fires, droughts, and floods eliminate vast quantities of desirable native plants, so that it seems almost a miracle that any are still to be seen anywhere.

With more and more people doing their own gardening, many gardeners are finding that the naturalistic type of planting is easier to care for and more rewarding than the more familiar rose garden or perennial border. Also, a more positive approach to wild flower conservation is now accepted, and lovers of native plants are anxious to establish wild flower gardens on their own places to which rare species in danger of extermination can be removed. Such a project is quite feasible, but a few principles must be well understood, and adequate preparation made, before starting a garden of this kind.

Although the establishment of wild flower gardens is to be encouraged, to accomplish anything of permanent value in the conservation of native plants, more must be known about propagating them. There is much yet to be learned, however, and the aim of this book is to present as much information as is now possible on this important subject.

The experience and advice of experts in the field have contributed greatly to the fund of information presented. We are especially grateful to Alfred Fordham, Plant Propagator at the Arnold Arboretum, Jamaica Plain, Massachusetts, for his help in preparing the section on plant propagation and for allowing the use of his notes prepared for classes at the Arboretum. Appreciation is extended to Will C. Curtis, of South Sudbury, Massachusetts, who has provided valuable data from personal experiment at "Garden in the Woods."

Gray's *Manual of Botany*, Eighth Edition, is the authority for the nomenclature of the plants listed, and *The New Britton and Brown Illustrated Flora . . .* was followed closely for botanical information and for ranges of plants.

Other reference books in constant use include: *Wild Flower Guide, Northeastern and Midland United States* by Edgar T. Wherry, *Field Book of American Wild Flowers* by F. Schuyler Mathews, *Kansas Wild Flowers* by William Chase Stevens, *Wild Flowers of the Northern States and Canada* by A. C. Quick, *Propagation of Alpines* by Lawrence D. Hills, *Flowers of the South, Native and Exotic* by W. F. Greene and H. L. Blomquist, *Growing Woodland Plants* by Clarence and Eleanor G. Birdseye, and *Wild Flowers and How to Grow Them* by Edwin F. Steffek.

The plant material covered in this book includes only showy species that would attract the interest of the amateur wild flower gardener. Plants too difficult or actually impossible to naturalize such as most orchids, are omitted, as are plants impossible to eradicate when once introduced. To reduce the volume of the book, no ferns, fern allies, grasses, rushes, or sedges are listed in the main section.

The plant ranges and seasons of bloom are only approximate, to allow for the wide latitude covered. For convenience, the heights of plants are given in feet and inches.

The order of presentation follows the arrangement of botanical families from cat-tails to composites, the botanical name at the left and the common name at the right of the page. Since the common names of plants are local and variable, the more dependable botanical name is given first.

Each plant description is concluded with notes on propagation. The term is used loosely to include such procedures as transplanting and division, which technically are not propagation.

The delightful illustrations prepared by Catherine R. Hammond add greatly to the value and appearance of the handbook, and the bibliography compiled by Persis Green is an excellent guide to further reading.

KATHRYN S. TAYLOR
STEPHEN F. HAMBLIN

The New England Wild Flower Preservation Society, Inc.
Horticultural Hall
Boston, Massachusetts

Planning the Wild Flower Garden

The subject of wild flower gardening must be approached from a standpoint entirely different from that of cultivated gardening. In planning a perennial border, for example, the average gardener presumably decides what plants he would like to grow and then goes about obtaining them with little thought as to whether any would not be suited to the new environment. The majority of cultivated plants *do* succeed reasonably well in any good garden soil, and if some do not survive, they can easily be replaced with no twinge of conscience that a choice native species has been sacrificed.

A wild flower garden is quite a different matter. The gardener should study the environment under which the plants he wants are growing. He has to realize that one growing naturally in very acid soil can never, by any bit of luck, be made happy in less acid soil. After investigating the soil and climatic conditions on his own place thoroughly, he can then try to choose those species he thinks will take hold in that situation. If he is conscientious in the matter, he may conclude that it would be useless to attempt many of the plants he most wanted, but he will nevertheless be able to acquire a beautiful garden containing wild flowers that will flourish as well as, and perhaps even better than, in the habitat from which they were taken.

There are two distinct methods of approach in developing a wild garden. The more common one is entirely artificial. The gardener may take some part of his grounds where no wild flowers are present and turn it into a naturalistic trail. Where conditions are entirely man-made, the choice of plant material may well include almost any plant that looks appropriate in the general plan. For instance, in Massachusetts, such a garden might contain *Mertensia virginica* from Pennsylvania, *Shortia galacifolia* from the Carolina mountains, *Erythronium* from the Far West, and *Dodecatheon* from the Midwestern prairies. All these would combine well with such local favorites as bloodroot, spring-beauty, yellow violet, and columbine.

The second method of approach is better from the standpoint of conservation. In this case the gardener has a definite natural habitat to start with, and restores to it, or adds to it, native plants that should occur in such a place. This limits the choice of plant material, but the gardener will get special pleasure from preserving and improving a natural landscape that will require little future maintenance because all the plants growing there are very much at home.

Every section of the United States has its characteristic vegetation that sets it apart from other regions in the country. Native plants give individuality to each state, and the variety and character of typical natural landscapes should be carefully studied by the gardener. A woodland habitat is a good example for illustration. It may be a coniferous forest, if in a cold climate, or it may be a deciduous or a mixed forest, if in a more temperate one. The soil in the coniferous forest is always very acid. The decay of organic matter on the forest floor proceeds slowly for this reason. Fungi that break it down are necessary to the life of plants found in such soil, and if removed to a less acid environment they will eventually die. The pink lady's-slipper is a typical example.

A mixed forest of oaks and evergreens is also very acid. Early spring sunshine filtering through the branches of the oaks allows wild azaleas, mountain-laurel, trailing arbutus, and hepaticas to come into flower before the expanding tree leaves exclude the sunlight for the summer. None of these plants would flourish in the slightly acid soil of the forest where maples, beeches, and more lime-loving vegetation are predominant.

Many wild flowers are not especially particular about soil acidity and will thrive in a variety of soils if other conditions are to their liking. The amount of sunlight or moisture available during the flowering period greatly affects the adaptability of some plants. For example, marsh-marigold grows actually in water when it blossoms in spring. Often the brooks by which it abounds dry up in summer, but this does the plants no harm. Dryness in the spring would be another matter. Hepaticas need filtered sunlight when in flower but can stand complete shade thereafter.

When planning a wild flower garden the existing vegetation is an important clue in choosing suitable plants for it. Quite frequently, when land is acquired for a new house, the buyer removes almost every vestige of plant life so that the ground can be graded and a lawn started. This is a mistake, because the plants originally there can tell him what sort of soil he has and what he can expect to grow. Sometimes there is one fine old specimen tree, perhaps an oak or white pine, proving that other oaks and pines must once have been there. Probably wild flowers found under oaks and pines could be restored to the area unless extensive cultivation has lessened the acidity. It is difficult to establish plants under lawn trees. When similar trees grow in the woods, none has so much root or branch spread, the shade is less thick, and the soil nutrients are not exhausted. If fallen leaves from under the lawn trees have been raked up and burned, the situation could hardly be more unfavorable.

The natural vegetation is often more attractive than exotics bought from a nursery. The landowner, therefore, should learn to appreciate what nature has given him without cost. In studying the existing vegetation, the trees, shrubs, and herbaceous plants found in the greatest numbers will tell most about growing conditions. Where no vegetation exists the problem becomes difficult, especially if the garden is to be shady, and if there are no mature trees and shrubs beneath which to plant the wild flowers. The determined gardener need not necessarily delay the start of his woodland garden until suitable woody plants have had time to become established. Many dealers in native plants prefer to grow them under lath or brush shades which can provide any degree of protection desired over the plants and which take nothing from the soil. Lath houses can be made most attractive, and the amateur can experiment happily in this way while waiting for his woodland to materialize.

While the soil affects the plants growing in it, the plants also change the character of the soil. It would be well to have soil samples tested at an agricultural experiment station to determine what elements are present and what should be added to the soil in addition to finding out the degree of acidity.

Sufficient organic matter in the soil is vital to the culture of wild flowers. It holds moisture, aerates the soil, and serves as a mulch to keep it cool and friable. It also maintains humidity around the plants. No wild flowers should ever be set out in any location leaving bare ground around them as in cultivated gardens. They need a ground cover of companion plants or decaying vegetation at all times. If the organic matter and ground covers were removed from the forest floor, the forest itself would soon deteriorate. In many sections native peat can be bought quite reasonably, and this, plus decaying leaves or compost from a compost pile, should be incorporated in the soil. The acidity of peat is variable, and in purchasing it one should learn its degree of acidity.

Organic matter in the soil is also vital from a biological standpoint. It furnishes food for the bacteria and countless other soil organisms which are responsible for making nutrients available to plants and for maintaining the efficiency of the soil. Soils cannot be fertile without the presence of organic matter.

Although the woodland wild flowers of spring are general favorites, there are desirable kinds for almost any location and time of year. In fact, the enthusiastic wild flower gardener can spend many exciting hours in the search for appropriate material.

When the gardener has decided on the type of wild flower garden he can create, he should visit as many areas similar to his own as possible and take copious notes covering every phase of the habitat. As previously stated, the dominant plants tell most about the character of the soil, amount of moisture, sunlight, and what companion plants to expect to find. After a little practice he will become familiar with a number of "key" plants which, by their presence or absence, give an obvious clue to prevailing growing conditions in an area. It is not enough to visit a habitat only when the plants are in blossom. The site should be checked regularly throughout a growing season to note any changes in environment that occur as the months go by. Changes in the amount of light and moisture are certain to take place.

The gardener must be willing to assemble for himself most of the pertinent data on the culture of many wild plants. If he relies for help entirely upon books and printed lists, the results will not be fully satisfactory. Growing conditions vary greatly even within narrow bounds, and the existing plants will readily prove this fact. Ground covers are especially good examples; no two states have the same ones in the same quantity, dominance, or luxuriance. For this reason, also, conservation lists intended for a wide area are unsatisfactory. No matter what a list recommends, no wild plants should be collected unless their numbers are greater than can readily be counted, and even then only a few plants should be taken. Sometimes plants on the "forbidden" list are very abundant in a locality. If so, it is ridiculous to prohibit collecting a few plants provided it is a species that can stand transplanting. Most of the orchids cannot be moved with any hope of success, and they should be let alone. The yellow and the showy lady's-slipper can be moved successfully by skillful and experienced gardeners. They will live for many years in favorable spots. *All* the others, including the pink lady's-slipper, will eventually die if removed from their special environment. It may take a few years, but they are doomed. If wild flower gardeners would refrain from buying them, their chance of survival in the wild would be greatly increased. There are records showing that the pink lady's-slipper has persisted for at least fifteen years when transplanted into new locations in areas *where these orchids were already present*, but this is an uncommon occurrence.

The subject of whether to collect or to buy plants for a wild garden is controversial. It is certainly poor policy to stop by the roadside to dig up coveted plants. They should be left for travelers to enjoy; also, it would be an embarrassing moment if the landowner or the state police should happen by in the middle of the operation. This is more likely to occur than one might think. Usually any serious wild flower gardener can make friends with some country dweller with plenty of the eagerly sought plants growing on his land. If only a few plants are taken, nobody should object to such procedure. Permission to dig them should always be obtained.

It is often safest to buy one's wild flowers, and, if possible, one should patronize a dealer who makes some effort to increase his stock by various means of propagation. A dealer who would withdraw from his general catalogue especially rare or difficult plants would benefit from the increased confidence of his customers. Many gardeners are not aware of the difficulties entailed in growing certain favorite wild flowers and would not buy them if they understood the matter. They see such plants offered for sale and buy them, little suspecting that they are probably throwing their money away. Dealers could help by listing the difficult species separately, making it clear that only experienced gardeners should try them. Many desirable and interesting plants are obtainable only from dealers, and it is not the purpose of this book to discourage the serious gardener from buying from them.

As the wild flower gardener gains experience and knowledge, he may increase the range of plants that he can grow by creating an imitation, in miniature, of a natural scene that gives him unusual pleasure. A group of rocks of the same general appearance can be laid together with crevasses between them to simulate a natural outcrop. This will provide a home for rock-loving species.

A tiny brook, perhaps with a waterfall, is a big addition to any wild garden where the cost of the water is not prohibitive. An artificial brook has the advantage that it never overflows in wet spring weather or dries out in summer. Flowers can safely be planted close to its edge with charming effect. A pool has many advantages. For example, one end can be bricked off with a leaky wall and made into a small bog. With a little imagination, there is practically no limit to the diversity of natural landscapes that can be included in a wild flower garden even if it is quite small.

If the facilities of a cold frame and cold greenhouse are available, it is possible to enjoy some of the best-loved wild flowers even if one has no place for a wild garden. British gardeners seem to be more appreciative of the value of North American plants as garden subjects than we are, and often display them to great advantage in alpine houses and greenhouses as well as in the garden.

The alpine house is a greenhouse, usually unheated, wherein alpines from high mountain ranges are brought into flower in pots. The alpine house must receive a maximum amount of light and air. The plants spend a relatively short period of time in it, however, the pots being plunged in a cold frame for much of the year. The North American wild flowers displayed in British alpine houses include *Houstonia caerulea* hybrids, *Cornus canadensis*, *Uvularia perfoliata*, *Lewisia* hybrids, *Cypripedium reginae*, and other favorites.

Many wild flowers can be grown in cold greenhouses in this country, too, especially some that are difficult in the wild garden. Such species as *Pyxidanthera barbulata*, *Lygodium palmatum*, *Epi-*

gaea repens, Gentiana crinita, and *Phyllitis Scolopendrium* were kept successfully for several years in a sun-heated pit because the moisture, sunlight, and soil requirements could thus be accurately dealt with. A large flat of arbutus growing in peat and sand blossoms heavily every spring and receives little care. It spends most of the year in a shaded cold frame. The flowers come very early and are doubly welcome.

Satisfying the Needs
of Wild Flowers

A woodland garden, unless in a naturally moist area, will probably require artificial watering during the summer. If the garden has been made on a slope, and if the soil is light and sandy, this will definitely be necessary. If possible, provision for an adequate water supply should be made when the garden is being planned, perhaps with underground piping; otherwise, the gardener with a dry, shady situation will have to get used to seeing lengths of hose lying about the paths for most of the summer, especially if the season is a dry one. A successful garden created under conditions of this sort may have the hose running for long periods almost daily to satisfy the needs of trilliums and other moisture-loving woodland plants that have been put there. They grow extremely well, however, because they never lack for water.

The woodland garden cannot exist without a constant mulch of decaying organic material. To supply a sufficient amount both a leaf mold pile and a compost heap are helpful. A leaf mold pile is easy to acquire. Oak and beech leaves are preferred, and they should be stacked in well-trodden layers at least two feet square, kept in bounds with chicken wire around the outside. As each layer of new leaves is added, it should be wet down with the hose. Dry leaves break down slowly, but moist ones decay fairly soon and should make excellent leaf mold in two years. If they are cut into smaller pieces with a rotary lawn mower and watered with a bacterial activator, such as Fertosan, they will break down in one season. Untold amounts of oak leaves along streets and highways are burned every fall. Some effort should be made to compost them before they go up in smoke.

Leaf mold is better for mulching than compost made of garden refuse. The refuse usually contains weed seeds which may germinate in incredible numbers in the moist, woodsy soil of the wild garden. Properly made compost is valuable, however, as a top-dressing for the entire wild garden, applied both in spring and fall. To make a satisfactory compost heap, garden refuse of varying coarseness should be stacked in layers at least four feet square. Never use all fine material such as grass clippings. Each layer of refuse should be 12 inches thick. A sprinkling of commercial fertilizer, such as 5-10-5, should then be watered into the layer. Even better, omit the fertilizer and water the pile with a bacterial activator, being sure that the whole layer is moistened. Each layer, as it is piled, should receive a thin covering of soil. If chicken or stable manure, wood ashes or seaweed are available, a thin layer of any of these can be added before covering with soil. The pile is built up in the shape of a pyramid and should be at least four feet high. The finished heap should be completely covered with a layer of soil. In addition, pieces of burlap or a sheet of black polyethylene plastic used as a final cover will help to retain moisture. The black plastic is supposed to help to retain heat, also. A heap made in this way need never be turned while it is breaking down.

It may happen that insufficient compost and leaf mold are at hand to mulch a new wild garden. Native peat or commercial peat moss can be turned into excellent mulch by thoroughly moistening a loose pile of the material with a "liquid compost" made by adding one teaspoonful each of Fertosan Myco stock solution and fish fertilizer to each gallon of water used. Untreated peat moss is a poor mulch because, in the process of breaking it down, the bacteria rob the plants of whatever nutrients may be in the soil.

Trilliums thrive in very old, rotted manure; so do arbutus and other choice ground covers. A one-inch layer should be sufficient. Orchids do not seem to like animal manure, no matter how old. They prefer rotted wood, which is also good for other wild flowers.

Sections of decaying logs partially sunk in the ground in a moist situation will encourage such ground covers as twin flower and bunchberry to trail over them.

Sometimes the layer of autumn leaves and pine needles becomes too thick for the wild flowers planted beneath them, and they are smothered. Maple leaves, in particular, will mat down. The excess should be removed to the compost pile. If the natural mulch is too thin for winter protection, evergreen boughs laid over the plants will safeguard them. By pruning evergreens, particularly yews, in early winter a good supply can be held in reserve.

Most wild flowers enjoy a light sprinkling of bone meal applied with the top-dressing of compost in the fall. The plants that require a neutral soil could be given a little ground limestone in addition.

The matter of providing the right degree of soil acidity or alkalinity in the woodland garden should be given attention. Acid soil contains an excess of hydrogen ions, the degree of acidity being expressed by the pH scale. At pH 7.0 the soil is neutral. The lower the number, the more acid the soil; pH 6.0 is ten times more acid than pH 7.0, pH 5.0 is 100 times more acid than pH 7.0, and so on down the scale. Few plants will grow below pH 3.5. A pH 7.5 to 8.0 is as alkaline as most lime-loving species require. Above pH 8.5, which is ten times more alkaline than pH 7.5, few plants can exist. The great majority of plants grow at a pH of about 6.5.

It is difficult to increase permanently the acidity of a slightly acid soil to an extremely acid one. It is soon changed back to its former state by earthworms, bacteria, and other soil organisms. The addition of sawdust, the needles of conifers, and oak leaves helps to some extent but cannot maintain the degree of acidity required by arbutus, bunchberry, shortia, and many others which want a pH from 4.0 to 5.0. If the soil is not naturally very acid, such plants will not succeed. Powdered sulfur or aluminum sulphate helps to increase acidity, but the proper amount of either to use should be determined by consulting an agricultural experiment station. For general purposes an excellent, inexpensive kit for testing soil acidity is obtainable. The results of this test will give the gardener a good idea of the degree of soil acidity and will guide him in the choice of suitable plant material.

Plants in the mixed oak and coniferous forest also need very acid soil, roughly not above pH 5.5.

The deciduous forest may provide moderately acid conditions, pH 5.5 to 6.5, or only slightly acid ones, pH 6.5 to 7.0, depending on climate, existing vegetation, and various other factors.

Plants needing definitely neutral or slightly alkaline soil prefer pH 7.0 to 7.5; pH 8.0 is the upper limit for plants in the range covered in this book. Some plants in the Far West tolerate even greater alkalinity. Soil alkalinity is increased by adding ground limestone.

One of the most pleasant of early spring chores is the gradual removal of the winter mulch. This should be done by hand, pressing back into the ground any plants that have been heaved out by winter thawing and freezing. Enough mulch should always be left so that no bare ground is visible.

Wild Flower Propagation

BY SEEDS

An essential procedure in the preservation of wild flowers is to learn how to propagate them. The ability to increase favorite wild flowers from seeds is an exciting and rewarding aspect of this type of gardening.

Some dealers offer seeds of native plants, but usually it is necessary to collect one's own. Few gardeners make a practice of gathering seeds, and much patient watchfulness is required to take them at the proper time. Unless one can frequently visit the plants from which the seeds are to be taken, the most satisfactory procedure is to tie a thin muslin bag over the flower head as the time nears when the seeds will be shed. This will save the loss of valuable seeds and avoid the disappointment of finding that dehiscence has occurred in one's absence. A good amount of seeds should be left on the plants to self-sow.

It is sometimes suggested that the seeds of wild flowers be broadcast along roadsides or wherever a spot seems favorable, but this is usually a waste of effort. In nature, only the smallest fraction of the seeds of choice plants succeeds in germinating and growing to maturity because of the many hazards encountered along the way.

After seeds have been gathered they are spread out to dry for a few days before storing. This drying period helps to keep them from becoming moldy. After being dried on sheets of paper, seeds still on stalks can be placed in paper bags tied loosely at the top and hung in a warm, dry place. Slow drying in this way is excellent. The seeds should always be cleaned before storage. Much of the debris can be removed with the fingers before running the seeds through fine wire screens for the final cleaning. Screens of several different mesh sizes are helpful where many kinds of seeds are to be processed. Fleshy fruits require crushing and soaking before the seeds are separated by screening or flotation. The cleaned seeds are then packeted in Manila envelopes, carefully labeled and dated. The packets are placed in screw-topped jars in the refrigerator until planting time. Refrigerated storage is not necessary with many seeds such as azalea and those of legumes.

The best time to plant wild flower seeds depends almost as much on the facilities of the gardener as on the character of the seeds. Many do not mature until fall, and few can be expected to germinate within a few days of sowing. From such a late sowing it would be difficult to keep any seedlings alive through the long winter without the protection of a greenhouse.

Seeds of many wild flowers have embryos that are immature when they are shed from the parent plant. An after-ripening period is necessary to overcome the dormancy of such seeds before germination can take place. This is done by holding the seeds in a cold, moist environment for periods varying from a month to a year, according to species, the process being known as cold stratification. The recommended temperature is 40° F. Various alpine seeds, as well as those of certain trees, such as flowering dogwood and magnolia, must also be given stratification.

Another group known as two-year seeds must overcome two kinds of dormancy before germination occurs. This is known as double dormancy, and two distinct treatments are required. One of the two types of dormancy is caused by a tough, impenetrable seed coat that must become water-permeable before the seeds are ready for the second treatment. This is brought about by exposing the seeds to a warm temperature during which the seed coat decomposes. They are placed in a plastic bag containing a mixture of moist (not wet) sand and peat at a room temperature with daily and nightly fluctuation to satisfy this requirement. The medium should be two to three times the volume of the seed. The bag is tightly closed with a rubber band. At the end of this period the hard coat will be water-permeable. Internal dormancy, already described, is the other type, and can be overcome by placing the bag in the refrigerator for about three months. Subjection to warm treatment always precedes the cold treatment. Top growth sometimes begins while the seeds are in the refrigerator. Some seeds show no germination until after both treatments. Others, such as the native lilies and viburnum, produce radicals (first roots) in the warm treatment, after which the dormancy in the shoot bud must be overcome by the period of cold. If stratified the previous fall, the seeds are planted outdoors in prepared beds in the spring. The seed may also be sown in prepared containers. In either case the entire contents of the plastic bag are planted.

Hard-coated seeds of the Pea Family can be soaked in warm water before planting. Those of *Cytisus* and *Genista* are treated by pouring boiling water over the seeds. The water is allowed to cool, but the seeds should be left overnight in it. The amount of water should be five times the volume of the seeds.

Cardinal-flower seeds will not germinate if kept in the dark after sowing. Certain annuals should be sown outdoors in the fall to make flowering plants for the next spring. These are known as winter annuals. Blue-eyed Mary, *Collinsia verna*, is an example.

When planting the seeds of wild flowers, not all should be sown at one time. With fresh seeds collected during the summer, part might be sown at once and the remainder in late winter or early spring. January and February are excellent months for starting seeds. They will germinate and grow with the lengthening days, which give more light for growth together with less darkness for trouble with fungi. Fluctuation in temperature between warm days and cold nights also aids germination. If the fall-sown seeds fail to germinate in due time, they should be subjected to alternate freezing and thawing. This helps to break the dormancy of the seeds. Two years should be allowed to elapse before concluding that the seeds are not going to come up. Sometimes a few will start the first year and still more will appear the following year.

A sun-heated pit or cold frame is helpful in raising wild flowers from seeds sown in fall or winter. A layer of plastic on either side of the sash can be used instead of glass. This provides an air space for increased insulation and makes the sash lighter. The sides of the frame should be high enough so that the surface of the soil inside can be above that of the surrounding ground. A soil depth of 8 to 10 inches of prepared compost is needed. A square of hardware cloth large enough when laid beneath the frame to reach partly up the sides will keep out rodents. The frame should not be in full sun, as part shade is best for seeds and seedlings. Lath shades will protect the seedlings if the frame must be in sun. Burlap bags loosely filled with leaves and placed over the plastic covers in severe weather will give added insulation and keep the sun from overheating the air inside when the frame remains tightly closed during the coldest part of the winter. If the soil is prepared for planting before cold weather sets in, seeds can usually be sown right in the frame in midwinter during a mild spell. This is the easiest method when many seeds are to be planted. A light mulch over the seed bed will prevent heaving of the soil; it should be removed as soon as any germination takes place.

Seed pans, clay or plastic pots and tin cans make good containers for sowing seeds. Cans have advantages that make them popular with amateur gardeners. Since they are not porous, they do not dry out for a long time; they take up much less room than pots and will not break if put out in snow to freeze. It is better to put each kind of seed in separate cans than to plant several different kinds in one large flat. The cans can be left in an out-of-the-way spot for as long as necessary and then be disposed of when no longer needed. It is often easier to plunge cans, flats, or pots of seeds in sand or ashes in a cold frame than to plant the seeds in it directly. The containers should be plunged to the rims and the sash or plastic frame should be put on for the winter. Burlap should be placed over the glass to keep out the sun. On warm days the frame should be opened slightly; the sash is permanently removed by early April.

If the cans are to be placed indoors for germination, a goodly number can be set in a large flat that is then elevated on other cans, out of reach of slugs that may eat off a whole crop of young plants in one night. If the supporting cans are set in dishes of water, even better protection is afforded.

Tin cans are prepared for planting as follows: Punch several holes in the bottoms of the cans (preferably of the Number 2 size used for fruit and vegetables, *not* the tall ones used for juices). A few small holes on the sides near the bottom give added drainage. Another small hole made with a nail as near to the top of the can as possible is used for tying a label to the can. This label, of wood or cardboard, if written on with indelible ink and sprayed with a plastic, will preserve the writing as long as the can is used. The name of the wild flower, the date of sowing, the date of germination, and the date of pricking off (when small seedlings are transplanted) should all be preserved on the label or in a notebook.

The procedure of sowing seeds is the same in all types of containers. An inch or two of broken flowerpots or pebbles is placed in the bottom, the amount depending on the depth of the container. This is essential to provide good drainage. The drainage material is then covered with a thin layer of sphagnum moss, peat moss, or dried leaves to keep the drainage from becoming clogged. Shredded oak or beech leaves are especially good because they never get soggy. Anything sufficiently coarse is suitable. This layer should be tamped down firmly, and moistened. A tamper that just fits into the container can be made of wood with a handle screwed to its center, and is a great time saver. The two ends cut off a wooden rolling pin make splendid tampers for tin cans and pots. The container is then filled with seed compost to within about two inches of the top. The compost is made up of two parts good fibrous loam, one part peat, and one part coarse sand put through a $\frac{1}{4}$-inch sieve. The container is then filled practically to the top with a sterile medium in which to plant the seeds. A 1-inch layer of sifted sphagnum moss may be used in which the seeds should be planted thinly. The moss is so light that it is forced up when the stand of seedlings is too thick. Then the new little roots dry up. A little fine sand treated with boiling water may be mixed with the moss to overcome this difficulty. Very small seeds need no covering, and larger ones are just covered from sight with more sphagnum. The container is then watered from below by standing it in water nearly to the rim. It is removed as soon as the surface looks damp. Plastic freezer bags are inverted loosely over individual containers or a large sheet of polyethylene may cover the lot. The containers are put in a light place but out of direct sunlight until germination takes place. As soon as any seedlings appear, the plastic is removed and the container is placed in full sun. If damping-off fungus occurs, due to overwatering or too thick planting, a soil drench such as Pano-drench 4 will save any seedlings that have not succumbed.

Some growers insist that the soil in the seed compost be sterilized to remove weed seeds and to discourage damping-off. When soil is sterilized, especially by amateurs, toxic conditions of which they are not aware may result. Many gardeners never sterilize the soil. If it is desired to sterilize the soil, however, a pan of it may be put in the oven set at 160° F. for half an hour. A knife blade is used to keep the door slightly ajar. A dairy thermometer thrust into the soil will help to check the temperature.

An extremely satisfactory sterile medium for many seeds is composed of two parts Perl-lome (a horticultural grade of perlite), two parts of Terralite (a horticultural grade of vermiculite), and one part of sifted sphagnum moss. After planting, the seeds are driven into close contact with the medium by the use of any small hand sprayer which allows the spray to be directed downward onto the seedbed with reasonable force. With small seeds this is very important. If Pano-drench is used instead of plain water, it gives additional protection to the seeds. The seedbed is moistened from below with a weak solution of fertilizer. One-fourth teaspoonful of Hyponex in a gallon of water gives excellent results. This is used for every watering, the strength being slightly increased as the seedlings grow. Various fertilizers are suited to this purpose, and the directions that accompany them should be carefully followed.

A light top-dressing of calcite chicken grit encourages good germination for lime-loving plants, or one of granite grit for others. This is particularly helpful when seeds of alpines are sown.

When preparing seed compost in a cold frame, the addition of a *small* amount of organic fertilizer will help to produce more sturdy seedlings. The seeds of many wild flowers can be sown in the shaded cold frame in May. Some of the seedlings will be large enough for moving to the wild garden by fall.

If wild flowers are thriving in the garden, they will self-sow generously if the ground around the plants is not disturbed. Many young seedlings are destroyed by cultivating around wild flowers unnecessarily. This rarely, if ever, should be done.

Seedlings in a seedbed must be pricked off into flats as soon as they can possibly be handled. They are generally set from 1 to 2 inches apart each way. Care should be taken that the tips of the roots are not bent upward in the process. The soil should not be too rich. If the seedlings are transplanted into individual peat pots, the roots need never be disturbed again, even when setting the plants out in the garden. The top of the pot should be sunk below the surface of the soil.

When raising wild flowers from seeds, the greatest mortality usually occurs after the little seedlings have been taken from the seedbed. The process of exposing them to more air and sunlight must be accomplished gradually. They also need full protection from heavy rainfall, yet they should never be left in too close an atmosphere so that they become spindly. Well-grown plants spend considerable time in a well-managed frame before they are moved to their final quarters. The gardener must be willing and able to give the seedlings this constant attention under suitable protection if his efforts are to succeed.

THE GLASS-JAR METHOD FOR SEEDS

A method of germinating seeds which has worked particularly well with gentians has been described by Dr. C. R. Worth of Groton, New York. Briefly, it is as follows:

Twelve-ounce peanut butter jars with screw tops are washed thoroughly.

Fill to 1 or 2 inches of the top with a mixture of 75 per cent peat and 25 per cent sand by bulk. Firm it with the thumbs.

Saturate the medium with a fungicide. Pano-drench is used by the author. Screw on the tops and let stand for two days. Remove the covers, invert jars on a rack, and drain excess moisture.

Plant seeds on surface of medium. Small ones need no covering. Cover large ones with treated sand and peat. Screw on the jar tops again and set jars in an unheated place out of direct sunlight.

Germination should take place during the next three weeks, but occasionally a year or longer is required.

Fringed gentians planted in March had scattered germination in early April but had heavy germination in the following February. The late March sowing was probably responsible for this. The seeds remained in the closed jars for nearly a year.

When seeds start to come up, replace the metal covers with glass lids tilted to admit air; give more light. Proceed as for seedlings in general.

FROM CUTTINGS

Every serious wild flower gardener will enjoy experiments in propagating wild flowers vegetatively. The following recommendations are intended for amateurs who do not have a greenhouse or bottom heat to use when rooting cuttings. The cuttings are to be kept outdoors until rooting has taken place.

When taking cuttings the timing is very important. The gardener must learn by experience to tell when the wood is in the right stage of maturity. This cannot be taught satisfactorily in a book. A *sharp* knife is required when taking cuttings; a clean cut heals better than a jagged one. Stainless steel knives are not sharp enough and safety razor blades are to be preferred to dull knives. If the cutting is quite woody the razor blade will be inadequate. Cuttings are best taken in the morning and should be put at once into a plastic bag with a few drops of water to keep them from wilting until they can be inserted in the medium. The cut end is usually treated with a root-forming hormone before inserting it. Rootone, or Hormodin in strengths 1, 2, and 3, is recommended. The cuttings should not be dipped into the main supply but into a small amount taken out for the purpose. Any of this not used should be discarded. When inserting the cuttings take care not to rub off the hormone in the process. Enough space should be allowed each one so that light can reach the medium and so that the cuttings do not touch each other. A thorough soaking with water will compact the medium around the cuttings.

The containers for cuttings may be flats, shallow boxes, clay pots, tin cans with drainage holes punched in them or, simpler still, a shallow excavation in the ground about 6 inches deep and framed with boards to keep the soil from contaminating the medium. If the cuttings are in containers they should be buried almost to the rim in the cutting frame. A shaded location should be chosen where the cuttings will receive maximum light without direct sunlight. The north side of a building or wall with unobstructed north light is ideal.

There are several media to choose from in which to insert the cuttings. *Coarse* sand is the generally accepted medium, and washed brick sand is the grade to ask for when buying it. Instead of using sand alone, a mixture of three or four parts sand and one of shredded Styrofoam or vermiculite may give better results. Another excellent combination is two parts sand and one part perlite. For plants needing acid soil, four parts sand and one of acid' peat would be suitable.

Success in handling cuttings depends almost entirely on how well the cuttings are covered. If the atmosphere becomes dry, due to air leaks, failure will result. Polyethylene film is the covering used. A stout framework is needed to keep the plastic well above the cuttings despite possible heavy snow. A strong wire with a rectangular mesh known as "turkey wire" is good, but any kind of wire support would probably work. After the framework is arranged over the cuttings, a sheet of polyethylene is laid over it large enough to throw soil over all the edges, thus excluding the outside air. The film can be held firmly around a flat containing only a few cuttings by anchoring it with snap clothespins to screw eyes inserted in all four sides of the flat.

The new little plants will need the protection of a cold frame for at least a whole season before being put into the garden. Cuttings are potted up when the roots are about ½-inch long, using a prepared potting mixture.

Cuttings are usually inspected at least every two weeks to determine whether watering is needed. They must never be allowed to dry out. In fall and spring thorough watering will be necessary; during winter, only when the medium is thawed and has become dry. At times the cuttings will freeze solid during the winter.

The cuttings are rooted when a gentle upward pull fails to dislodge them. Fall-rooted cuttings should be left in the medium until spring. Those which callus in the fall and root in the spring should be left until well rooted. When rooted cuttings are large enough to be transferred to individual pots they must be taken gradually out of the humid atmosphere to which they are accustomed. First replace them in a shaded frame covered with plastic. Remove it on cloudy days and at night, covering again in the morning. A few days will be needed to complete the change to a normal atmosphere.

SOFTWOOD CUTTINGS

Many wild flowers, such as *Phlox divaricata*, can be increased by softwood cuttings of the basal growth taken in June. They root well if not too immature. The cuttings are of half-ripened shoots of new growth of perennials taken just as they are commencing to harden. The shoots should snap when bent. The cuttings are 3 to 5 inches long, and the cut is made just below a node, which is where a leaf joins a stem. The bottom leaves that would be buried in the medium are carefully cut off. Either Rootone or Hormodin 1 is used for softwood cuttings.

There are two general classes of summer cuttings. Softwood is that which is still growing. Greenwood is that which has nearly ripened. Short, lateral growths usually make the best cuttings. They may have from two to five buds, and are taken from July to September, the timing depending on the season, whether hot and dry or rainy and cool.

HARDWOOD CUTTINGS

Hardwood cuttings are made from completely dormant mature wood which has finished its growth for the season. They are taken after the weather has become cool. Those taken in early September may root by late fall; those taken in October will callus that fall and root the next spring. There are two groups of hardwood cuttings.

A) Deciduous hardwood cuttings. Example: shrubby-type dog-
woods.

These are taken after the leaves have fallen. They may be 6 to
8 inches long and not less than ¼-inch in diameter. The lower cut
should be below a node. The cuttings are tied in bundles and buried
in the ground beneath a thick mulch of hay or leaves or are stored
in a cool place (40° F.) in moist peat, sawdust, or sphagnum moss
until spring. They are then planted deeply in a nursery row with one
set of buds above ground level.

B) Evergreen hardwood cuttings.

1. Broadleaf hardwood cuttings. Examples: inkberry, rhododendron.

This type of cutting is of special interest since many of the
choicest wild flowers are evergreen woody plants. As a general rule
evergreens root much more slowly than deciduous material. Healthy
tip cuttings of the previous season's growth are usually made. Cutting below a node is not important. All foliage is removed from the
portion of the cutting to be inserted in the medium. Hormodin is
used according to directions. Care in spacing and watering is ob-
served as with other types of cuttings.

It is particularly gratifying to root cuttings of bearberry and trailing arbutus. January cuttings of both of these plants have rooted almost 100 per cent in a cool, moist, shady place without bottom heat.
Nevertheless, gentle bottom heat is a great help in rooting all woody
plants. Heating cables intended for almost any size of flat or frame
are now available. Arbutus and bearberry root best if rather long
cuttings are taken, going back far enough on the plant stems to
include a small bit of the root. The underside of the stem should be
scraped in several places, and this portion should be dusted with
Hormodin 3. The cuttings should be pinned down to the medium on
either side of the wounded areas. Discarded bobby pins are useful
for this operation. Copper wire bent into hairpins 6 to 8 inches long
is still better where depth of medium allows it. A sheet of polyethylene is tightly secured around the flat after it has been watered. The
cuttings must be kept cool and out of strong light. In the spring the
flat is placed in a shaded cold frame, where it should probably remain for a full year. During this time the roots that formed on the
scraped places and tips of the stems should fill the flat. The rooted

cuttings may then be set into their permanent positions. Cuttings must never dry out during the entire operation.

2. Narrowleaf evergreen cuttings. Examples: arbor-vitae, juniper, yew.

Most of these root readily after the wood has been ripened by a few autumn frosts. Either large or small cuttings are suitable. Large cuttings can include several years' growth. Those of yew and arbor-vitae 18 inches long, taken in October, have rooted well.

In the case of hemlock and spruce, cuttings of the previous season's growth would be used. These are sometimes quite short.

ROOT CUTTINGS

Some wild flowers impossible to transplant because of tap roots may be increased from root cuttings. Butterfly-weed and flowering spurge are examples of such plants. Pieces of the root about ¼-inch in diameter are cut in pieces 2 to 3 inches long and buried ½-inch deep in flats in a moist medium composed of one part loam, two parts peat, and three parts coarse sand. They are usually placed horizontally in the medium, but some do better if set upright. If placed upright, the end of the cutting nearest the crown of the plant should be at the top. Cuts are made with the tops straight and the bases slanted to avoid setting them the wrong end up. Root cuttings are made in winter in the greenhouse or in early spring in a cold frame. They are also sometimes inserted in ordinary soil in the open. If planted outdoors in the fall they should be well mulched during the winter.

BY DIVISION

Perhaps the easiest way to increase wild flowers is by division. This method applies to plants with extensive root systems that can readily be torn apart into small sections to start new plants. Each division must have a growing point. This is done in early spring as new growth starts. Plants that make strong clumps too thick to be torn apart can be cut into pieces with a sharpened sod cutter or a spade.

Some plants produce offsets which should be pulled away from the parent plant as early as possible after they have grown enough roots to support themselves. When taking offsets of iris species, a sharp knife is needed to make a straight cut through the old rhizome from which the offsets have grown. This is done after flowering when the offsets have made roots. Dodecatheon is an example of a plant increased by offsets.

It is not wise to separate plants into small pieces during their active growing season. If a plant must be moved at that time it should be replanted at once without being further disturbed. Autumn division of wild flowers is not desirable because few new roots are made at that season and the divisions will die or be heaved out of the ground during the winter. Even such plants as mertensia and dicentra are most safely divided in earliest spring, although there may be no flowers that season.

BY LAYERING

Flexible branches and stems of some shrubs and ground covers can be increased by layering. A sliver of bark is removed from the underside of the branch where the roots are to form. The wound is dusted with a root hormone. A shallow trench is then dug, into which the wounded portion of the branch is placed. It is covered with soil and either pegged or weighted down to hold it in place. The new plant should not be severed from the parent until the following spring. This is a good way to increase arbutus.

Trailing plants are often difficult to move. A common mistake has been to dig up trailing roots of ground pine, fringed polygala, and the like and set them immediately into their new home. They usually disappear in a relatively short time. If clumps of these plants are dug up carefully, they can be transferred to flats filled with soil in which the plants were growing. Existing roots should be carefully curled around and arranged in the confined space. The container is then placed in a shaded frame until it has become filled with new roots.

Small bits of almost any type of wild flower with a few roots attached or newly purchased specimens with bare roots can be put into a sand bed containing coarse sand or with the addition of a fifth part loam. This method is also helpful in establishing small rock ferns. The medium should never dry out or be too wet and should not receive direct sunlight until new roots have formed.

BY SPORES

When propagating ferns from spores the gardener should understand a little about fern structure. Ferns do not set seeds but are increased from spores enclosed in fruiting bodies, called sori, usually borne on the back of the fern frond. The fronds that do not bear sori are called sterile fronds. The fertile fronds must be collected when the spores are ripe. This varies with different species. If the spores cannot be planted at once, the fronds may be stored in smooth paper packets in the refrigerator.

Various types of containers, media, and treatments are suggested by those who raise ferns from spores. Two methods are given below:

1. Two-inch clay flowerpots are sterilized in boiling water for twenty minutes. When cool they are filled with sphagnum moss through which boiling water has been poured. The pots are inverted in plastic containers fitted with tight covers. The spores are sown directly on the inverted pots and covered tightly. A little water should stand in the bottom of the containers to prevent drying out. The containers are set out of direct sunlight at room temperature. When the spores germinate they are treated as in Method 2.

2. Pots are filled with soil containing a third each of loam, leaf mold, and sand to within ½-inch of the top. A layer of brick dust or crushed flowerpots is placed on the soil. Boiling water is then poured through the pots. When they have cooled, pieces of fern fronds bearing the spore cases are laid on the moist surface. The pots are covered with polyethylene or a sheet of glass, the pots then being placed in a pan of water in the shade. In a few weeks small green patches called prothalli will appear. These are left undisturbed until the true young fern plants have grown on the prothalli. These are pricked off into flats of woodland soil while very small and kept for at least a year in a shaded cold frame.

Gardeners who are seriously interested in propagating ferns should consult *American Ferns* by Roberts and Lawrence. Although now out of print, the book is available in many libraries. The whole subject is covered completely from a scientific standpoint.

COLLECTING PLANTS FROM THE WILD

Wild flowers should be dug with as much soil as possible adhering to the roots. When properly dug they take up considerable space, and only relatively few plants should be taken. They should be wrapped in wet burlap, newspapers, or be put in polyethylene bags to protect them from light and air. If they cannot be replanted at once, they require frequent inspection to see that they are not too wet or too dry. When in a confined space plants can rot quickly.

A good-sized hole should be prepared for each plant in the new location. If the existing soil is thin and poor, compost and other organic matter must be added, especially for woodland plants, at this time. Each plant should be well watered and, even in the woods, some sort of shade over the plants for a few days will help them to adjust to their new surroundings. Several waterings will be necessary during the first few weeks if no rainfall occurs. Sometimes it means carrying water for some distance, a back-breaking chore. A mulch of partially rotted leaves tucked around a plant or used lightly to cover a sod of arbutus or other choice ground cover will help them to become established.

A further precaution would be to protect each planting with a large piece of chicken wire or to erect a wire collar around each plant. Rabbits and woodchucks make immediately for new plantings, perhaps because a new flavor has been added to the accustomed menu. These animals have eaten hepatica and fringed gentian flowers and the new growth of arbutus when the wire protection was removed even for one night. Only failure will result if new plants are set out and left without adequate water or protection on the assumption that they are wild and can therefore shift for themselves.

The plants should have the same exposure that they enjoyed in the wild. Most spring wild flowers get a little sun while they are in blossom, and they must not be planted under evergreens. They can be put at the edges of evergreens. When conditions can be duplicated under which plants were flowering in their natural habitat, the chance for success will be greater.

Spring is generally considered the best time for transplanting most wild flowers. Asters and various other composites *must* be moved at that season. Lilies are moved in the fall. Actually, most plants can be taken at almost any season if the gardener is skillful and experienced.

Wild Flowers by Family

TYPHACEAE Cat-tail Family

Members of the Cat-tail Family have ribbon-like leaves and two kinds of flowers, staminate and pistillate on the same plant. There are no petals.

Typha angustifolia Narrow-leaved Cat-tail

The tall grass-like plants grow in close clumps from creeping rootstocks in swamps and wet places. Long, narrow, swordlike mostly basal leaves are 3 to 5 feet long. The dense brown flower spikes are in two sections, the upper male, the lower female, blossoming from late May to July. They persist as heads of brown downy seeds.

This plant is found from Nova Scotia and Ontario south to South Carolina, Missouri, and Nebraska, largely in shallow acid or alkaline waters, and is somewhat rare. It is the best species for bog gardens and pools.

PROPAGATION   The creeping rootstock divides readily in the spring or summer.

T. latifolia   Common Cat-tail

This species is larger in every way than *T. angustifolia* and is much too vigorous for small water gardens. The flower spike has no break between the two sexes of flowers. It blossoms from late May to July.

T. latifolia is found in marshes and shallow water from Newfoundland to Alaska, south through the United States into Mexico.

PROPAGATION   Same as for *T. angustifolia*.

ALISMATACEAE
                          Water-plantain Family

These are aquatic or marsh plants with basal, usually long-petioled leaves, erect or floating. The flowers are in whorls around a scape.

Sagittaria latifolia   Arrowhead

This is another water plant with arrow-shaped leaves, growing abundantly along muddy margins of sluggish streams and still ponds, in shallow water, from Canada to Mexico. The delicate flowers with three white petals are borne in widely spaced whorls of three on leafless stalks from July to September. The dry seeds are in a globose head. The size and shape of the leaves vary greatly among the different plants, which may grow nearly 5 feet tall. This arrowhead is not suited to small pools because it spreads rapidly. To succeed it must be planted well below the water line.

PROPAGATION By seeds planted in
autumn in flats of mucky soil submerged
a little beneath the water. Transplant once
before moving to permanent quarters.

Arrowheads may also be dug at any
time during the summer and held down
with stones until rooted into their new
location.

There are several smaller species better
suited to garden pools and tubs, the best
of which is S. *Engelmanniana,* reaching a
height of 2 feet. It has very narrow leaves.

A R A C E A E   Arum Family

The Arum Family contains mostly moisture-loving plants with the flowers fused together in a fleshy spike called a spadix, often
surrounded by a hood or spathe which sub-
tends it.

Acorus Calamus   Sweetflag

An aromatic plant, this species has narrow, erect sword-like leaves 2 to 5 feet long.
The flowers are borne on a scape resembling
the leaves, prolonged into an erect green
spathe. The spadix, which grows out at an
angle from the side of the two-edged stem,
is covered with tiny yellowish-brown flowers
in June and July. The plant has a pungent
odor and taste. It is suitable for large water
gardens.

A. *Calamus* is found beside small streams
and in wet ground from Nova Scotia and Quebec to Minnesota and Alberta, south to Florida, Texas, and Colorado.

PROPAGATION By seeds, rarely seen,
but at times, in September.

By division of the roots, at any time in
the growing season.

Arisaema atrorubens   Jack-in-the-Pulpit

This is the common species in New England. The plant sends up two large long-stemmed, three-parted leaves on long petioles, about 2 feet tall, which overshadow the pulpit that is produced at the fork of the leaf stems. The flowers are on the spadix within the pulpit, blossoming in spring, and in the fall there are clusters of bright red fruits. The color of the pulpit varies from green to purple and brown.

This plant is found in woods and swamps in a variety of soils, from New Brunswick and Quebec to Manitoba, south to South Carolina, Missouri and Kansas.

PROPAGATION   By seeds sown outdoors in the fall. Self-sows readily. Young plants move easily, all season.

A. triphyllum, Small Jack-in-the-pulpit, is a more southern species.

Orontium aquaticum   Golden Club

This attractive small water plant is not found in colder climates. It has floating, long-petioled dark green leaves from a deep-seated, creeping stem. In early spring it sends up a long snaky scape topped by a golden-yellow spadix on which the little yellow flowers are thickly clustered. The fruit is green. The species sometimes lives through northern winters, where it is a treasured addition to the water garden. In warmer climates, however, it spreads too rapidly for garden pools.

O. aquaticum is found in shallow water on the margins of ponds from southern Massachusetts and New York to Florida and Kentucky.

PROPAGATION   By division in the spring.
By seeds collected in the late summer and planted in a pot set in water.

Calla palustris   Wild Calla

An interesting plant found growing in the mud of shallow water or creeping in bogs in cold, acid soil, this is a welcome addition to the bog garden or swampy area. The plant has long, slender stems with a few heart-shaped leaves and solitary small white "calla lilies" in early summer. The clusters of bright red fruits, in late summer, resemble those of Jack-in-the-pulpit, but are smaller. It is not always easy to find a congenial spot for wild calla. It will not take hold in running water but is easy where the water is still and constant. The plant moves around a little every year.

This plant is found from Quebec to Minnesota and Alberta, south to Florida, Texas, and Colorado.

PROPAGATION   By division, in April or May.

By stem cuttings planted in wet mud in summer.

By seeds planted when they are ripe. They should be removed from the pulp.

Peltandra virginica   Arrow-Arum

The stream-side wild garden and the quiet pond depend for much of their interest on the foliage plants of different shapes and textures which give special beauty to the water garden. The arrow-arum is a desirable plant of this type for shallow water, and is particularly valuable for the small pool because it does not spread. The plant makes a stout clump of thick, fibrous roots. The handsome arrow-shaped shining leaves with long petioles are pinnately veined. In early summer a spadix is produced bearing groups of inconspicuous flowers, the whole surrounded by a green spathe with wavy, inrolled edges. The green seed capsule forms under water.

This plant grows about 18 inches tall and occurs from Maine to Florida, west to Michigan.

PROPAGATION   Since the plant is never abundant, it is best to buy specimens for the wild garden.

By seeds, squeezed from the pulp in the fall and sown at once.

Symplocarpus foetidus   Skunk-Cabbage

In earliest spring the yellowish flowers appear set on a knob-shaped spadix, close to the ground, surrounded by an interesting shell-like purple, red-and-green-mottled and -blotched spathe. After the flowers have faded, the plant makes large clumps of light green cabbage-like leaves which hide the clustered red berries. The plants are very deeply rooted and long-lived, preferring moderately to slightly acid soils.

This plant is found in swamps from Quebec and Nova Scotia to North Carolina, west to Minnesota and Iowa.

PROPAGATION By seeds sown in August. Small plants may be dug in the spring.

COMMELINACEAE
Spiderwort Family

These plants have jointed leafy stems and clusters of three-parted flowers that wither quickly.

Tradescantia virginiana   Virginia Spiderwort

Spiderworts are often seen in old gardens. They are sure to grow, and are effective when in flower. However, in summer the untidy foliage detracts from their appearance. The plants grow in erect clumps, 1 to 2 feet tall, with long narrow leaves, their bases clasping the stem. The flowers, which last but part of one day, have three petals, purple or white, in terminal umbels, blossoming from June to August.

This plant grows in moist fields and rich woods in neutral soil and it will flower in sun or shade. It is found from Connecticut to Wisconsin, south to Georgia, Missouri, Florida, and Texas.

PROPAGATION   By division in the spring.
By seeds sown in August. It self-sows readily.
By cuttings taken in the summer.

PONTEDERIACEAE
Pickerelweed Family

These aquatic plants have thick stems, creeping in mud, rather large solitary leaves and bilateral flowers in bracted spikes.

Pontederia cordata   Pickerelweed

The small pool or bog is no place for this rapidly increasing, strong-growing plant. It sends out fleshy cord-like roots which take hold readily in the mud beneath the shallow waters of ponds and streams. The plant is usually seen in large colonies and is beautiful when seen from a distance. It has erect long-petioled leaves, heart-shaped at the base, and spikes of violet-blue short-lived flowers on a one-leaved stem. The species grows about 2 feet tall and blossoms throughout the summer.

This plant is found on muddy shores from Nova Scotia to Ontario, south to Florida, Missouri, and Oklahoma.

PROPAGATION   By division in the summer while in bloom. Lift with spading-fork. The newly set plants should be anchored with stones.

LILIACEAE   Lily Family

The Lily Family contains many of our most beautiful native plants. The flowers, usually regular, have six divisions of three petals and three petal-like sepals, and the leaves have parallel veins characteristic of the monocotyledons. The family differs from the Amaryllis Family in the position of the ovary. It is superior in the Lily Family.

Aletris farinosa   Colicroot

Growing from a basal rosette of pointed leaves, this species sends up slender leafless stems, 1 to 2 feet tall, bearing a spike-like raceme of small tubular white flowers that are mealy on the outside. It is the most common of the colicroots, blossoming in June and July, and desirable for the summer wild garden where the soil can be kept strongly acid.

This plant is found in full sun in dry or moist sandy soil and barrens from Maine to Florida, west to Wisconsin, Minnesota, Arkansas, and Texas.

PROPAGATION   Easily transplanted at any time, where abundant.

Allium cernuum   Nodding Onion

The flowering onions belong in most wild gardens and should be better known. They have long, narrow basal leaves and, usually, leafless stems crowned with umbels of white, pink, or purplish flowers. They all have a strong onion odor.

This species has flat soft leaves and a flower stalk about 1 foot high which curves over at the top with umbels of nodding pale pink flowers in July and August.

A. cernuum is found in dry woods and on rocky slopes in neutral or moderately acid soil from New York to British Columbia, south to Georgia, Missouri, and Texas.

PROPAGATION   By seeds sown in the early spring, collected in autumn.

By division of the bulbs in the fall.

A. stellatum   Wild Onion

This species has thick, hard leaves grooved the whole length. The bright lilac-pink flowers are held upright and they are pretty. Since it blossoms in July and August, this is an especially desirable plant for the wild garden. It grows about 2 feet tall.

A. stellatum is found on prairies, rocky hills, and barrens, in neutral to slightly acid soil from Saskatchewan to Ohio, south to Missouri, Kansas, and Texas.

PROPAGATION   Same as for *A. cernuum.*

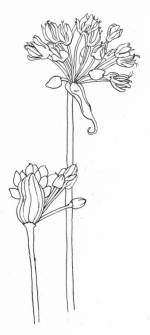

A. tricoccum   Wild Leek

This onion has large flat leaves like a lily-of-the-valley. These appear in early spring, and wither before the flower stalks appear in June and July. The whitish flowers are in an erect, flattened umbel on a stalk 1 foot high. This species often makes large colonies in rich woods from Quebec to New England and Minnesota, south to North Carolina and Tennessee.

PROPAGATION   Same as for *A. cernuum,* but seeds are few, and division of the bulb cluster as flowers fade is more desirable.

Chamaelirium luteum
                    Devil's-bit or Fairy-wand

Not well known, this more southern plant has a basal rosette of flat, lanceolate leaves and an erect stem, 1 to 4 feet tall, with several smaller leaves. The plants are of two sexes; the male plant has a flower stalk with a feathery, spike-like raceme 4 to 10 inches long, of small, fragrant white flowers tinted yellow because of the many stamens; the female ones are pure white in a shorter, more slender spike, the stalk also being more leafy. They blossom in June.

This plant is found in moderately acid, moist rich soil from western Massachusetts to Georgia and from Michigan south to Mississippi and Arkansas.

PROPAGATION   By seeds, kept wet, and sown in the fall.

By transplanting, which is easy, where abundant.

Camassia scilloides
> Wild Hyacinth or Eastern Camass

There are five species of Camassia in North America, four of them restricted to the western states. They are cultivated in eastern gardens, however, and, with their long, loose racemes of large pale blue, lilac, or white hyacinth-like flowers, are very striking.

Eastern camass has many narrow-oblong, mostly basal leaves. The star-like six-parted flowers are in a long raceme from 6 to 20 inches in height, blossoming in late April and May. It is a long-lived species and does not require an acid soil. It does well in the semi-shady wild garden.

This plant is found on prairies and in moist, open woods in Pennsylvania, West Virginia, west to Wisconsin and Kansas, south to Georgia and Texas.

PROPAGATION   By seeds sown in the fall.

Clintonia borealis   Bluebead-Lily

This plant prefers a cold northern climate where it may be seen in large colonies by the edges of rich moist woods and bogs and extending into subalpine meadows. It does fairly well in a milder climate, however, if the soil is strongly acid and peaty, but never produces so many flowers or berries as in its natural habitat. The plant has two, three, or four large oval dark glossy green leaves with hairy margins, somewhat resembling those of lily-of-the-valley. These sheath the base of the flower stalk, which is about 8 inches high. In May and June, nodding greenish-yellow flowers in loose terminal umbels appear, followed in late summer by clusters of showy large blue berries.

C. borealis is abundant in wet northern woods from Labrador to Manitoba and Minnesota, south to New Jersey, Pennsylvania, and Indiana; also in the Carolina mountains.

PROPAGATION   By seeds separated from the pulp in October and sown at once.
By division of the roots in the spring.
Where abundant, large sods may be transplanted in the spring.

C. umbellulata   Speckled Bead-Lily

A more southern species, this plant resembles *C. borealis* in general habit. The umbels of flowers are greenish-white spotted with purplish-brown, and do not nod. It is a much less common plant than the preceding, but easier to grow since it enjoys a rich moist soil only moderately acid. It flowers in May and June.

This species is found in rich mountain woods from New York and Ohio along the uplands to Georgia and Tennessee.

PROPAGATION   Same as for *C. borealis.*

Disporum lanuginosum
                    Yellow Mandarin or Fairybells

Another wild flower with nodding bell-shaped flowers, this plant grows 2 to 3 feet tall with the stem forked and bearing several stemless, oblong alternate leaves. In late spring greenish flowers nod from the upper leaf axils. This species resembles the Uvularia in habit but differs in that the fruit is a smooth red berry. It grows on wooded slopes in neutral to slightly acid soil and is desirable for the spring wild garden.

This plant is found in rich woods from Ontario, Ohio, and New York south to Georgia and Alabama, chiefly in the mountains.

PROPAGATION   By seeds removed from the pulp in autumn and sown at once.

Erythronium americanum
                    Fawn-Lily or Dog's-tooth-Violet

In early spring, in rich moist woods and
wet meadows, one frequently comes upon
great patches of small pointed, mottled
leaves close to the ground. Here and there in
the patch handsome nodding yellow bells appear on stems a few inches high, between two
brown-mottled leaves which grow up from a
deep-seated bulb. When transplanted into the
wild garden flowers are usually not borne for
several years. The gardener must wait until the
bulbs are deep enough in the ground and large
enough to flower. After a wait of about ten
years, transplanted bulbs now bloom heavily
in the author's garden. The foliage disappears
in June.

This plant is found in neutral or moderately acid soil from New Brunswick to Florida and from Ontario and Minnesota south
to Arkansas and Oklahoma.

PROPAGATION   By removing offsets in
    early spring or when dormant.
        By seeds sown outside or in a container.
    Seeds are rarely produced. Remove small
    bulbils and plant 3 inches deep.

E. albidum   White Trout Lily

This species, more common in the woods
of the Midwest, blooms soon after transplanting. It prefers a neutral soil. All the western
Erythroniums have this habit, making them
especially desirable for the wild garden. The
var. *mesochoreum* has white flowers, un-
mottled leaves, and grows on the prairies
rather than in woods. It prefers slightly acid
soil.

PROPAGATION   Same as for *E. ameri-
    canum.*

Helonias bullata   Swamp-pink

A splendid plant for the small bog garden, swamp-pink grows from a flat rosette of
oblong basal evergreen leaves. The stout
hollow scape, 1 to 2 feet tall, with bract-like
leaves, bears a dense terminal raceme of small
pink flowers in April and May. The plant prefers a strongly acid, humus-rich soil.

This species grows in bogs and swamps
from New Jersey to Virginia on the Coastal
Plain and in the Blue Ridge Mountains. It is
hardy in Massachusetts gardens.

PROPAGATION   By seeds sown in flats
    in the fall.

    May be transplanted where abundant.

Lilium canadense   Canada Lily

The native lilies are among the most impressive of wild flowers. Anyone who in early
summer has ever suddenly come upon a
stand of Canada lilies in some wet northern
meadow will never forget the fairy-like
beauty of the pendulous yellow bells thickly
spotted with purple-brown. It is the most
graceful of the lilies. The plant often grows 6
feet tall with several whorls of oblong leaves
around the stem and with the flowers arranged
in a perfect candelabrum, their petals slightly
recurved, and blossoming in June and July.

L. canadense prefers a cold situation and
is found in moist meadows and copses from
Quebec and Maine to Minnesota, south to Alabama and Indiana. It grows in neutral or
slightly acid soil.

PROPAGATION   By scales. Dig plants in
    the fall. Remove small scales at base of
    bulb and plant ½-inch deep in a cold
    frame. Replant the large bulbs.

    By seeds sown outside, 3 to 4 inches
    deep in neutral loam.

L. Grayi   Gray's Lily

This southern species is smaller in every way than the preceding. The flower is reddish-orange with darker spots.

It is found in meadows and swamps in the mountains of Virginia, North Carolina, and Tennessee.

PROPAGATION   Same as for *L. canadense.*

L. michiganense   Michigan Lily

In late June and July on the moist prairies from Ontario to Manitoba, south to Tennessee and Arkansas, colonies of Michigan lily are occasionally seen, growing to a height of 2 feet. Somewhat intermediate between Canada and Turk's-cap lilies, the red-orange, spotted, strongly reflexed flowers are borne singly or in umbels of one, two, or three. The plant sends out a horizontal rhizome produced annually. In this way it multiplies and forms colonies. It is excellent for the wild garden.

L. philadelphicum   Wood Lily

This lily is extremely difficult to establish in a wild garden. It apparently is short-lived, and never found long in the same place. It is an erect plant, 2 to 3 feet tall, with the leaves in whorls of four to seven. The red-orange flowers spotted with purple toward the base are upright in clusters of from one to five and they blossom from June to August.

This species is found in sun or part shade in dry, open woods and thickets from New Hampshire to North Carolina, west to Kentucky. It requires strongly acid soil.

PROPAGATION   Same as for *L. canadense* except that it needs acid soil on the dry side.

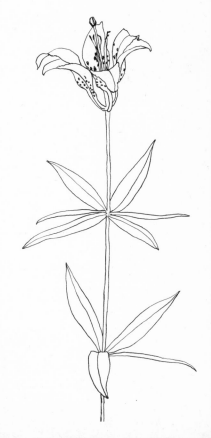

The best method of propagation is by scales.

Seeds sown in a polyethylene bag in the fall of 1958 stayed at room temperature, forgotten, until the fall of 1959. When found, practically all the seeds had made both roots and tops but no little bulblets. The seedlings were transferred to flats of peat and sand in a sun-heated pit, and in the spring of 1960 they were in good shape. If these reach flowering size they will make quite a planting.

L. Catesbaei is the similar Southern Wood Lily with red, widely spreading petals. It grows in swamps from North Carolina to Florida and Alabama.

L. superbum   Turk's-cap Lily

A beautiful species with completely reflexed petals which expose the handsome brown stamens to full view, this lily does well in wild gardens, often growing 8 feet high. The principal leaves are whorled, the upper ones being alternate. The showy, nodding red flowers spotted with maroon at the base are in panicles of three to many, and blossom in July and August. This species likes a warmer climate than Canada lily and is found in wet meadows and low ground from Georgia and Alabama, north to Massachusetts and New York, west to Minnesota. It occurs most often near the coast and needs a moderately acid soil.

PROPAGATION   By seeds sown in acid soil in the fall.

By scales separated and planted in the spring.

Maianthemum canadense

> False Lily-of-the-Valley or
> Wild Lily-of-the-Valley

A common and readily grown ground cover which will do well in heavy shade, this species covers large areas. The little plants have two or three oval, mostly basal leaves which appear in early spring. The tiny white flowers with four petals blossom in small erect terminal racemes only a few inches high, in May. In the fall there are clusters of small pale red berries.

This species is found in moist woods in moderately acid, humus-rich soil throughout Northern America and in the mountains to North Carolina.

PROPAGATION The berries may be planted in the fall.

Transplants easily if good sods are taken.

Medeola virginiana Indian Cucumber-root

Although this is not a showy plant, it has a place in the shady wild garden in moderately acid soil. The slender stem, 1 to 2 feet tall, has a whorl of five to nine long-ovate leaves near the middle and three ovate ones around the top of the stem. These subtend a sessile umbel of small recurved pale greenish-yellow flowers blossoming in May and June, which become purple berries in the fall.

This plant grows from Maine to Minnesota, southward.

PROPAGATION By seeds separated from the pulp in September and sown at once.

Melanthium virginicum   Bunchflower

A southern bog plant, bunchflower is quite imposing when it blossoms in June and July. The plant has stout, erect stems, 2 to 5 feet tall, with many narrow oblong leaves. The tiny greenish flowers are in a large branched panicle well above the leaves.

This plant requires a peaty, strongly acid soil and grows in swales and wet meadows from Florida to Texas, north to New York, Illinois, and Iowa.

PROPAGATION   By seeds sown in the fall.

Nothoscordum bivalve   False Garlic

This little plant has the general habit of the Allium without the onion odor. It has grass-like basal leaves above which the flower stalk, 1 foot tall, bears a flat cluster of starry white flowers with a yellow eye, in spring. It is suitable for the woodland wild garden in neutral, rich soil.

N. bivalve is found in open sandy woods and prairies, preferably in moist soil, from Florida to Mexico, north to Virginia, Indiana, and Nebraska.

PROPAGATION   By seeds sown in the fall.

By offsets taken from the mother bulb in the spring.

Polygonatum biflorum   Solomon's-seal

This is one wild flower which almost everybody knows, although the plant is not in the least showy. It grows from a slowly creeping knotted rhizome. The numerous alternate ovate-oblong leaves are somewhat clasping and are arranged on either side of the smooth, arching stems which are from 1 to 2 feet tall. The small greenish-white bells drooping on slender peduncles from each leaf axil are inconspicuous. They may be solitary or two-flowered, blossoming in May and June. The fruits are blue-black berries.

This species grows in slightly acid soil in rocky woods and thickets from Maine to Florida, west to Michigan, Iowa, and Nebraska. It is an excellent ground cover in woodlands.

PROPAGATION   By seeds sown as whole berries, or mashed, in autumn.

By transplanting in the spring where abundant.

P. canaliculatum   Great Solomon's-seal

This impressive plant is splendid for the shady wild garden. The strong, arched stems may be 4 feet tall. The drooping bells are in clusters of two, three, or four, flowering in May and June.

This species is found from New Hampshire, Michigan, and North Dakota south to Georgia and Texas. It prefers slightly acid to neutral soil.

PROPAGATION   By seeds separated from the pulp and sown in the fall.

By division in the spring only.

Smilacina racemosa   False Spikenard

A conspicuous plant usually seen in colonies in rich woods, this species has arching leafy stems 2 to 3 feet tall. The alternate ovate hairy-edged leaves are sessile, and the tiny white flowers are in a feathery terminal panicle, blossoming in June. The attractive fruits are small whitish, speckled berries in clusters, turning red in fall.

This plant is easily grown in moderately acid soil in the shady wild garden. The range is from Nova Scotia to British Columbia, south to Georgia and Arizona.

PROPAGATION   By division in the spring.

By seeds separated from the pulp and sown in the fall.

S. stellata   Starry False Solomon's-seal

Similar to the preceding species but much smaller, being only 1 foot tall, this plant has fewer but larger white flowers at the tip of the stem, in May. The light, blue-green leaves are downy beneath and clasp the zigzag stem. The plant probably does best in neutral soil but is not particular about shade and moisture. It will spread by underground stems into large patches.

This species is found from Newfoundland to British Columbia, south to New Jersey, Virginia, and Missouri, and in the west to California.

PROPAGATION   Same as for *S. racemosa*, but the creeping stems are readily divided.

Stenanthium gramineum Featherbells

Suitable for a southern bog garden or for moist, strongly acid soil, this interesting plant has basal leaves which are long and narrow, with somewhat smaller ones alternate on the stem that may reach a height of 6 feet. This robust form is often cultivated. The small white flowers, with pointed petals and sepals soon becoming greenish in color, blossom in very large terminal panicles, in summer.

This plant is found in mountain woods from Pennsylvania, Indiana, and Missouri south to Florida and Arkansas. It is hardy in New England.

PROPAGATION   By seeds separated from the capsules in the fall and sown at once.

Streptopus amplexifolius var. *americanus*
Twisted-stalk

This plant has a leafy forked stem from 2 to three feet in height. The smooth ovate leaves clasp the stem. The open bell-shaped, solitary or paired, greenish-white nodding flowers are on slender stalks conspicuously twisted near the middle and borne in the leaf axils in June and July. The fruits are red berries.

The plant grows in cold moist woods in acid soil and occurs from Greenland to Alaska, south to New England, New York, Michigan, and Minnesota, in the mountains to North Carolina and in the Rockies to Arizona.

PROPAGATION   By division in the early spring.

By seeds separated from the pulp and sown at once.

S. roseus   Rosybells

This species is much like the preceding but with pink flowers on slender stalks kinked near the middle. They blossom from May to July. The leaves are sessile and do not clasp the stem.

This plant is found in rich woods in moderately acid soil. There are three varieties of the species which are practically identical, found over the northeastern half of North America, extending in the mountains to North Carolina; also in the Pacific states and western Canada.

PROPAGATION   Same as for *S. amplexi-folius.*

Trillium   Trillium

These lovely spring wild flowers are among the easiest to identify and are also easy to introduce into wild gardens. The name refers to the general make-up of the plant. It has three leaves whorled around a solitary stem with a single terminal flower having three white or colored petals and three green sepals. It is impossible to pick the flower without also removing the leaves, and this may cause the death of the tuber-like rhizome. All species blossom in the spring.

T. cernuum   Nodding Trillium

The stem of this species is from 6 to 18 inches tall, the leaves without much petiole. In May and June the flower is borne on a short stalk which curves downward, almost hiding the nodding white flower beneath the leaves. The plant does well in the moist wild garden.

This species prefers moist woods and swamps in moderately acid soil. It is found from Newfoundland and Quebec to Pennsylvania and Delaware.

PROPAGATION By seeds sown in March ½-inch deep in leafy soil, or sown outside in fall, as soon as ripe, removed from the pulp but still wet.

By division in the summer before the roots go dormant.

T. erectum   Purple Trillium

This species sometimes sends up several stout stems as much as 2 feet tall, making very strong clumps. The leaves are broad and overlapping. The long flower stalk bears a dull red or dark purple flower well above the leaves which has a disagreeable odor. The species may also have yellow or white flowers that lack the unpleasant smell.

T. erectum grows in rich cool woods of varying acidity and moisture. It is found from Quebec and Ontario to Massachusetts and Ohio, south to North Carolina, Georgia, and Tennessee.

PROPAGATION Same as for *T. cernuum*, but division is possible, and seedlings are often abundant.

T. grandiflorum   Great or Snow Trillium

Perhaps the most beloved of the trilliums, this species has a single stem 6 to 18 inches tall, with three broad, pointed leaves, rounded at the base, without petioles. The long flower stalk is erect, the pure white petals much longer than the green sepals, turning pink with age. This is the only trillium that does not want an acid soil. It will form large colonies in favorable situations. The trilliums respond to a yearly mulch of very old manure, rotted wood, compost, or leaf mold.

This species grows in rich moist woods in neutral or slightly acid soil. Its range is from Quebec and Maine to Minnesota, south to Pennsylvania, Ohio, Indiana, and Arkansas, and in the mountains to Georgia.

PROPAGATION   By seeds separated from the pulp, and sown at once.

By division, but rarely to be tried, as the rhizome has few offsets.

This species sometimes produces double or four-parted flowers, in which case the plant can be propagated by making a shallow incision under the pointed bud at the top of the rhizome, in late spring. Little offsets appear around the wound and can be transplanted the second year.

T. nivale   Dwarf White Trillium

This delightful little plant should be seen more often. It is an extremely early species, almost the first wild flower to blossom. It grows about 4 inches high. The small white flowers have petals less than an inch long and blossom in March and April.

T. nivale is found in rich woods and on shaded ledges in slightly acid to neutral soil and should do well in a shaded rock garden. The range is from Pennsylvania and Kentucky to Minnesota and Iowa.

PROPAGATION   Same as for *T. cernuum.*

T. sessile   Toad Trillium

This species is more curious than beautiful. The very dark red or yellow flowers have small erect petals and are sessile, resting directly upon the leaves, which are also sessile and mottled with brown. An easy plant for the wild garden in light soil in partial shade, flowering in April and May, its natural home is in moist neutral soil in rich woods, ranging from Pennsylvania to Missouri, south to Virginia, Tennessee, and Arkansas.

PROPAGATION   Same as for *T. cernuum.*

T. undulatum   Painted Trillium

This is a difficult species and should not be tried in the average wild garden. It requires cold peaty, strongly acid soil and is often found in swamps. In this species the wavy-edged white petals are strongly marked with a crimson V at the base. It flowers in May and June.

This species is found in cold wet woods from Quebec and Ontario to New Jersey and Pennsylvania, south in the mountains to Tennessee.

PROPAGATION   Same as for *T. cernuum,*
     but with much moisture and highly acid
     soil.

Uvularia perfoliata   Bellwort or Merry-bells

A favorite, dependable wild flower, this bellwort is suitable for the average wild garden where the soil is only moderately acid.

The plant grows in erect leafy clumps with forked stems about 2 feet tall. One to four smooth oblong gray-green leaves clasp the stem below the fork. At the tip of each fork there is one nodding pale corn-yellow bell-shaped flower about an inch long which blossoms in May and June. The fruit is an interesting fleshy winged capsule with few seeds.

This plant is found in moist woods from Quebec and New England south to Florida, Tennessee, and Ohio.

PROPAGATION   By division in the early spring or when dormant in the fall.

By seeds separated from the capsule and sown in autumn.

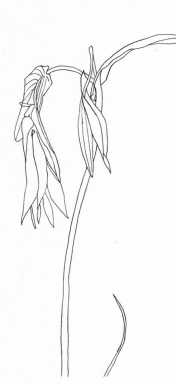

U. grandiflora   Great Merry-bells

This is the more common species west or south of New England. The flowers are bright yellow, blossoming in April and May, and the leaves are finely hairy beneath.

U. grandiflora prefers a neutral or limy soil and is found in rich woods from Quebec to Minnesota, south to Connecticut, West Virginia, Tennessee, and Oklahoma.

PROPAGATION   Same as for *U. perfoliata.*

U. sessilifolia   Wild-oats

The sight of this little bellwort always recalls a childhood belief that the "wild oats" sown by questionable citizens were in some way connected with this innocent flower. It is a good addition to the spring wild garden, making great patches in moist woods. The narrow oval deep-green leaves, grayish beneath, are sessile. The one or two straw-colored flowers on slender drooping stalks near the tip of the angled stem appear in April and May.

This is an excellent ground cover under deciduous trees. It grows 1 foot tall.

This plant is common in moderately acid open woods from New Brunswick to North Dakota, south to New England, Georgia, and Missouri.

PROPAGATION Same as for *U. perfoliata*.

Veratrum viride False Hellebore

This coarse, poisonous perennial, from 3 to 5 feet tall, is a good accent plant in the moist wild garden. The short broad, ribbed, clasping leaves are alternate up the stem in three rows, and wither early. The uninteresting yellowish-green flowers are borne in a terminal panicle in June and July.

V. viride is found in swamps and wet woods from Quebec to Ontario, south to North Carolina and from Alaska to Oregon.

PROPAGATION Transplants with difficulty in spring.

Yucca filamentosa Adam's Needle

For an imposing effect in dry sandy soil there is no better plant than yucca. This species has long, leathery evergreen leaves with loose threads on the margin and with a sharp needle-like tip. The leafless flower stalk, which may be 8 feet tall, bears a panicle of many drooping white flowers in June and July.

This species grows from a huge woody root, thriving in pure sand, and is found near the coast from Maryland to Georgia. It is often cultivated in northern gardens.

PROPAGATION By side shoots from the main plant.

By root cuttings. If seed is produced, it germinates as readily as that of onions.

Y. glauca   Soapweed or Beargrass

This smaller species forms leafy multiple crowns of narrow, blue-green, evergreen bayonet-shaped leaves. In June and July small greenish-white bells blossom in a long spike on a woody leafless stem 4 feet tall. It is sometimes seen in eastern gardens.

Y. glauca is found on dry prairies of the Midwest.

PROPAGATION   Same as for *Y. filamentosa.*

AMARYLLIDACEAE
Amaryllis Family

This family is closely related to the Lily Family, differing primarily in its inferior ovary.

Agave virginica   False Aloe

In regions not subjected to subzero temperatures, false aloe would add interest to a sunny, sandy wild garden. It has the century plant's characteristic rosette of fleshy sword-shaped leaves, sometimes with spiny teeth, but deciduous in autumn. In summer, night-fragrant greenish-yellow flowers are borne in abundance in a loose slender spike at the summit of a tall scape up to 6 feet high.

This plant is found in poor dry soil from North Carolina to Ohio and Missouri, south to Florida and Texas.

PROPAGATION   By seeds sown in the spring after collecting in the autumn.

By division in the spring.

Hymenocallis occidentalis   Spider-Lily

This is an excellent species for cultivating on the borders of ponds in southern gardens. The plant has long sessile basal leaves and in August it bears a terminal umbel of large white sessile flowers with six linear spreading divisions on a scape 2 feet tall. The flowers are unique and interesting because of the conspicuous membrane which joins the stamen filaments and forms a broad inner crown.

This plant is found in wooded swamps from Indiana and Missouri south to the Gulf. It would be hardy somewhat farther north.

PROPAGATION   By division in the spring.

Hypoxis hirsuta   Stargrass

This delightful small perennial grows 6 inches tall from a tiny corm-like rhizome and is found in dry open woods and fields in acid soil. It has grass-like, hairy, erect basal leaves and bright yellow star-like flowers on slender leafless stalks either singly or in an irregular umbel of two to six, flowering in June and occasionally through the summer.

H. hirsuta is found from Maine to Manitoba, south to Georgia, Mississippi, and Texas.

PROPAGATION   By division of offsets.
By seeds, but rarely has the gardener the luck to find them.

Zephyranthes Atamasco   Zephyr-Lily

In early spring in southern meadows and damp clearings, especially where the grass has been mowed, these small white lilies, about 3 inches tall, with several narrow shining leaves are often produced in great profusion.

This plant is found in moist woods and meadows from Virginia to Alabama. It is doubtfully hardy where the ground freezes deeply.

PROPAGATION   By division in early summer when the bulb is growing.

By seeds sown in April in leafy soil.

Z. candida

Like Atamasco, but fall flowering.

PROPAGATION   Same as for Z. *Atamasco*.

IRIDACEAE   Iris Family

Members of this popular family are easily identified. The flower parts are in threes. Their bases unite into a long tube that connects with an inferior ovary. Irises have mostly erect basal sword-like flattened leaves and grow from rhizomes, corms, bulbs, or fibrous roots.

Iris cristata   Crested Iris

Although all the native irises are without beards on their falls, thereby being unlike the familiar bearded iris of perennial gardens, there are two dwarf species whose falls bear a fringy yellow crest. This crested iris with handsome lavender-blue flowers over 2 inches across reaches a height of about 6 inches. It spreads by running, wiry stems and makes large mats when thriving. It is hardy in northern gardens.

This species is found in rich moist woods and on rocky and sandy slopes in neutral or moderately acid soil, in sun or shade, from Maryland to Oklahoma and Georgia. It flowers in April and May and is a perfect species for the. spring wild garden in a variety of locations.

PROPAGATION   By division of stolons in spring.

By seeds but the hidden capsules are not easily seen.

I. lacustris   Dwarf Lake Iris

This is a similar but smaller species, and needs both moisture and coolness. It is native to the wet sands of the Great Lakes Region in neutral soil.

PROPAGATION   Same as for *I. cristata*.

I. fulva   Copper Iris

This strong-growing species is an example of the famous Louisiana irises, considered among the most remarkable in existence. There are many species and hybrids. This species is slender with bright green leaves, and in May and June it bears a flower stalk 2 feet tall with two or three terminal red-brown flowers borne well above the foliage. It is excellent for the moist wild garden.

I. fulva is found in ditches and swamps in neutral or moderately acid soil from Illinois and Missouri to Georgia and Louisiana.

PROPAGATION   By division in the spring or after flowering.

By seeds sown in pots; keep wet.

I. prismatica   Slender Blue Flag

A desirable species for a really moist small wild or bog garden, this plant slowly forms small colonies of slender wiry stems, 2 feet tall, with narrow grass-like leaves. In June and July there are one or two flat blue-violet flowers, about three inches across, with yellow sepal bases.

This species is found in marshes and damp meadows near the coast from Nova Scotia to Georgia. It needs acid sandy or peaty soil.

PROPAGATION   By seeds sown in fall or spring.

By division in the spring or after flowering.

May be transplanted where abundant.

I. Pseudacorus   Yellow Iris

This robust European immigrant has escaped from gardens over a wide area. It makes strong clumps of long wide leaves on the margins of streams and ponds. The large yellow terminal flowers come in May on stems over 3 feet tall. This is an indestructible plant for the water garden, but will also grow in dry ground.

PROPAGATION   By division in spring or fall.

By seeds. It self-sows widely.

I. verna   Dwarf Iris or Vernal Iris

A dwarf southern species, it is found in dry pinelands and moist sandy open woods in very acid soil. The solitary lavender-blue flowers are but a few inches above the ground and close to the foliage. Each fall bears a bright orange band. The flowers appear in

April and May. The old leaves are leathery
and the black, wiry roots are attached directly
to the crown of the plant without any conspicuous length of rhizome.

This species is found from Georgia to Mississippi, Kentucky, and Pennsylvania, being
most abundant on the Coastal Plain.

PROPAGATION   By division in July. Cut
through the old rhizome after flowering
when the new offsets show roots.
Leave old plants undisturbed.

I. versicolor   Blue Flag

As large and robust as *I. Pseudacorus,* this
species makes large colonies in wet meadows,
casting a purple haze on the spring landscape when they are in flower. The plants are
erect with abundant dark green foliage and
showy terminal purple blossoms in May and
June. They are easily grown in the moist wild
garden.

This species is common in neutral to moderately acid soil in marshes and wet meadows
from Newfoundland to Manitoba, south to
Virginia and Minnesota. There are similar
more southern species.

PROPAGATION   By division in spring.
By seeds. It self-sows freely.

Sisyrinchium angustifolium   Blue-eyed Grass

When a wet meadow is filled with stiff
little clumps of this plant in full bloom, it is a
charming sight. They are seldom over 1 foot
tall and blossom in May and June. They have
narrow blue-green leaves, flat stems, and small
rich blue six-parted flowers in loose clusters,
each flower lasting but a few hours.

The plant requires wet soil in full sun, and grows from Newfoundland, Ontario, and Minnesota south to Pennsylvania and Indiana.

PROPAGATION   By division in spring or fall.

By seeds sown in late winter.

ORCHIDACEAE   Orchid Family

The flowers of the orchid family are in six parts. There are three sepals, two of them united in most cases, two similar lateral petals, and a third petal markedly different from the others, called the lip. The fruit is a capsule with thousands of dust-like seeds, few of which germinate.

The orchids are desperately in need of intelligent handling on the part of wild flower gardeners. Their culture, for many species, is still a mystery. This is particularly true of species demanding very acid soil. Many are presumably short-lived even in nature.

Cypripedium acaule   Stemless Lady's-slipper

This species is mentioned because practically every wild flower gardener tries to grow it, only to lose it within a year or two. It is a waste of time to plant this orchid in areas where none are already growing. There are probably exceptions to this statement, but they are few.

The plant has two hairy basal leaves close to the ground. The flower has a pink moccasin-shaped lip with red veins, the other petals and the sepals being bronzy. It blossoms in May.

This species requires very acid soil and grows in dry woods, swamps, and bogs from Newfoundland and Quebec to Alberta, south to New Jersey and Indiana, and along the mountains and the Coastal Plain to South Carolina and Alabama.

PROPAGATION   Some claim success by planting seeds in soil from around the parent plants mixed with *old* decayed pine needles, peat or leaf mold, and sand.

By division in spring and placed where plants of this species are already growing.

C. *Calceolus* var. *pubescens*
Large Yellow Lady's-slipper

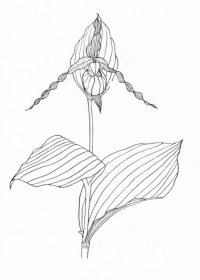

Very satisfactory in the wild garden, this beautiful orchid makes large crowns which will increase in size and persist for many years. It is a leafy plant with a stem from 18 to 24 inches tall. It has broad ovate leaves and terminal flowers; the lip is pale yellow, and the sepals and lateral petals are greenish-yellow to purplish-brown.

This species is found in bogs and moist deciduous woods in slightly acid or neutral soil, flowering in May. Plants in the wild garden respond to an annual top-dressing of rotted wood, compost, or leaf mold. The range of this species is from Newfoundland to northwest Canada, south to South Carolina, Louisiana, and New Mexico.

PROPAGATION   By division in spring. Plant in neutral or slightly acid, loose humus-filled soil. Keep shaded.

C. *Calceolus* var. *parviflorum*
Small Yellow Lady's-slipper

This species is similar to the preceding, but smaller. The sepals and spiraled lateral petals are bronzy, while the lip is bright golden yellow, about an inch long, marked with purplish lines.

This species requires cold wet rich neutral to moderately acid soil and part shade. It flowers in May and June and is found throughout Canada and the northeastern states, south in the mountains to Alabama and westward.

PROPAGATION   Same as for *C. Calceolus* var. *pubescens.*

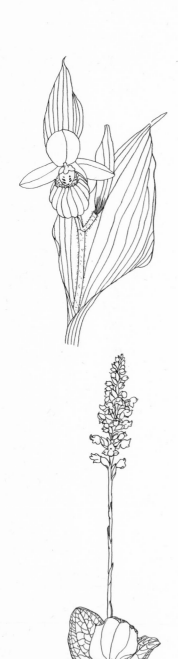

C. reginae   Showy Lady's-slipper

Fortunate, indeed, is the wild flower gardener who can provide a congenial environment for this lovely orchid. It grows in swamps and wet woods in neutral soil and may reach a height of 30 inches. The plant is rather coarse with a hairy, leafy stem. The white flowers with a bright pink lip are solitary or in small groups, blossoming in June and July. Old plants form large clumps and live for many years. The north side of a building or stone wall makes a suitable place for this plant if the right soil and amount of moisture have been provided.

This species is found from Newfoundland and Quebec to North Dakota, south to North Carolina, Georgia, and Missouri. It is mostly a northern species.

PROPAGATION   Same as for *C. Calceolus* var. *pubescens.*

Goodyera pubescens
                    Downy Rattlesnake-plantain

Very noticeable in winter, this plant forms mats of dark green ovate leaves with white veins in dry acid pine and oak woods. In July, little white tubular flowers with a small lip are borne in dense, many-flowered racemes on a downy stalk from 6 to 15 inches tall. The foliage is more important than the flowers.

This species is found from Newfoundland to Minnesota, south to North Carolina, Alabama, and Missouri.

PROPAGATION   By division at any time in the growing season.

By cuttings taken in the fall and planted in a cold frame or cool greenhouse over winter.

ARISTOLOCHIACEAE
Birthwort Family

This family contains plants with entire heart-shaped leaves and aromatic sap. The reddish brown flowers have three sepals, the petals being obsolete.

Asarum canadense   Wild Ginger

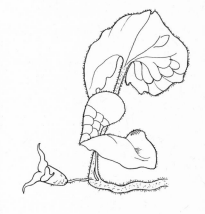

An easy and satisfactory ground cover for a woodland wild garden in slightly acid to neutral soil, this low hairy plant, a few inches high, grows from creeping fleshy underground stems with two large kidney-shaped deciduous leaves, about 6 inches wide at their tips. The curious solitary brown-purple flowers, borne close to the ground in the forks between the leaf stalks, are not easily seen. They blossom in April and May.

This species is found in rich woods and on shaded calcareous ledges from Quebec to Minnesota, south to North Carolina, Kentucky, and Illinois.

PROPAGATION   By division in the spring.

By cuttings of the rhizomes inserted in sand and peat.

By transplanting, where abundant.

A. virginicum   Heartleaf

This southern species is hardy in northern gardens. It has broad heart-shaped evergreen leaves, smaller than the preceding, in
thick crowns. The leaves are often mottled.

This plant occurs in acid leaf mold in
sandy, peaty, or rocky woods from Virginia to
South Carolina and Tennessee.

PROPAGATION   Same as for *A. canadense.*

A. europeaum, the European wild ginger,
with roundish, shining, evergreen leaves, has
long been a favorite garden plant and should
be used with the above species.

PHYTOLACCACEAE
Pokeweed Family

This is a family of coarse plants almost
shrub-like in growth, with branched groups
of small flowers with five sepals, the petals
being obsolete.

Phytolacca americana   Common Pokeberry

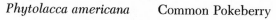

Once established in the wild garden in
rich moist soil, pokeberry self-sows and often
forms colonies of stout woody plants that may
grow more than 5 feet tall. The plant has
smooth, alternate leaves. In July, long erect
racemes of greenish to purplish or white flowers are borne which later droop down under
the weight of the dark purple fruits, much
loved by birds. The thick roots and the mature
foliage are poisonous when eaten.

PROPAGATION   Young plants may be
transplanted.

Birds are sure to sow seeds for new
plants.

It often comes in on newly disturbed
ground.

Seeds may be separated from the pulp and sown in the fall.

PORTULACACEAE
Purslane Family

This family includes herbs with succulent leaves which are usually opposite. The flowers, mostly with five petals, may be regular, or not entirely so, the sepals sometimes fewer than the petals, the stamens often of an indefinite number. The stamens are opposite the petals when of the same number.

Claytonia virginica   Spring-beauty

One must make trips to the woods in very early spring to see this delightful little plant at its best. It sends up simple stems, 4 to 6 inches high, from a small tuber, each stem bearing a pair of opposite narrow leaves and loose racemes of five-petaled pink flowers with deeper veining. The plant is a splendid ground cover for the spring wild garden.

This species covers large areas in rich open woods and grassy thickets in a variety of soils from Newfoundland, Saskatchewan, and Minnesota, south through New England and the mountains of North Carolina to Georgia, Louisiana, and Texas.

A rough, semishaded bank separating two city houselots, in eastern Massachusetts, has the finest carpet of spring-beauty imaginable. It is an almost unbelievable sight in early spring.

PROPAGATION   By division in the spring or fall.

By seeds sown as soon as ripe. The plant self-sows.

C. caroliniana is similar with wider leaves and fewer flowers.

CARYOPHYLLACEAE
Pink Family

These plants have smooth stems and swollen joints, with opposite leaves, smooth, entire, and usually narrow. The flower parts are mostly in fives.

Lychnis Flos-cuculi   Ragged-Robin

Although introduced from Europe, this slender plant, escaped from old gardens, deserves a place in the moist, sunny wild garden. It is downy below, slightly sticky, and has a few narrowly lanceolate leaves widely spaced. The ragged flowers, deeply four-lobed, are a clear shade of pink, and blossom in June and July. The plant is becoming more common in the wild.

PROPAGATION   By seeds sown in the spring.
      By division in the spring.
      By cuttings taken in the summer.
      Easily transplanted where abundant.

Saponaria officinalis   Bouncing-Bet

Suitable for planting in sunny, gravelly waste places in a large wild garden, this common perennial, introduced from Europe, grows about 2 feet tall. The plant has oval leaves and dense clusters of pale pink flowers, about an inch across with five shallowly notched petals. It flowers over a long period in summer. The plant spreads rapidly from underground stems.

PROPAGATION   By division in the spring.
      By seeds sown in the fall.

Silene caroliniana Wild Pink

This tufted little plant has loose clusters of clear pink flowers with sticky hairs on the sepals. It grows from 4 to 9 inches high and blossoms in May. The rather small leaves are oblong. It is a desirable species for dry banks in the wild garden and is especially attractive planted with *Viola pedata.* It is not a long-lived plant.

This species is found on dry rocky and sandy slopes in moderately acid soil in North and South Carolina.

The variety *pensylvanica,* which is similar, occurs north to southern New Hampshire, Ohio, and Tennessee.

PROPAGATION By seeds sown in the early spring.

By division in the spring.

By large softwood cuttings in late summer.

S. regia Royal Catchfly

A species found in dry soils on the prairies and in open woodlands from Ohio and Missouri, south to Alabama and Georgia, this short-lived but showy plant has sessile, finely downy leaves and rather long narrow terminal panicles of scarlet flowers, blossoming in July. It grows from 3 to 4 feet tall.

PROPAGATION By seeds sown in the spring.

S. virginica *Fire-Pink*

Another southern species with large bright red flowers, fire-pink has stems about 1 foot tall. It blossoms in spring and summer in open

woods, thickets, and on sandy slopes in neutral or moderately acid soil.

This species is found from Ontario to
Minnesota, south to Georgia, Alabama, and
Oklahoma.

PROPAGATION   By seeds sown in the
early spring.

By cuttings taken in the later summer.

N Y M P H A E A C E A E Water-Lily Family

This family includes aquatic plants with
coarse, creeping stems, floating leaves, and
large solitary flowers with few sepals and
numerous petals grading into stamens. The
seeds are large and plentiful.

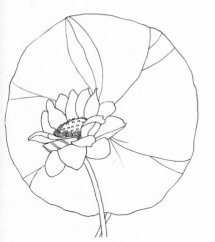

Nelumbo lutea   American Lotus

This strong-growing aquatic has round,
shield-like leaves, 1 to 2 feet across, raised
above the water on long petioles, the stem
attached centrally. It has pale yellow solitary,
many-petaled flowers, over 6 inches across,
also carried high above the water. They appear
in summer. The fruiting receptacle is funnel-
shaped and much appreciated for dried flower
arrangements. The roots run widely in water
at least 2 feet deep and do well if not crowded,
so that the plant is useless in small pools and
tubs. Unfortunately muskrats eat the tubers.

This plant is found in ponds and quiet
streams from Florida to Texas, northward,
locally, in widely separated areas.

PROPAGATION   By rooted runners in
May, which soon make new tubers.

Nuphar advena   Yellow Pond-lily or Cow-lily

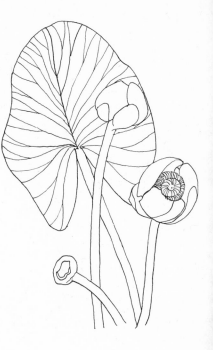

Another aquatic not suited to small pools, this species has large floating heart-shaped leaves sometimes held above the water on rounded petioles, the plant creeping forward slowly by stout rootstalks. The solitary round-ish deep yellow flowers are 3 inches across, have five or six incurved sepals and tiny petals, the disk of the stigma pale green and promi-nent in the center of the flower. It blossoms from June to August and is good for large ponds where the water is at least 2 to 4 feet deep.

This plant is found from Florida to Texas, north to New England, Ohio, Michigan, Wis-consin, and Nebraska.

PROPAGATION   Collect the rhizomes in May and June or later and anchor them with rocks until established.

Nymphaea tetragona   Pygmy Water-lily

This species should be used in small pools and tubs. It is a little plant growing from small erect tubers in shallow water from 1 to 2 feet deep. The small thin floating leaves do not hide the water and the little nonfragrant white flowers are open from noon to about 5:00 P.M., blooming throughout the summer.

This plant is found in cold ponds and lakes from Maine and Ontario to Michigan and Idaho, northward.

PROPAGATION   By seeds, which must be kept wet.

By transplanting if the plants are suf-ficiently abundant.

There are various other species of water-lilies useful for the large water garden.

N. odorata

Fragrant Water-lily or Pond-lily

This highly desirable aquatic will grow in shallow water from 1 to 2 feet deep and is splendid for medium-sized pools. The plant has round leaves and solitary floating, very fragrant flowers with many petals. The flowers are usually white but are occasionally pale pink and beautiful, blossoming in July and August and opening only in the morning. Muskrats eat the tubers.

This species is found in quiet waters from Newfoundland to Manitoba, Minnesota, and Michigan, south on the Coastal Plain to Florida and Texas.

PROPAGATION   Transplant in summer or fall, weighting down the roots until established.

RANUNCULACEAE

Crowfoot Family

This is a large family many of whose members have handsome dissected leaves. The flowers may have many petals or none, with the sepals often colored like petals. The sepals, petals, numerous stamens, and few or many pistils are all distinct and separate from one another.

Aquilegia canadensis   Wild Columbine

These graceful, erect plants, from 1 to 2 feet tall, have long-stemmed, mostly basal, compound leaves, two or three times divided, the leaflets lobed. The large nodding flowers have five yellow petals culminating in red spurs and five red sepals. Common in dry woods and on rocky cliffs and ledges in a variety of soils, this is one of the easiest and most desirable species for the spring wild garden in part shade. If given too rich and

moist soil, the plants lose their delicate appearance and grow more like cultivated columbine in the perennial border; they are also
more short-lived. They prefer moderately to
slightly acid soil.

This species is found from Nova Scotia to
Saskatchewan, south to Florida and Texas.

PROPAGATION   By seeds in spring or
    fall. The plant self-sows freely.

Actaea pachypoda
                White Baneberry or Doll's-eyes

The baneberries are very useful in the
shaded wild garden because they are easily
grown and attractive at all times. They are
bushy woodland plants, 2 feet or more tall,
with large compound, three-, four- or five-
parted leaves, the leaflets toothed and lobed.
The small white flowers, borne in May and
June, are in short thick terminal racemes followed by berry-like fruits.

White baneberry has china-white berries with a purple spot at the tip on a thick
fleshy red stalk. Sometimes the berries are a
pinkish red.

This plant is found in rich woods and
thickets, often in neutral soil, from Quebec to
Ontario and Minnesota, south to Georgia and
Oklahoma.

PROPAGATION   By division in the spring.
    By seeds sown in the fall, separated
    from the pulp.

A. rubra   Red Baneberry

This species is similar to white baneberry,
the leaflets not so deeply cut or sharply
toothed. The red berries are in thick clusters
on slender wiry stalks. In the wild garden the
two baneberries with blue cohosh and golden-

seal would make a striking grouping of berried plants with beautiful foliage.

Red baneberry is found in rich woods in moderately acid soil from Labrador and Newfoundland to Alaska, south to Connecticut, New Jersey, Indiana, and Iowa, west to Arizona.

PROPAGATION   Same as for *A. pachypoda*.

Anemone patens var. *Wolfgangiana*
Pasque-flower

The most showy of American species of anemone, this beautiful wild flower should be in every spring wild garden. The large solitary purple blossoms, 2 inches across, are on hairy stalks about 8 inches tall, appearing in early spring. The hairy basal leaves are much cut into slender divisions. The numerous feathery fruits give the plant its other common name of prairie smoke. This species grows in sun on plains and hillsides in dry soil. When once established it should not be disturbed.

This species is found from Alaska to Texas, extending east on dry barrens to Wisconsin and Illinois.

PROPAGATION   By seeds sown as soon as ripe or in the early spring. Before sowing remove the plumy tails.

By root cuttings taken in the late summer. These should be at least ⅛-inch in diameter and 1 inch long. The tips should protrude from the soil.

A. quinquefolia
Windflower or American Wood Anemone

Windflowers are known to all who roam the woods in early spring. The slender plants,

3 to 5 inches tall, have creeping, white root-stocks. The leaves are few, mostly near the base, with three, four, or five pointed lobes. They are pinkish when unfolding. The stem leaves are in whorls which form a kind of involucre below the flower. The size and position of the stem leaves varies with different species and helps in identifying them. In the windflower they are similar to the base leaves, but smaller. The flowers are solitary and nodding, their drooping sepals white or pinkish, four to nine in number.

This species is found in open woods and thickets from Nova Scotia to Georgia, west to Ohio and Kentucky. It blossoms in April and May. It often occurs in moderately acid soil.

PROPAGATION   By seeds sown as soon as ripe.

By root division in the spring.

By stem cuttings in the fall.

A. *caroliniana*   Carolina Anemone

This attractive southern representative of the anemones is a tuberous rooted perennial and grows 1 foot tall. The basal leaves are deeply three-parted, the segments being irregularly divided and deeply cut. The involucre occurs much below the middle of the flower stem. The blossoms are solitary with ten to twenty narrow sepals which are white to rose in color. Since the plant prefers dry stony ground, it is suitable for rock gardens.

This species blooms in April and May in countless numbers on dry prairies, barrens, and calcareous gravel soils from Indiana to South Dakota, south to Louisiana, Texas, and Georgia.

PROPAGATION   Same as for A. *quinquefolia*.

Anemonella thalictroides   Rue-Anemone

This beautiful slender, wiry-stemmed little plant, 3 to 6 inches tall, which springs from a cluster of tuberous roots, is not a true anemone. It has one compound basal leaf resembling a tiny meadow-rue, and a whorl of stem leaves, smaller than the basal one, below a cluster of white flowers. The blossoms have five to ten sepals on long, fragile pedicels, flowering in May and June.

The plant is found in moderately acid soil, in open woods, from Maine to Florida, west to Minnesota and Oklahoma. The flowers of western plants are pinker in color.

PROPAGATION   By seeds sown outside or in containers, in the fall.

Large clumps may be divided after the foliage has died down.

A. canadensis   Meadow Anemone

This anemone, which blossoms in June, is taller and coarser in habit than the fragile species of early spring. It is desirable for the large wild garden. This plant grows into large patches in moist meadows, roadside ditches and open woods. The broad leaves are deeply three-, four- or five-parted, hairy and sharply toothed. The stem leaves are similar, but sessile, and are at the base of the solitary long-stalked flowers, which have five white sepals, many stamens, and are often more than an inch across. The plant grows 2 feet high and makes a good companion for the pale magenta wild geranium which it resembles in general size and habit of growth. Both are best adapted to truly wild spots in the garden and, although desirable, cannot easily be kept under control.

This species is found in a variety of soils from Quebec and Nova Scotia, south to New Jersey and Pennsylvania, west to Colorado.

PROPAGATION   Same as for *A. quinque-folia,* and usually spring division is adequate.

Other strong-growing, summer-flowering species of anemone are the thimbleweeds. These have insignificant flowers with five or six greenish white sepals set on long stems. The central cone of the flower is thimble-shaped and later becomes a cottony mass of seeds. Thimbleweeds have little decorative value for the wild garden with the exception of *A. riparia,* the riverbank anemone, with large white flowers and smoother stems and leaves than similar species. This plant is found from Quebec to Michigan and Minnesota, south to Connecticut and Maryland, in open woods and on rocky banks.

Caltha palustris   Marsh-Marigold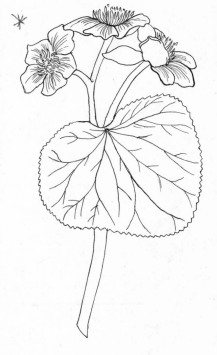

In early spring, wet meadows, swamps, and brooksides become gay with the shining bright gold flowers of marsh-marigold. This species has alternate smooth roundish, toothed leaves which are mostly basal. The flowers with five to nine sepals are clustered at the top of hollow stems up to 2 feet tall. The plant disappears in summer. If put where the ground is very wet, in spring, it can become fairly dry later in the season without suffering.

This plant is found from Labrador to Alaska, south to South Carolina, Tennessee, Iowa, and Nebraska.

PROPAGATION   By division in the early spring or after flowering.

By seeds sown in wet soil as soon as they are ripe. It self-sows freely.

By transplanting at any time, where abundant.

C. americana   American Bugbane

This species grows only 3 feet tall. It has smaller leaves than those of *C. racemosa*. The flowers appear in late August and September, often taken by frost before they finish blooming. It is a beautiful species for the wild garden and for cultivated borders.

This plant is found in moist woods, chiefly in the mountains, from Pennsylvania and West Virginia to Georgia and Tennessee.

PROPAGATION   Same as for *C. racemosa*.

Cimicifuga racemosa
           Black Snakeroot or Black Cohosh

Often used as a background plant in the perennial border, this species should be similarly used in the shaded wild garden where there is room for very large specimens. This is an erect plant often reaching a height of 8 feet. The large compound, two or three times ternately divided leaves are noticeable throughout the season, and the long wand-like racemes of small white flowers, from July to September, blossom at a time when there is little to see in the shaded garden.

This species is found in moderately acid soil in rich woods from western Massachusetts to Ontario, south to Georgia and Missouri.

PROPAGATION   By division of the large crowns in spring.

By seeds sown in frames, ½-inch deep, in the fall.

Clematis virginiana   Virgin's-bower

There are many opportunities in the wild garden to make good use of this desirable woody vine which supports itself by a twist in the leaf petiole. It clambers over walls and bushes to a length of 30 feet. In late summer the small white flowers with four sepals are borne in panicles from many leaf axils, the opposite, compound leaves of three leaflets being coarsely toothed. The plumy seed clusters are also attractive in the fall. The vine seems to have no bad habits and is easier to keep in bounds than groundnut which grows in similar places. The two vines can well be used together in a large, sunny garden.

This species is found in moderately acid soil from Nova Scotia and Quebec to Manitoba, south to Georgia and Louisiana.

PROPAGATION   By seeds sown in the spring or fall, first removing the plumes.

By layering the long stems.

By transplanting in spring, where abundant.

C. ochroleuca   Leather Flower

There are various species of native clematis which do not climb. This one has opposite, rounded leaves on stems from 1 to 2 feet tall. The solitary terminal nodding flowers are dull yellow to purple, blossoming in April and May. The plumy fruits have tails of a brownish-yellow color.

This species is found in acid, gravelly soils, in thickets and on rocky slopes from southern New York to Georgia.

PROPAGATION   By seeds sown in the fall. Remove the tails before planting.

Coptis groenlandica   Goldthread

In May and June, damp mossy woods and bogs are starred with the little solitary white flowers of goldthread. This small evergreen creeps by little yellow roots. It has shining three-parted, lobed leaves on stems a few inches high. The flower has five, six, or seven sepals. It is an excellent plant for the large or small bog garden and will grow in sun, although it prefers some shade, and acid soil.

This plant is found from Greenland to Manitoba, south to New Jersey, the mountains of North Carolina, Tennessee, and to Iowa.

PROPAGATION   By seeds, sown in fall.
By division in spring.
Where abundant, large sods transplant well.

Delphinium exaltatum   Tall Larkspur

The native perennial larkspurs are mostly to be found in the southern and western sections of the country. They are similar to the garden sorts. This species may grow 6 feet tall with numerous leaves three, four, or five times cleft. The blue or white flowers are in a loose, slender raceme. The upper sepal of the flower is prolonged into a spur. It flowers in July and August in slightly acid soil.

This species is found in rich woods and thickets from Pennsylvania to North Carolina and Alabama, west to Ohio and Tennessee.

PROPAGATION   By seeds sown in the fall or spring.
By division in the spring.

D. carolinianum   Carolina Larkspur

This is a downy, more slender plant than the preceding, not exceeding 2 feet in height. The brilliant sky-blue flowers blossom through May, June, and July. It grows in dry woods, and on prairies and sand hills from Illinois and Missouri to South Carolina, Florida, and Texas.

PROPAGATION   Same as for *D. exaltatum*.

D. tricorne   Rock Larkspur

This is a common species in the prairie states. It is especially desirable for the wild garden because it blossoms in early spring, beginning in April. The flowers are blue or violet, sometimes variegated.

This species grows 2 feet tall in open woods, thickets, and by roadsides and on calcareous slopes from Pennsylvania to Minnesota and Nebraska, south to Georgia and Oklahoma.

PROPAGATION   By seeds sown in the fall or spring.

By division of the tuberous roots.

Hepatica americana   Round-lobed Hepatica

Among the earliest of spring wild flowers, these dainty blossoms with five or more blue, rose, or white sepals emerge from their furry buds on the first warm days. The low plants have thick basal leaves with three or rarely five rounded lobes, the new ones appearing after the flowers have faded. There are three conspicuous bracts behind the flowers. Hepaticas grow in dry, moderately acid soil in deciduous woods and need some sun when blossoming. They grow on wooded slopes and should be in every spring wild garden.

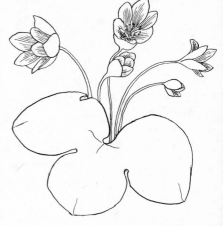

This species is found from Nova Scotia to Manitoba, south to Florida, Alabama, and Missouri.

PROPAGATION   By division after flowering.

By seeds. It self-sows readily.

H. acutiloba   Sharp-lobed Hepatica

This hepatica forms much stronger clumps than the preceding, and often grows on limestone soil. Actually, it is somewhat indifferent to soil reaction. The leaves have three sharp-pointed lobes, and the pale-colored flowers are more numerous than those of *H. americana*.

This species is found in rich woods from Maine to Minnesota, south to Georgia, Alabama, and Missouri.

PROPAGATION   Same as for *H. americana*, but in neutral soil.

Hydrastis canadensis   Golden-seal

This plant has a thick knotted yellow rhizome which in April sends up a single heavily veined round basal leaf, palmately cut into broad sharp-toothed lobes, and a hairy stem, two-leaved near the summit, terminated by a solitary greenish-white flower. This is followed by a close head of orange-red berries in late summer. The root having medicinal value, the plant has nearly been exterminated. This is an unusual selection for the wild garden in partial shade and in moist rich neutral or slightly acid soil.

Golden-seal is found from Vermont to Michigan and Minnesota, south to Virginia, Tennessee, and Arkansas.

PROPAGATION   By seeds sown in moist, sandy soil in the fall or early spring. Cover with a slight mulch.

By division of the roots in early spring or fall.

Ranunculus   Buttercup

The buttercups are too weedy to include in any but the largest of wild gardens. Many of them are introduced species and are even greater pests than the native ones. Lesser celandine, *R. Ficaria,* is an outstanding example of an introduced pest in moist soils, although it is quite attractive when in flower.

R. bulbosus   Bulbous Buttercup

This European native grows from a bulblike root to about 1 foot tall. The three-parted leaf, each division three-lobed and deeply notched, and the stem are hairy. The deep yellow flowers have five, six or seven petals, blossoming from May to July. The plant is common in fields and meadows over a wide area.

PROPAGATION   By seeds. It self-sows widely.

Easily transplanted. Move the corms in the late fall.

The double-flowered form of *R. bulbosus* is often seen in cultivated gardens. It is very pretty if kept under control.

R. septentrionalis   Swamp Buttercup

This representative native buttercup is confined to swamps and low wet ground. The deep yellow flowers are fully an inch across, blossoming from late April to June. The hollow stem, 2 to 3 feet tall, is quite smooth. The leaves with three leaflets, each three-lobed, are long, narrow, and without teeth near the top of the stem. The stems are stoloniferous after flowering .

This species is found from Labrador to Ontario, south to Texas, Arkansas, Kentucky, and Virginia.

PROPAGATION   This plant self-sows, and increases by its stolons.

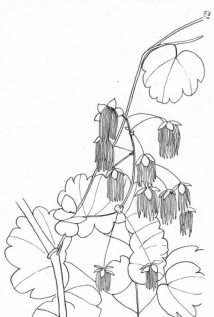

Thalictrum dioicum   Early Meadow-Rue

This plant is grown almost entirely for its feathery, handsome foliage, as the flowers are insignificant. It reaches a height of 2 feet and makes an airy, graceful ground cover for large areas under deciduous trees. The compound leaves are much divided, and in spring there are loose panicles of small greenish or purplish flowers. It grows in a variety of soils.

This species is found from Quebec to Manitoba, south to South Carolina and Alabama, west to Missouri and Kansas.

PROPAGATION   By seeds in the summer.
By division in the spring.
By transplanting where abundant.

T. polygamum   Tall Meadow-Rue

A splendid wild flower for summer flowering, this decorative plant, sometimes 10 feet tall, has beautiful compound leaves repeatedly divided in threes. It is remarkable for its plumy clusters of white flowers without petals but with many conspicuous threadlike stamens. It should be planted in the sunny swamp garden.

This species is found in wet meadows from Labrador to Ontario, south to North Carolina, Tennessee, and Indiana.

PROPAGATION   By seeds gathered and sown in September.
By division in the spring.
By cuttings of side shoots in summer.

BERBERIDACEAE   Barberry Family

The members of this family included here have large, handsome leaves and flowers with few petals.

Caulophyllum thalictroides   Blue Cohosh

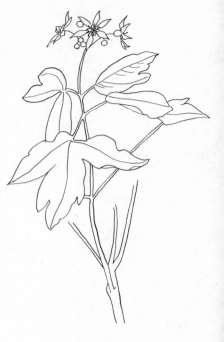

This smooth, erect plant reaches a height of 2 feet. The stem seems to form a stalk for one large, thrice-compound leaf, with lobed leaflets, borne above the middle, and another smaller leaf just below the little panicle of dull greenish yellow flowers which blossom in spring. These are followed by attractive large blue berries late in the season. The plant is permanent and easily grown in rich moist woods, often in neutral soil. It is an excellent companion for the red- or white-fruited baneberries.

This plant is found from New Brunswick to Ontario and Manitoba, south to Alabama and Missouri.

PROPAGATION   By seeds stratified over winter. The plant self-sows.

By division in the spring or fall.

Diphylleia cymosa   Umbrella-leaf

Each spring this plant sends up from creeping root stalks a very large two-cleft, cut-lobed, and rounded umbrella-like leaf on a stout petiole; if a flowering stem, which may reach a height of 3 feet, it has two similar, smaller, more deeply two-cleft alternate leaves, peltate near one margin, terminated by a cyme of six-petaled white flowers. These blossom in May and June. The fruits are blue berries in a cluster.

This plant is found in cool mountain woods and along streams from Virginia to Georgia. It does well in more northern gardens.

PROPAGATION   By division in the spring.

By seeds, separated from the pulp and sown in the fall.

May be transplanted, where abundant.

Jeffersonia diphylla   Twinleaf

A much lower and smaller plant than the two. preceding, this species has basal leaves about 1 foot tall, deeply divided into two leaflets. The solitary white flowers with about eight petals are borne in spring on leafless stalks shorter than the leaf petioles and last but one day. The seed capsule is interesting, jug-like, the top opening like a lid when the seeds are ripe. This is an easy and unusual plant for the spring wild garden, in open woods, in acid, slightly acid, or neutral soil. It makes good-sized clumps and is permanent.

This plant is found from New York and Ontario to Iowa, and south to Alabama.

PROPAGATION   By division in August or early spring.

By seeds shaken from the capsule and sown in the fall or very early spring.

Podophyllum peltatum

May-apple or Mandrake

This species is not well suited to a small wild garden because it spreads too rapidly. It is easily grown in moist open woods and clearings, often beside railroad tracks. The plant, 12 to 18 inches high, has large umbrella-like leaves with seven, eight, or nine lobes supported by the stem in the center. The flowering stem has a pair of terminal, deeply three- to seven-parted leaves and a solitary white flower with yellow stamens and six to nine petals. The fleshy fruit is yellow, appearing in August.

This plant grows under deciduous trees, in thickets and pastures, in neutral, acid, or slightly acid soil, from Florida to Texas, north to Minnesota and Ontario.

PROPAGATION   By division of the roots at each joint, in summer. Treat like cuttings.

By seeds removed from pulp and stratified as soon as ripe in early fall.

PAPAVERACEAE   Poppy Family

Poppy Subfamily

This subfamily comprises delicate plants with milky or yellow juice, alternate leaves, and large flowers with two or three sepals, soon falling, and four to twelve petals.

Sanguinaria canadensis   Bloodroot

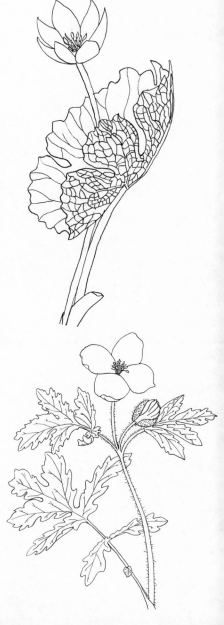

There are few wild gardens in which bloodroot cannot be made to grow. The vigorous plants have short horizontal rhizomes, containing an acrid red-orange juice, which send up a large blue-green basal leaf that is deeply wavy-lobed and usually disappears during the summer. The solitary white flowers are on leafless stalks a few inches high and blossom from late March to May. They last a very short time. The plants often spread into thick mats.

This plant is found in rich neutral or moderately acid soil from Quebec to Manitoba, south to Nova Scotia, Pennsylvania, Kentucky, and Kansas.

PROPAGATION   By seeds sown in the spring or fall. It self-sows freely.

By division in the spring or summer.

The double form is of exceptional beauty and is more robust in every way. The double pure white flowers resemble small peonies.

Stylophorum diphyllum   Celandine-Poppy

Those who are acquainted only with the coarse and weedy celandine are agreeably surprised when they see a similar-looking plant in a wild garden bearing quite large yellow poppy-like flowers. These are produced in few-flowered clusters on leafy stalks about 1 foot tall. This low perennial has leaves that are whitish beneath and divided into five, six, or seven deeply-cut wavy lobes. The bright yellow poppies have four petals and flower in April and May. In its native habitat this plant self-sows freely and can become very weedy.

This long-lived plant is found in rich neutral leaf mold from Pennsylvania to Michigan and Wisconsin, south to Tennessee and Arkansas.

PROPAGATION   By seeds, shaken from the capsules and sown in September.

By division of the roots in the spring.

By root cuttings in the summer.

Fumitory Subfamily

The Fumitory Family has small bilateral flowers in racemes. There are two minute sepals and a flattened, closed corolla with four petals in two pairs, the outer larger, and one or both spurred or sack-like at the base.

Adlumia fungosa   Allegheny-vine

This slender biennial vine climbs by leaf-stalks to a height of 10 to 15 feet. The fern-like leaves are thrice-divided, and the narrow tubular purplish-pink flowers are in drooping clusters, blossoming all summer. The plant makes an attractive rosette its first year, elongating the second season.

This plant is found in moderately acid soil in mountain woods from Quebec to Wisconsin, south to Delaware, Tennessee, and Indiana.

PROPAGATION   By seeds sown in the spring or fall. The plant self-sows.

Corydalis aurea   Golden Corydalis

A very useful and desirable plant for the wild garden, this species blossoms in sun or shade, day in and day out, the whole summer long. The plants are about 1 foot tall with bright green, much divided basal leaves and leafy flower stalks with groups of golden-yellow bilateral blossoms at the branch tips, the corolla one-spurred at the base.

This species is found on rocky calcareous banks or in sandy soil from Quebec to Manitoba, south to Pennsylvania, Michigan, and Minnesota.

PROPAGATION   By seeds. The plant self-sows widely and provides all the seedlings one can use. Old clumps become quite large, so that it is difficult to know whether the plants are biennial or perennial.

C. sempervirens   Pale Corydalis

A pretty biennial for dry rocky places in the sun, this plant sometimes forms large clumps before it dies. In its first year it makes conspicuous rosettes of much-divided gray-green leaves. The second season it sends up smooth branching flower stalks, from 6 to 12 inches high, bearing clusters of clear pink flowers tipped with yellow, through much of the summer. Often these plants grow with wild columbine, making an interesting combination.

This species is found in dry rocky woods in moderately acid soil throughout northern North America and down the Appalachians.

PROPAGATION   By seeds sown in the late winter. Plants self-sow freely.

By transplanting young rosettes, where abundant.

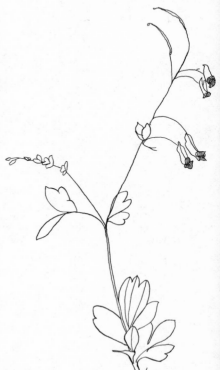

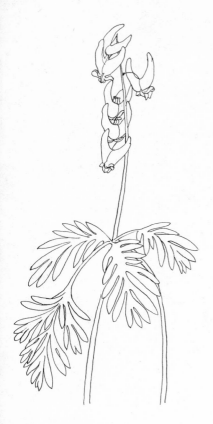

Dicentra cucullaria   Dutchman's-breeches

In early spring this delicate wild flower pushes through the soil and bursts into bloom with surprising speed. After flowering, it disappears as quickly as it came. It makes clumps of finely cut pale green basal leaves. The slender, arching flower stalks, sometimes growing almost a foot tall, have three to twelve nodding white flowers with cream-colored crests and with two spurs at the base forming the "breeches." The plant grows from a collection of white grain-like tubers crowded together into a scaly bulb, and prefers rich deciduous woods and neutral soil. Often when transplanted to the wild garden there are clumps of leaves but no flowers. A dusting of ground limestone around the plants will usually correct this difficulty.

This species is found from Quebec to Minnesota, south to North Carolina, Arkansas, and Kansas.

PROPAGATION   By division of the clustered bulbs in July or early spring. This is best done in a flat of leaf mold.

By seeds which should be sown in late summer and allowed to stratify through the winter.

D. eximia
Turkey-corn or Wild Bleeding-heart

A common garden perennial, this species is remarkably handsome used as a ground cover between clumps of shrubbery under deciduous trees. It blooms more or less all summer and does not die down until winter comes. The plant is quite bushy with finely cut basal leaves 1 foot long. The long flower custers, 18 inches in height, have many drooping narrow "hearts," pale pinky-purple in color. The white form is now much planted.

This species is found in moderately acid soil in dry or moist mountain woods from New Jersey to Pennsylvania and West Virginia, south to North Carolina and Tennessee.

PROPAGATION   By division in April or July.

By seeds, sown in August or later. Usually it self-sows.

D. canadensis   Squirrel-corn

This delightful little plant is a small sister to Dutchman's breeches. It grows from a little tuber like a kernel of yellow corn and is found in rich woods in neutral soil. The finely cut basal leaves are gray-green in color. In April and May, curious nodding flowers with a heart-shaped base are produced on leafless stalks 6 to 8 inches tall. They are greenish white tinged with pink, the larger petals expanded into rounded spurs, the smaller bearing yellowish crests; they are fragrant.

This species is found from Quebec to Minnesota, south to North Carolina, Tennessee, and Missouri.

PROPAGATION   By separation of the tubers in early spring or while dormant in summer. Sift the soil to find the yellow tubers.

By seeds sown in February or in the fall.

CRUCIFERAE   Mustard Family

The members of this family have flowers with four sepals and four petals, their blades spreading in a symmetrical cross, to which the family name refers. Few are desirable in the wild flower garden.

Dentaria diphylla   Toothwort

A low creeping ground cover for shade in
moist woods, this plant prefers a cold climate
but does quite well in a warmer one. The basal
bright green leaves are palmately divided into
three leaflets and are sharply toothed. There
are two similar, nearly opposite leaves part
way up the smooth stems. The white flowers,
pinkish below, are borne in loose terminal
clusters in April and May.

This desirable plant for the woodland
wild garden is found in moderately acid soil
from Quebec and New Brunswick to Minnesota, south to Pennsylvania, Ohio, and Indiana; also through the mountains to Georgia
and Alabama.

PROPAGATION   By seeds gathered in
July and sown at any time. Keep wet.

By division of the rootstocks in the fall
or spring.

Cardamine pratensis
                    Lady's-smock or Cuckoo-flower

Wherever there are meadows and fields
that are wet in the springtime, this attractive
little perennial will surely make itself at home.
The slender, tufted plants send up leafy stems
a foot high. There are many basal leaves with
numerous pinnate leaflets. The small white or
pinkish flowers blossom in slender, erect racemes in May and June. There is also a double
form. The plant is naturalized from Europe
but is also native in some of its forms.

PROPAGATION   By seeds in summer. The
plant self-sows freely.

By transplanting at any time.

Draba arabisans   Whitlow-grass

In the northern states there are many species of draba. These are low plants, some annual, some perennial, with small white flowers in erect little racemes. This species is very similar to the familiar garden arabis, hence its name. It makes loose rosettes of paddle-shaped leaves with flowering stems from 4 to 16 inches tall, appearing in May and June. When in fruit the stems are limp and untidy. It is a good subject for rocky ground in the wild garden.

This plant ranges from Newfoundland to Ontario, south to New England, New York, and Michigan.

PROPAGATION   By seeds gathered in early summer and sown at any time.

SARRACENIACEAE
Pitcher-plant Family

The plants in this family have rosettes of curious, tubular leaves containing water which traps and drowns insects, then digests them. The solitary flowers have five petals.

Sarracenia purpurea   Pitcher-plant

This is an indispensable plant for the sphagnum bog in the wild garden. The beautiful mottled, pitcher-shaped leaves spread out radially from the root. They are hollow with a wing on one side. The interesting large nodding flowers, borne on leafless stalks, are reddish-purple in color and appear in June and July, being about 1 foot tall. These plants must be grown in acid peat bogs in sun.

This species is found from Labrador to Florida, west to Minnesota. It is the only northern species.

S. flava, Yellow Trumpets, found from Virginia southward, has long, erect yellow-green pitchers and yellow flowers. It is a much taller plant, growing 2 feet high, and is very handsome.

PROPAGATION   By seeds sown as soon as ripe in moist peat in pots set in water. Cover with a polyethylene bag. The seeds will germinate in one to two years.

Where abundant, young plants may be transplanted.

By division of old clumps.

CRASSULACEAE   Orpine Family

The plants in this family are small and succulent with four- or five-petaled flowers in flat-topped clusters.

Sedum acre   Mossy Sedum or Wallpepper

In summer this introduced plant will cover large areas in sandy or rocky soil with its fleshy pale green narrow leaves and its clusters of small, deep yellow flowers on short, erect stems. It will even grow on sea-beaches. It should not be planted where it can crowd out more desirable natives.

PROPAGATION   It spreads and self-sows rapidly.

S. ternatum   Stonecrop

This native prostrate sedum is a small species found on rocky ledges and in stony woodlands. It is quite attractive. The small five-petaled flowers grow on horizontally spreading branches, and the small, fleshy leaves are in whorls of three on the stem.

This species is found on damp, often calcareous rocks and mossy banks from New York to Michigan and Illinois, south to Georgia and Tennessee.

PROPAGATION   By seeds. It self-sows. May be easily transplanted, where abundant.

SAXIFRAGACEAE   Saxifrage Family

Closely related to the Rose Family, the members of the Saxifrage Family may have alternate or opposite leaves. The flowers have five petals.

Saxifraga virginiensis   Early Saxifrage

This plant makes a small rosette of rather broad ovate small leaves. It hugs rocks on normally dry, sunny hillsides, which, however, are usually dripping with water when the tiny starry white flowers appear in earliest spring on stems only a few inches tall.

This plant is found on dry or wet rocks and gravelly slopes of varying acidity, in sun or shade, from Quebec to Ontario and Minnesota, south to Georgia, Tennessee, and Missouri.

PROPAGATION   By seeds collected in July and sown at any time.
By division in the spring.

Astilbe biternata   False Goat's-beard

This is a tall perennial herb with large alternate leaves, two or three times ternately divided, the leaflets cut and toothed. It is a large edition of the astilbes cultivated in perennial borders. The tiny white flowers are in large terminal panicles on stems from 5 to 8 feet tall, blossoming from May to July.

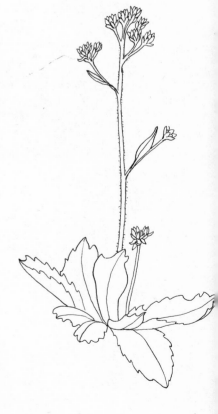

This plant requires wet soil and is found in moist woods in the mountains from Virginia to Kentucky, south to Georgia.

PROPAGATION   By division in the spring.
By seeds collected from the capsules in the fall and sown at any time.

Heuchera americana   Alumroot

The heucheras are associated with rocky ground, in nature, and therefore fill an important place in the wild rock garden. There are several similar species, all with handsome rosettes of basal geranium-like leaves from which, from April to June, slender flower stalks arise bearing panicles of insignificant greenish or white flowers. The leaves of this species are mottled with dark reddish bronze, especially as winter approaches.

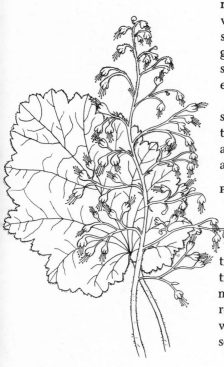

This species prefers shaded calcareous slopes and rocks, and grows from Connecticut to Ontario and Michigan, south to Georgia and Oklahoma. It grows also in moderately acid soil.

PROPAGATION   By division in the spring or fall.
By seeds sown at any time.

H. villosa, a more southern species, is particularly desirable because of its clouds of tiny white flowers which appear in late summer and fall on many stalks arising from the rosette of shining green leaves. There are few woodland flowers that bloom so late in the season.

Mitella diphylla   Bishop's-cap or Miterwort

As a ground cover under deciduous trees in rich neutral soil this plant is unexcelled. It has many heart-shaped basal leaves, the whole plant being hairy. The flower stem is from 6 to 12 inches tall with a pair of small opposite leaves in the middle of the stem. Each tiny flower has five beautifully fringed petals and is on a short pedicel distinctly separated from the others in the slender raceme. In May and June a colony of miterworts in full bloom on the forest floor is fairy-like in its charm.

This plant is found in rich moist woods, often in neutral soil, from Quebec and Ontario to Minnesota, south to Virginia, Alabama, and Missouri.

PROPAGATION   By division in early spring.

By seeds which germinate quickly if sown as soon as ripe.

By softwood cuttings in summer.

Parnassia glauca   Grass-of-Parnassus

This interesting little wild flower has small basal evergreen leaves in a rosette and solitary cream-white flowers, delicately veined with green, on stems 6 to 12 inches tall. It blossoms in August and September and must have very wet limestone soil and sun.

This plant is found in calcareous bogs and wet meadows from Quebec and New Brunswick to Saskatchewan, south to Virginia, Ohio, Iowa, and South Dakota.

PROPAGATION   By seeds sown in a peaty mixture in late winter. Expose to freezing or snow. If possible mulch the newly set out seedlings with soil taken from around the parent plants. May be sown in late summer.

By division in early spring, using soil from around the parent plants.

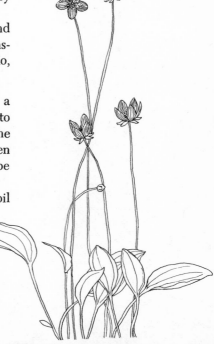

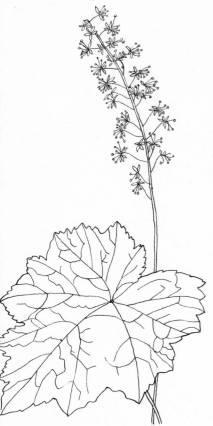

Tiarella cordifolia

False Miterwort or Foamflower

The rosettes of foamflower leaves resemble those of heuchera but are smaller. The plant sends out runners in summer. In spring, clouds of small white feathery flowers are borne in erect racemes on leafless stalks a few inches tall. This is one of the best spring wild flowers for the shady garden and is easily grown under deciduous trees in rich moderately acid or neutral soil. If a clump is planted in a shaded cold frame in soil rich in leaf mold, the runners will root everywhere and the new little plants can be lifted and potted, to be planted outside the following spring.

This plant is found from Nova Scotia and New Brunswick to Ontario and Michigan, south to Georgia and Alabama.

PROPAGATION   By   division   in   the spring.

By seeds sown when ripe in the late summer.

It may be transplanted, where abundant.

ROSACEAE   Rose Family

This large family contains many trees and shrubs. The leaves are alternate, usually accompanied by stipules. The regular flowers have five sepals, five petals, numerous distinct stamens, and one or many pistils. The sepals and petals are usually inserted with the stamens on the edge of a disk which lines the calyx-tube.

Aruncus dioicus   Goat's-beard

Although attractive in the perennial border, this imposing plant is breath-taking when

seen at its best in rich woods and ravines. The plant has a few large two or three ternately compound leaves without stipules, and may reach a height of 5 feet. In June and July, thousands of tiny white flowers are borne in many loose, drooping terminal panicles. The sexes are borne on different plants. It is easily grown in the partly shaded wild garden.

This plant is found in rich moist woods from New York south to Georgia and Missouri.

PROPAGATION   By division in spring. By seeds which germinate easily.

Dalibarda repens   Star-violet or Dalibarda

Not a well-known wild flower, this small stemless plant, 3 to 6 inches high, is found in wet woods in strongly acid soil. It creeps below the ground and is a tiny relative of the blackberry. The simple rounded leaves are all basal, and the solitary little white flowers, raised above the leaves, blossom from June to August. Later, flowers without petals are produced which contain the clustered seeds. Seed production is rare, however.

This plant is found from Nova Scotia to Minnesota, south to North Carolina, Ohio, and Michigan.

PROPAGATION   By spreading rootstocks. By division, or by cuttings, in summer. They should be planted in flats of acid leaf mold, kept moist.

Duchesnea indica   Indian Strawberry

An Asian plant, this species has established itself in moist waste places from Florida to Oklahoma, north to Connecticut, Ohio, and Iowa. It is slender and strawberry-like, with

many runners, the leaves divided into three leaflets, the flowers with yellow petals, one from each leaf axil, borne during much of the summer. The bright red berries are insipid. The plant is an excellent ground cover for sunny places in the wild garden.

PROPAGATION   From rooted runners, as if a strawberry.

By seeds, sown in the berry in August.

Filipendula rubra   Queen-of-the-prairie

A tall species from the West, the plant has large pinnately compound leaves, the terminal leaflet larger than the others, and seven-, eight-, or nine-lobed. The compound flat terminal clusters of small deep-pink flowers appear in June and July, the plants reaching a height of 5 to 6 feet. It is a very satisfactory species or the summer wild garden but will not succeed in dry soil. When thriving, it sends out many creeping rootstocks. It prefers neutral or slightly acid soil.

This species is found in moist sunny meadows and prairies from Pennsylvania to Michigan, south to Georgia and Kentucky, and has escaped from northern gardens.

PROPAGATION   By division in spring.

By cuttings of the rootstock in summer.

F. Ulmaria   Queen-of-the-meadow

This species, introduced from Europe, has white flowers. The terminal leaflet is round in general outline and three-, four-, or five-lobed, the leaves being generally pale below.

PROPAGATION   Same as for *F. rubra.*

Fragaria vesca   Woodland Strawberry

This is the wild strawberry beloved by children. It is a slender, leafy plant, the leaves quite erect. The small clustered white flowers are followed by long conical berries.

This plant is found in fields and by roadsides in moderately acid soil from Quebec and Newfoundland to Michigan, south to Pennsylvania and Illinois.

PROPAGATION   By transplanting newly rooted runners.

F. virginiana is the commonest wild strawberry. It occurs throughout our range and grows in rough dry pasture lands. It is the parent of the garden strawberries.

Geum canadense   White Avens

The geums are grown as much for their leaves as for their flowers. They all have compound leaves, the terminal leaflet very large and lobed, the others much smaller. The least showy are those with white flowers. This species resembles a tall strawberry plant without runners. The white flowers are on branched stems, about 2 feet tall, appearing in June and July.

This species is found in neutral or slightly acid soil in dry or moist woods from Nova Scotia to Minnesota, South Dakota, and south to Georgia and Texas.

PROPAGATION   By division in spring only.

By seeds sown at any time.

G. rivale   Purple Avens

This moisture-loving plant has nodding cap-shaped flowers with short dull yellow petals and a purple calyx. It is an interesting and dependable plant for the bog garden, and flowers in May and June, in sun or part shade, in slightly acid soil.

This species is found in bogs and wet meadows from Newfoundland and Quebec to Alberta, south to New Jersey, Indiana, and Michigan.

PROPAGATION   By seeds sown in very early spring.

By division in spring or summer.

The majority of geum species with yellow flowers prefer cold climates.

Gillenia trifoliata   Bowman's-root

An unusual and easy plant for the wild garden, this species grows about 3 feet tall. It has pointed leaves divided into three sharply and irregularly serrated leaflets with a pair of tiny narrow stipules at the base of the petiole. The narrow-petaled white flowers are in loose panicles, blooming in May and June.

This plant grows in moderately acid soil in dry or moist upland woods, especially in the mountains, from Ontario to Delaware, North Carolina, Alabama, and Kentucky.

PROPAGATION   By division in spring only.

By seeds gathered in early fall and sown at any time.

Potentilla argentea   Silvery Cinquefoil

A low much-branched plant with deeply cut silvery palmate leaves, this European weed is well suited to covering dry sunny banks. The small yellow flowers are insignificant.

PROPAGATION   By seeds sown at any time. It self-sows.

There are other useful yellow-flowered potentillas, some upright and some trailing.

P. tridentata

Three-toothed or Wine-leaved Cinquefoil

Although native to rocky hilltops and exposed mountain summits, this thoroughly delightful ground cover, only a few inches high, often does extremely well in full sun in the cool rock garden. It has shining evergreen three-parted leaves, each leaflet three-toothed at the apex. The leaves turn a beautiful wine-red in fall. The small white flowers are in flat-topped clusters blossoming from June to August. The plant needs a cool peaty and sandy soil that is very acid.

This species is found in northern North America and along exposed mountains from New England and New York to Georgia, and from Minnesota and Michigan to Iowa and North Dakota.

PROPAGATION   By division in spring in gritty soil.

By cuttings in a dryish frame. Cut the underground stems into short pieces and plant them in flats of gritty soil in August and September.

By seeds gathered in early fall and sown in containers.

Rosa acicularis   Prickly Rose

The wild rose of cold regions, this species grows about 4 feet tall and has stems with many scattered needle-like prickles and bristles. The leaves have three to seven leaflets and are smooth above, mostly downy below. The pink flowers are usually solitary and appear in June. The seed hips are smooth and oblong to pear-shaped.

This species is found in thickets and on rocky slopes, often in acid soil, from New England, New York, Michigan, Minnesota, and South Dakota to Colorado.

PROPAGATION   By suckers, which usually are abundant. Dig in spring.

By seeds removed from the hip; sow or stratify at once.

R. blanda   Smooth Rose

The only native rose without prickles, except for a few around the base of the plant, this species has dull pale green leaves of five to nine leaflets, coarsely toothed, especially above the middle. The pink flowers are solitary or in clusters, and bloom in June on plants up to 6 feet tall. The oblong hips are soft and dull red.

This species is found in dry woods and on prairies and dunes, in neutral or acid soil, from Quebec to Manitoba, south to New York, Pennsylvania, Indiana, and Missouri.

PROPAGATION Same as for *R. acicularis*.

R. carolina   Carolina Rose

The dwarf species rose of our eastern states, growing only 2 feet high, this plant sends out many creeping rootstocks. The leaves have five leaflets, dull green above and pale below. The pink flowers are mostly solitary, appearing in June. The globular hips are smooth and red.

This species is found in dry rocky, sunny pastures in moderately acid soil from Nova Scotia and New England to Michigan, Wisconsin, Florida, and Texas.

PROPAGATION Same as for *R. acicularis*, but the creeping roots divide readily.

R. palustris   Swamp Rose

The tallest of wild roses, this one may grow 8 feet high, suckering widely. The stems have stout, paired prickles. The dull green leaves with five to nine leaflets are downy below. The pink flowers are single or in small corymbs, and appear from late June through July. The flattened hips are globular, smooth, and red. This is the only bog-loving native rose, and it will not grow in dry sandy soils. It is the latest native rose to bloom.

This species is found in swamps and marshes from Nova Scotia to Minnesota, south to the Gulf of Mexico.

PROPAGATION Same as for *R. acicularis*.

R. setigera   Prairie Rose

This is the only climbing native rose species. The arching stems with few stout decurved thorns, or unarmed, reach a length of about 15 feet. The root does not sucker. The large leaves of three to five leaflets are ovate, with the terminal one long-stalked. The pink flowers are in large terminal clusters from late May to July. The hips are small, smooth, and red.

This species is found along thickets and fence rows from Ontario to Ohio, Iowa, and Kansas, south to Georgia, Louisiana, and Texas.

PROPAGATION   By seeds as for *R. acicularis,* as it cannot be divided.

By layering the long stems.

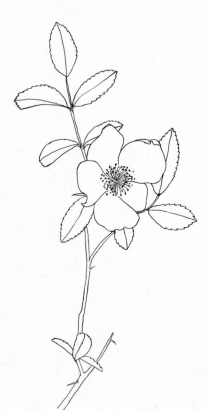

R. virginiana   Virginia Rose

A plant of medium size, less than 6 feet tall, the stems have stout paired thorns below the stipules, but few bristles. The leaves have five to eleven dark green leaflets, shining above, and there are bright pink flowers clustered at the ends of the twigs in June. The hips are smooth and red.

This species is common in moist or dry soil from Newfoundland to Pennsylvania and Virginia.

PROPAGATION   Same as for *R. acicularis.*

The above species are representative of the many native wild roses throughout our range.

Sanguisorba canadensis   American Burnet

An especially useful wild flower because it blooms in the fall, this species deserves more attention. The plant has handsome basal pinnate leaves with 13 to 21 toothed leaflets and grows 3 to 5 feet high. The stem leaves become progressively smaller. The little whitish flowers are in dense spikes and are very noticeable in marshes and wet meadows in late summer and early fall. The plant should be in every wet garden. It needs an acid soil.

This plant is found from Newfoundland to Manitoba, south to New Jersey, Pennsylvania, and Indiana and in the mountains to South Carolina.

PROPAGATION   By division in the spring. By seeds gathered from the spikes in autumn and sown at any time.

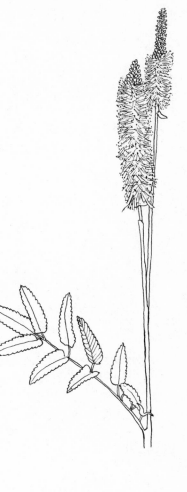

Spiraea alba   Meadow-sweet

A slender bushy shrub about 4 feet tall, this is a common plant in low wet ground. The alternate leaves are finely toothed, and the fragrant small pinkish-white flowers are borne in rounded panicles throughout the summer.

S. latifolia is similar, the leaves more coarsely toothed, the twigs purple-red in color.

These species range from Newfoundland to Michigan, south to Georgia, and west to Missouri and South Dakota. *S. latifolia* is more common near the coast.

PROPAGATION   By division in spring.

S. tomentosa   Hardhack or Steeple-bush

Another erect shrub about 5 feet tall, this plant is also common in wet fields from Nova Scotia to Quebec and Minnesota, south to North Carolina, Tennessee, and Arkansas. It is most abundant near the coast. The sharply toothed leaves are oblong and very white or brown-woolly below. The small rose-colored flowers are in long narrow "steeples" borne well above the leaves from July to September. This is available in a white-flowered form.

PROPAGATION   By division in the spring. Transplants readily, where abundant.

Waldsteinia fragarioides   Barren Strawberry

An attractive but seldom seen ground cover for moist wooded slopes in moderately acid soil rich in humus, this plant has long-stalked basal leaves with three broad, toothed leaflets. The pale yellow flowers, about ½-inch across, are on bracted scapes about 8 inches tall. It is a good companion plant for hepaticas.

This plant is found in moist or dry woods from Maine and Quebec to Minnesota, south to Pennsylvania and Indiana and at high elevations.

PROPAGATION   By division in fall.

By seeds sown in the early spring, collected in the early fall.

LEGUMINOSAE   Pea Family

The Pea Family contains many genera which are of value to the wild flower gardener. Some are upright in habit, like lupine, but the

majority have weak stems which trail on the
ground or climb over other plants, often
smothering them. They have mostly flowers
shaped like those on garden pea plants and
pinnately or palmately compound leaves which
add much to their beauty.

The plants should be given no better
growing conditions in the garden than they
enjoy in the wild; otherwise, they may lose
their desirable characteristics and become real
pests.

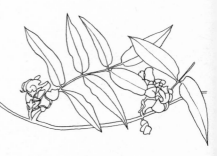

Apios americana   Groundnut or Potato-Bean

This is a vine which should be planted
only where there is ample room for it to climb
at will over weeds and bushes. It grows to
about 8 feet in length, has leaves with three to
nine leaflets and short, dense racemes of fragrant purple-brown pea flowers from July to
September. In the South the racemes are usually longer. The seed pod is small and contains a few tiny beans.

This plant is found in moist woods and
rich thickets from Quebec to Minnesota, South
Dakota and Texas and from New England to
Florida.

PROPAGATION   The root has a series of
potato-like tubers which transplant readily in spring and are difficult to eradicate
thereafter. The plant also self-sows.

Baptisia alba   White False Indigo

The wild indigos are as well adapted to
the wild garden as they are to cultivated flower
beds where they are more commonly seen.
They make upright, bushy plants about 3 feet
tall with attractive foliage. This species, like
the yellow wild indigo, *B. tinctoria*, with a

more northerly range, is found in dry open woods, pinelands, and clearings, in acid soil, from Virginia and Tennessee to Florida. It flowers in late spring. The white blossoms are in long, erect racemes borne well above the foliage. The leaves have three narrow leaflets. The seed pod is erect and very slender.

PROPAGATION   By division in early spring.

The plants will self-sow once they become established.

Remove the small seeds from the capsules in early fall. Sow at any time.

B. leucantha   Prairie-False Indigo

This is similar to white false indigo but is larger and stouter in every way. The leaves turn black when dry, unlike the preceding species, which remain green. The seed pods are oblong and drooping. This plant grows in moist, often neutral, soil. It flowers in early summer and is found in mid-America.

PROPAGATION   Same as for *B. alba.*

B. leucophaea   Plains-False Indigo

Unlike the two preceding species, this is a downy, hairy plant with creamy-white flowers in downward-arching racemes, often a foot in length. The seed pod is downy and ovoid. The plant is less than 3 feet tall with a characteristic silver sheen from the silky hairs that cover the stems and leaves. It occurs in sandy soil on the prairies from Michigan to Arkansas and south to Louisiana, flowering in April and May.

PROPAGATION   Same as for *B. alba.*

B. australis   Blue False Indigo

This handsome, well-branched plant is the species common to perennial borders. It has broad oblong blue-green leaves with three leaflets and indigo-blue flowers in erect racemes. The leaves turn black when dried. The seed pods are large, black, and bladdery, containing many small yellow "beans." By far the most showy of the baptisias, the blue false indigo grows along moist stream banks and in rich soil, flowering in late spring.

The plant is native from Pennsylvania to Kentucky and Indiana and southward to Georgia. It has become naturalized in New York and Vermont.

PROPAGATION   Same as for *B. alba;* very readily from seeds.

B. tinctoria   Yellow Wild Indigo

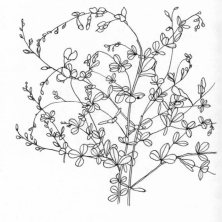

A familiar sight in dry acid sandy fields over much of the eastern United States are the extremely bushy clumps of yellow wild indigo growing to a height of from 2 to 3 feet. The small blue-green leaves, with three leaflets, remain in good condition until frost, when they turn black. The deep yellow flowers are also small and are in sparse clusters at the ends of the branches, appearing in June and July. The small pea pods are inflated and contain little yellow seeds. The plant is a desirable addition to the dry wild garden, as it can survive conditions of real drought.

Another name for this plant is horseflyweed. In past days work horses were often seen with branches of it stuck into their bridles behind their ears, ostensibly to keep the flies away.

PROPAGATION   Same as for *B. alba,* principally from seed.

Cassia marilandica   Wild Senna

This is one of the most useful members of the Pea Family for wild gardens and it should be seen more often. It is a strong-growing perennial which sometimes reaches a height of more than 6 feet. The compound leaves have 10 to 18 pale green leaflets, and in summer there are yellow flowers with five nearly equal petals in both terminal and axillary clusters. Since they are only very slightly irregular, they are quite different from conventional pea flowers, which are definitely bilateral. The clustered seed pods are long, brown, and flat, with many oblong seeds.

This species is found in both moist and dry open woods and thickets from Pennsylvania to Iowa and south to Florida and Texas.

PROPAGATION   From seeds sown in spring or fall.

C. fasciculata   Partridge-Pea

A wild garden where the soil is poor and sandy and where few other desirable plants could be expected to grow is a suitable location for the partridge-pea, an erect annual varying in height from 1 to 2 feet. The sensitive, feathery leaves have 10 to 15 pairs of narrow oblong leaflets that fold together when handled. The large deep yellow flowers with five regular petals, usually with a purple spot at the base, are in small clusters above the leaf axils and bloom from July to September. The seed pods are slender and flattened.

This species flourishes in sandy soils from Massachusetts to southern Minnesota and south to Florida and Texas.

PROPAGATION   From seeds planted in a sandy area.

Centrosema virginianum   Butterfly-Pea

This twining pea vine with stems about 3 feet long frequents sandy woods and barrens from New Jersey to Tennessee and south to Florida and Texas. It is not found in northern gardens.

The leaves have three leaflets and the large pea flowers are borne in July and August on short stems from the leaf axils, one to four in a peduncled raceme. The seed pod is long, slender, and flat, with many seeds.

PROPAGATION   Plant seeds in the spring.

Clitoria mariana   Butterfly-Pea

This is another rather short pea vine, similar to *Centrosema,* for dry woods and barrens found from Long Island and New Jersey to Illinois and southward and westward to Florida and Arizona.

The leaves have three smooth leaflets. One or two showy pale blue flowers with large upper petals are produced in the upper leaf axils in summer. In August, smaller flowers that do not open are followed by long, flat pods with several sticky seeds.

PROPAGATION   From seeds sown in the spring.

Coronilla varia   Crown-Vetch

In addition to native members of the Pea Family desirable for the wild garden, there are several introduced species which deserve attention. Perhaps the best of these is crown-vetch, a perennial with sprawling stems, pinnately compound leaves with 11 to 21 leaflets, and attractive heads of rose-pink clover-like flowers produced in great abundance from June to August.

This plant grows by roadsides and in sunny wastelands and must not be pampered. It was originally cultivated and is now common from Maine to North Carolina and westward to Missouri.

PROPAGATION   Easily raised from seeds or from sections of the root left in the ground. Also by division.

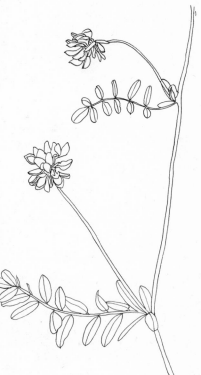

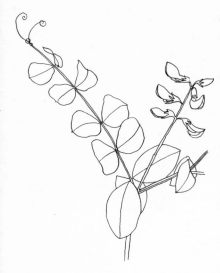

Lathyrus japonicus   Beach-Pea

The beach-pea is a desirable species for seashore gardens only. It is found in salty soils near the coast from Canada to New Jersey, and makes a useful ground cover for sand dunes.

This species is a trailing vine with a tendril at the tip of each pinnate leaf. The leaflets number from four to ten and are blue-green in color. The violet-purple flowers are produced in compact racemes from the upper leaf axils in June and July but are not particularly showy.

PROPAGATION Since the beach-pea transplants with difficulty, it should be raised from seeds sown in moist sand where it is to grow.

L. latifolius   Everlasting Pea

This European perennial plant has escaped from cultivation and is a useful addition to the wild garden. The long creeping stems will trail or climb as desired. The large bright rose-pink or white flowers are in many-flowered racemes and bloom during much of the summer. The roots do not spread, so that the plant stays where it is set.

PROPAGATION Easily raised from seeds and readily self-sows.

Lotus corniculatus   Birdsfoot-Trefoil

Still another European perennial trailing pea desirable for a ground cover, found in sunny fields and by roadsides, is the yellow-flowered birdsfoot-trefoil. It has leaves with 5 leaflets, the basal pair simulating stipules. The small flowers are solitary or in umbels on long erect peduncles and bloom much of the summer.

This plant grows from Newfoundland to Minnesota and south to Virginia and Ohio, being especially common in New York State.

PROPAGATION   Small plants can be transplanted or it may be raised from seeds as if a clover.

Lupinus perennis   Wild Lupine

This lupine is one of the most beautiful of wild flowers and, in spring, often covers large areas of dry sand nonfertile acid soil in coastal regions from Maine to Florida and from Minnesota to Louisiana. The plant is erect in habit and grows abouth 2 feet tall. The round leaves are palmately divided into seven to eleven narrow leaflets. The flowers, usually blue-purple but sometimes pink or white, are in long terminal racemes. The seed pod contains many round seeds which ripen early in July.

PROPAGATION   Seeds must be collected when barely ripe and should be planted at once in some of the soil from around the base of the parent plant. The young seedlings are easily transplanted, but it should be done while they are still small. Mature plants have deep woody roots, and it is a waste of time to try to move them.

L. polyphyllus   Wild Lupine

This is the lupine of the Northwest. It may grow 5 feet tall. The leaves have more leaflets than *L. perennis*. It also prefers a more moist soil, and has escaped eastward into northern New England.

Trifolium spp.   Clover

The clovers are too well known to need description, but several of the annual species should not be overlooked. The yellow-flowered hop-clovers, of which *T. agrarium* is an example, and the fuzzy-headed rabbit-foot-clover, *T. arvense,* are neat and pleasing in their habits and blossom all summer in poor dry soil. These species are all introduced annuals from Europe.

PROPAGATION   From seeds only.

Petalostemum villosum   Hairy Prairie Clover

Several similar species of prairie clover are found on sandy, western prairies and hills from Michigan and Montana to Texas and New Mexico. They are erect plants with slender stems from 2 to 3 feet tall. Hairy prairie clover has leaves with 13 to 19 narrow oblong leaflets which are very silky-haired. The small rose-purple clover-like flowers are densely clustered in long narrow cylindric terminal spikes, and bloom in July and August. The small pods contain one or two seeds.

PROPAGATION   From seeds sown in spring; division of the plants is difficult.

Phaseolus polystachios   Wild Bean

The familiar vegetable garden bean is a close relative of this perennial climbing bean found in dry open pine and oak woods and sandy thickets from New Jersey, southern Illinois, and Nebraska to Florida and Texas.

The leaves have three broad, pointed leaflets, and the twining stem is very rough to the touch. The small purple flowers, about ⅓ of an inch long, grow in slender racemes from the leaf axils, flowering in summer, and are followed by long, drooping pods with flattened seeds.

The pink wild bean, *Strophostyles hel-vola,* is a similar perennial trailer with larger flowers, dull pink in color, on long stalks from the leaf axils. The leaves have three lobed leaflets. These two beans are less aggressive than the groundnut, which spreads too rapidly for a small wild garden.

PROPAGATION These may be grown like garden beans from collected seeds.

Psoralea Onobrychis Scurf-pea

The several species of scurf-peas are more familiar on the western plains and prairies than in the northeastern states. *P. Onobrychis* is an erect plant found in rich woodlands and moist prairies from Ohio to Missouri and in the mountain woods of western Virginia to eastern Tennessee and western South Carolina.

The plant grows about 3 feet tall and has long axillary spires of small pale blue pea flowers in June and July. The leaves have three bright-green broad ovate leaflets. The wrinkled pods contain one seed each.

PROPAGATION Young seedlings are readily transplanted, or seeds may be sown where the plants are to grow.

Tephrosia virginiana Hoary Pea

This upright pea has stiff silky-haired stems from 1 to 2 feet tall. The compound pinnate leaves with 17 to 29 oblong leaflets are silk-haired below. Large pink and buff flowers in compact terminal clusters appear in June, the plant forming strong clumps in open woods and sandy fields in full sun. It is desirable for the summer wild garden in acid soil.

This plant occurs from New England to Wisconsin and south to Florida and Texas.

PROPAGATION   The woody roots of old plants may be cut apart in the spring. Collected seeds may also be planted at the same season, or sown at once in the fall.

Thermopsis mollis   Bush-pea

A favorite subject for the perennial border and one equally desirable for the late spring and summer wild garden is the bush-pea. It grows in stout clumps 3 feet tall. The softly downy oblong leaves have three leaflets with short stipules at the leaf base. The yellow pea flowers are in long, close terminal spires and they bloom in May and June. The pods are short, narrow, and erect, containing several yellow "beans."

This species is native to dry soils in mountain woods from Virginia and Georgia to Alabama. It is often grown in northern gardens.

PROPAGATION   By division in spring and from seeds sown in spring or fall.

T. caroliniana   Bush-pea

This is a taller species found in the mountains of North Carolina; it is also common in northern gardens. It is the better species of the two, resembling a tall yellow lupine reaching a height of 5 feet.

PROPAGATION   Same as for *T. mollis.*

Melilotus alba   White Sweet Clover

This tall bushy, branching plant was brought from Europe, and may grow 6 feet tall. The leaves have three leaflets, and the small white flowers, shaped like those of pea plants, bloom in long, erect racemes for most of the summer.

This plant is a biennial and is suitable for large waste areas. It prefers neutral or alkaline soils. It often grows with yellow sweet clover, *M. officinalis,* a similar plant with yellow flowers.

PROPAGATION   From seeds. It self-sows widely.

Vicia Cracca   Tufted Vetch

Another introduced legume which makes a good companion for crown-vetch is tufted vetch. This plant produces tangled masses of weak stems in meadows and fields. The leaves have eight, nine, or ten pairs of narrow, dark green leaflets with a terminal tendril. The numerous small deep purple pea flowers are crowded in long one-sided axillary racemes for most of the summer.

PROPAGATION   Self-sows freely. The black thread-like roots may be divided.

OXALIDACEAE   Wild-Sorrel Family

The plants in this family have compound basal or alternate stem leaves with their blades divided into three inversely heart-shaped leaflets. The five-parted flowers are solitary or few in a cluster.

Oxalis montana   Common Wood-Sorrel

A ground cover for very acid soil in cold moist woods, this plant grows from slender creeping roots to a height of 6 inches. The three-parted leaves, again divided, are long-petioled. The solitary flowers have white notched petals with red veins and blossom in spring and early summer. Cleistogamous flowers are borne later in the season. This species is not suited to the average wild garden.

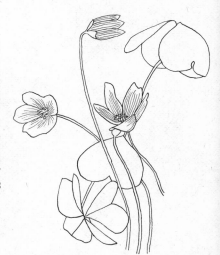

O. montana is found in deep humus-rich woods from Quebec to New York, Wisconsin and Saskatchewan, south in the mountains to North Carolina and Tennessee.

PROPAGATION   By division in the spring only.

O. violacea   Violet Wood-Sorrel

This oxalis has few-flowered clusters of lavender-purple blossoms on leafless stalks, 4 to 6 inches high, borne well above the foliage in May and June. It spreads rapidly by runners from clusters of small bulbs.

This species is found in open woods and grasslands, in slightly acid soil from Massachusetts to Minnesota, south to Florida and Texas.

PROPAGATION   By division of the bulbs in the spring.

GERANIACEAE   Geranium Family

This small family has symmetrical flowers of five sepals and five petals, the fruit a cylindric capsule prolonged into a beak eventually splitting at the base. The leaves are often palmately divided.

Geranium maculatum
                    Cranesbill or Wild Geranium

Although a common wild flower, this plant is especially attractive when grown in large colonies with such plants as the Canada anemone. It has mostly rough-hairy basal leaves on long petioles that are deeply five-lobed. A single pair of similar, smaller leaves appears on the unbranched stem well below the clusters of large rosy-purple flowers. This geranium flowers in May and June and will cover large areas in moist shady situations in a variety of soils.

This species is found from Maine to Manitoba, south to Georgia, Missouri, and Kansas.

PROPAGATION   By seeds sown in the spring or fall.

By division in the spring.

G. Robertianum   Herb-Robert

This annual plant has deeply cut toothed leaves and small lilac-purple flowers. It often appears, uninvited, and blooms more or less all summer. It grows in rocky woods and thickets. Seed is the only method of increase.

POLYGALACEAE   Milkwort Family

Members of this family are small plants with bilateral flowers that have five sepals, the two lateral ones enlarged and petal-like, and three petals connected in a tube, the lower one ending in a pouch crested at the tip.

Polygala paucifolia   Fringed Polygala

A charming but difficult evergreen ground cover in acid humus-rich soil, this low creeping plant has clusters of ovate leaves at the tops of stems about 3 inches high. The irregular flowers in small clusters somewhat resemble small magenta-pink orchids. They blossom in May and June. A white form is very rare.

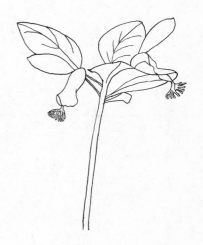

This species is found in moist rich woods from Quebec and New Brunswick to Saskatchewan, south to New York and Wisconsin, and through the mountains to Georgia.

PROPAGATION   By seeds in early spring, collected in summer.

By stem cuttings taken in the summer.

P. Senega   Seneca-snakeroot

This interesting little plant is not showy. It grows in small clumps up to 20 inches tall with many little leaves on the unbranched stems. The tiny whitish flowers are in dense racemes, blossoming in May.

This species is found in dry rocky, mostly calcareous areas from New Brunswick to Alberta, south to Georgia and Arkansas.

PROPAGATION   By softwood cuttings in summer.

EUPHORBIACEAE   Spurge Family

The plants of this family contain a milky juice, often highly acrid. The flowers are much reduced. They consist of a cup with several petal-like marginal lobes, within which stalked groups of stamens or of three carpels arise.

Euphorbia corollata   Flowering Spurge

This erect leafy plant, which grows from 2 to 3 feet tall, is occasionally seen in perennial borders. It has many alternate, linear stem leaves, and the clusters of tiny flowers are surrounded by five white petal-like bracts, appearing in July and August.

This species grows in dry fields, woods, and prairies in a variety of soils from New York to Minnesota, south to Florida and Texas.

PROPAGATION From cuttings of basal shoots in the summer, or division of the roots in spring.

By seeds in late winter, gathered in late summer.

E. Cyparissias   Cypress Spurge

Introduced from Europe, this plant covers the ground along dry roadsides in waste places where nothing else grows. It should not be planted unless with this purpose in mind. The plant has many very narrow yellow-green leaves and terminal flat-topped clusters of small greenish-yellow flowers with broad yellow floral leaves turning reddish with age.

PROPAGATION By division in the spring. There is apparently no seed.

BUXACEAE   Box Family

This family comprises perennial herbs, but mostly trees and shrubs with simple, alternate, or opposite leaves and small flowers without petals in spikes or heads.

Pachysandra procumbens Allegheny-spurge

This native pachysandra is an interesting and little-known ground cover. The plant sends up fleshy stems, about 6 inches tall, from creeping rootstocks with the deeply toothed leaves crowded toward their summits. Although evergreen in the South, the leaves are deciduous where winter temperatures fall to zero. The scented small white flowers with long stamens are quite showy, blossoming in terminal spikes, in April and May, before the leaves are fully grown.

The species is found in rich calcareous woods from Kentucky to Florida and Louisiana.

PROPAGATION   By division in the early spring. Include a bud with every division.

BALSAMINACEAE
Touch-me-not Family

This family has bilateral, two-lipped flowers with three sepals, the lower one a petal-colored spur, and five petals. The leaves are alternate and toothed.

Impatiens capensis   Jewelweed

This erect fleshy annual is a pale green watery plant growing 2 to 3 feet tall. The leaves are elliptical and entire. The axillary flowers are deep orange, spotted crimson, blossoming from July to September. The fruit is a fleshy capsule that throws out its seeds when touched. The plant is easily established in the large moist wild garden, and self-sows everywhere. It is too weedy to put with choice plants.

This species is found in a variety of soils, including acid swamps from Newfoundland to Alaska, south to Florida and Oklahoma. *I. pallida* (pale jewelweed) is clear yellow in color, without spots, and prefers calcareous soil in sun or shade.

PROPAGATION   By seeds only, gathered in early autumn and sown in the spring.

MALVACEAE   Mallow Family

Members of the Mallow Family are easily identified by the column or tube made by the stamens united by their filaments around the pistil in the center of the flower. The round cheese-shaped seed receptacles are also characteristic. The regular flowers have five petals, and are usually in shades of rose or white. The alternate leaves are palmately veined.

Callirhoë involucrata Poppy Mallow

A plant native to dry sunny plains and prairies from North Dakota to Wyoming, south to Oklahoma and Texas, it has, nevertheless, escaped eastward and is now planted in many gardens, both wild and cultivated.

The plant has a deep tap-root and widely creeping stems on which the rounded, five-, six- or seven-parted, toothed leaves are well spaced. The large solitary flowers on axillary or terminal peduncles are a bright magenta-purple, making gay patches on the landscape from June to August. The plant is very drought-resistant.

PROPAGATION By seeds sown in the spring or fall. The deep root cannot be divided, and the trailing stems do not root into the ground.

Hibiscus militaris
Halberd-leaved Rose-Mallow

This coarse perennial may grow to 6 feet in height with smooth stout upright stems. The large smooth long-petioled leaves are triangular in outline, the upper ones with a lobe on either side of the base. The pinkish flowers have purple centers and are a little smaller than those of rose-mallow. They are clustered in the leaf axils much like hollyhocks, and flower from July to September.

This species is found in marshes and shallow water on the Coastal Plain from Pennsylvania to Florida and Texas, and north, in the interior, to Ohio and Minnesota.

PROPAGATION   From seeds sown at any time.

Small plants can be moved, but take only from areas where abundant.

H. palustris   Swamp-Rose-Mallow

Although found, in nature, mostly in salt marshes along the coast, this striking perennial will grow very well in garden soil that is not too dry. It is one of the standbys of the wild or cultivated garden in late summer. The tall leafy stems are often more than 6 feet high. The large, broadly ovate leaves are on long petioles, and the very large clear pink flowers are in terminal clusters blooming, one at a time, over a long period from midsummer to fall. This hibiscus starts to grow very late in the spring, and makes big clumps which live for years. Red and white color forms are in gardens.

This species is found from Massachusetts to Virginia and inland to Indiana, often in neutral soil. It sometimes escapes from cultivation.

H. moscheutos has creamy white petals with dark red centers. It is a more southern species found from Maryland to the Gulf, inland to Ohio and Indiana.

PROPAGATION   By seeds, gathered in the fall and sown at any time.

By division of the large clumps in the spring.

Where abundant, young plants may be easily transplanted.

By cuttings taken in the summer.

Malva moschata   Musk-Mallow

This plant, introduced from Europe, is desirable for the summer wild garden. An escapee from cultivation, it is now common along roadsides and in waste places, especially in the northern states. It extends southward to Virginia and Missouri.

The plants are from 2 to 3 feet tall, with slender, downy, branched stems. The rounded basal alternate leaves are somewhat lobed. The upper stem leaves are deeply five-lobed, and in their axils short clusters of rose or white flowers with five deeply notched broad petals are borne from June to August. The plant has a musky odor.

PROPAGATION   Small plants are easily moved in spring.

By seeds. The plants self-sow freely.

CISTACEAE   Rockrose Family

This family contains herbs and shrubs, and the members described here have radially symmetrical yellow flowers with five petals, in cymes.

Helianthemum canadense   Frostweed

This slender bushy plant with small oblong leaves on erect stems, about 1 foot tall, is suitable for the dry, sunny wild garden. The showy solitary flowers, with petals which soon shed, are borne in late spring and summer. They are in loose terminal racemes followed later by numerous insignificant flowers without petals crowded on short axillary branches. In late autumn, frost crystals form about the

shrubby stem bases. It is thought to be a
short-lived species and, under cultivation, may
produce mostly the insignificant type of flowers.

This plant is found in dry, sunny, nonfertile acid soil, often in pure sand, from
Maine to Minnesota, south to North Carolina
and Illinois.

PROPAGATION   By seeds, gathered in
the fall and sown at once or the next
spring.

By cuttings or layering.

Hudsonia tomentosa
Poverty-grass or Beach-heath

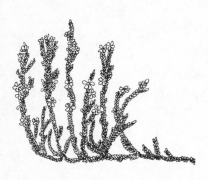

This densely tufted plant with alternate
evergreen scale-like woolly leaves is covered
in late spring and summer with delicate small
yellow flowers produced in the leaf axils.

It is impossible to cultivate this species
except on sandy slopes and dunes along the
seacoast or in the Great Lakes area.

Its range is from New Brunswick to Virginia and along the Great Lakes to Minnesota.

PROPAGATION   Although a perfect plant
for the seaside garden, it is almost impossible to establish either by division or
by seed. Layering is probably the best
method. It self-sows widely in sandy
places.

VIOLACEAE   Violet Family

This genus is so large and varied that even
the expert wild flower gardener finds it difficult to name the species correctly.

The irregular flowers have five petals, the
two lateral frequently bearded at the base, the
lower one usually with a spur. Some species

are stemless, the leaves and flowers coming directly from the root; others are leafy-stemmed. They all blossom in spring.

Many stemless species produce no seeds from their showy flowers but bear hidden buds beneath the foliage, during the summer, which contain the seeds. These are called cleistogamous flowers.

A few examples, only, of the different types of violet are listed:

Stemmed Violets

Viola canadensis   Canada Violet

This erect, leafy-stemmed species grows about 1 foot tall, the leaves being heart-shaped. The white flowers produced in the upper leaf axils have a yellow eye and are shaded with lilac on the back of the petals.

This species is found in neutral to moderately acid soil in cool moist woodlands and slopes from Newfoundland to South Carolina, westward.

PROPAGATION   By division in the fall. By seeds. (They need winter ripening.) By cuttings of shoots from the base of the plant after flowering.

V. conspersa   American Dog-Violet

This species produces numerous leafy stems about 7 inches tall; the basal leaves are kidney-shaped. The light blue-violet flowers are on slender peduncles raised high above the leaves. The plant grows in moist woodlands and meadows from Quebec and Nova Scotia to Minnesota, south to South Carolina and Missouri.

PROPAGATION   Same as *V. canadensis;* division in spring is easy.

V. rostrata   Long-spurred Violet

This species, similar to the preceding, has spurs ½ inch long. It is found in rich, often calcareous, woods, in deep humus, from Quebec to Michigan and Wisconsin, south to Georgia and Alabama.

PROPAGATION   Same as for *V. canadensis.*

There are similar branched species all with toothed stipules at the base of each leaf.

V. pubescens   Downy Yellow Violet

When once established in the spring wild garden, this dependable violet is a long-lived treasure. It is a leafy-stemmed plant about 1 foot tall, the stem leaves broad and downy. The small yellow flowers, veined purple-brown, are borne in terminal clusters.

This species is found in deep rich, deciduous dry woods in neutral or slightly acid soil from Nova Scotia to North Dakota, south to North Carolina, Georgia, and Oklahoma.

PROPAGATION   Plants self-sow freely; pick the seed capsules in July.

V. pensylvanica   Smooth Yellow Violet

This species is similar to the above but quite smooth. It is found in damp open woods and on cool, shaded rocky slopes in neutral or slightly acid soil from Nova Scotia to Manitoba, south to Georgia and Texas.

PROPAGATION   Plants self-sow freely. Catch the ripe pods before they open in July.

Stemless Violets

V. blanda   Sweet White Violet

This little violet grows everywhere in swamps, wet meadows and sometimes in drier areas from Quebec to Minnesota, south to the mountains of South Carolina and Georgia. It has rounded heart-shaped leaves, slightly scalloped, hairy above, and very small sweet-scented white flowers with purple veins. The young stems are red.

PROPAGATION   Plants self-sow freely, and may be divided readily.

V. lanceolata   Lance-leaved Violet

This smooth plant has narrow linear-lance-shaped leaves, slightly scalloped, and small white flowers veined purple. It grows in open bogs, wet meadows, and on shores of ponds from Nova Scotia to Minnesota, south to Florida and Texas.

PROPAGATION   Same as for *V. blanda.* It is readily divided, and the runners are easily layered.

V. primulifolia   Primrose-leaved Violet

This species, similar to the preceding, has paddle-shaped leaves flat on the soil. The plant prefers moist, moderately acid clay soil in full sun. Its natural range is similar to that of *V. lanceolata.*

PROPAGATION   Same as for V. blanda.

V. cucullata   Blue Marsh Violet

In wet meadows and bogs, in sun or shade, this is an abundant species. The blue-violet flowers are on long stalks well above the heart-shaped leaves.

This violet is found from Quebec and Ontario to Missouri and Georgia.

PROPAGATION   Same as for *V. blanda.*

V. odorata   Sweet or English Violet

Although not native, this intensely fragrant small violet adds much to the pleasure of a wild garden. In earliest spring quantities of pale lavender, white, deep purple, or rosy flowers perfume the air, often blossoming again in the fall. The small leaves are broadly heart-shaped, and the plant spreads from leafy stolons as well as from seeds. It is easily kept under control.

V. papilionacea   Common Blue Violet

This extremely weedy species resembles *V. cucullata* except that the leaves are larger and the flowers more richly colored. It seeds itself so prolifically and makes such large clumps of foliage that it has no place among choice wild flowers. The Confederate violet with grayish-white flowers veined with blue is a form of this species.

V. pedata   Pansy-Violet or Bird-foot-Violet

Probably the handsomest of all the violets, this species grows in full sun in clayish or sandy, nonfertile acid soil. It will not live in good soil, but it thrives along gravely railroad embankments. The plants are low and hidden in May by the many large, flat-faced blue-violet flowers, the two upper petals a deep, velvety purple, the tips of the orange anthers very prominent in the center of the flower. The dull green leaves are cut into three, four, or five segments, these being again divided and toothed. A form without the dark upper petals is common, and an albino form may be found. This is our only native violet with flat pansy-like form.

This species is found from Maine to Minnesota, south to Florida and Texas. There may be some autumn bloom.

PROPAGATION Move plants immediately after blooming, cutting a section out of the center of the plant. The cut should be 4 inches deep and 1½ inches from the crown. Make a clean sharp-sided hole and leave it open. Severed roots on its inside surface will give rise to many new plants.

By root cuttings planted upright with the top end at soil level.

This species has no cleistogamous flowers, but must increase in nature from its seed.

V. palmata   Wood Violet

Another species with deeply cut but hairy leaves and deep violet flowers, this plant is found in woodlands, shaded calcareous ledges, and rich soil from Massachusetts to Minnesota, south to Mississippi and Florida.

There are various cut-leaved species confusing to identify.

PROPAGATION By division.

By seeds, gathered from ripe unopened capsules in summer.

V. septentrionalis   Northern Blue Violet

This violet, similar to the weedy blue violet, is much less of a spreader and therefore a better subject for the wild garden. Its range is from Newfoundland to British Columbia, south to Virginia, Wisconsin, Nebraska, and Washington.

PROPAGATION   Same as for *V. palmata*.

V. sororia   Woolly Blue Violet

A very common violet in meadows and open woods, in full sun, it seldom exceeds 3 inches in height. The whole plant is downy, the ovate leaves thick, dark green and close to the ground. The deep purple flowers are on short stems. This violet will grow in poor sandy soils, too dry for most native species. This species is found from Quebec and Maine to Minnesota, south to North Carolina and Oklahoma.

PROPAGATION   It self-sows freely, and is readily transplanted in spring.

V. rotundifolia   Round-leaved Yellow Violet

One must go into cold coniferous woods very early in the spring to find this cheerful little violet in flower. The plant is dwarf, with large round leaves close to the ground, becoming still larger after the small bright yellow flowers have faded. This violet can be grown only in wet acid soil, in shade.

This species is found from Quebec and Maine to Ontario, south to Pennsylvania and in the mountains to South Carolina and Georgia.

PROPAGATION   It self-sows, and is increased only from its natural seedlings. It does not divide readily.

CACTACEAE   Cactus Family

The plants in this family have enlarged fleshy stems with minute spine-like leaves. The showy flowers mature to a fleshy edible fruit.

Opuntia humifusa   Prickly-pear

Since this cactus has few spines, it is a good species for the small wild garden. The plant has flat stems with large oblong joints. The big solitary clear yellow flowers with many petals are produced on the edge of the joints in July and August. The pear-shaped reddish succulent fruit remains on the plant all winter.

This is the only species hardy in southern New England. It grows in full sun on poor, often neutral soil from southern Massachusetts to Minnesota, south to South Carolina, Missouri and Oklahoma. There are several western species of opuntia, most of them being extremely spiny, a few of them hardy to much frost.

PROPAGATION   By seeds sown in flats in spring, the fruits collected in autumn. By division of the joints in spring.

LYTHRACEAE   Loosestrife Family

A family of strong-growing, leafy-stemmed herbs or shrubs, the flowers mostly have four, five, or six sepals united into a tube, four, five, or six petals, four to twelve stamens, and two united carpels.

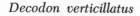

Decodon verticillatus   Water-willow

It is easy to recognize this shrubby perennial because of its long leafy stems which arch out over the water for a length of 3 to 4 feet, in swamps and along streams. Numerous lance-shaped leaves are opposite or in whorls of three or four, and the small bell-shaped rose-purple flowers with five petals are in dense clusters in the upper leaf axils, blossoming in July and August. Though it is an excellent plant to hold the bank along streams, it is not suitable for a small garden.

This plant is found from New England south to Florida and Louisiana and north in the Mississippi Valley to Illinois and Indiana.

PROPAGATION   The tips of the long branches are self-rooting and are easily separated from the parent plant in early summer.

By division of the old plants in the spring.

Lythrum alatum   Winged Loosestrife

This native lythrum is more common to the prairies of the Midwest than to eastern habitats. It grows 2 to 3 feet tall with wand-like four-angled stems and narrow, mostly alternate, leaves. The deep purple-magenta flowers are solitary in the upper leaf axils, and blossom from June to September. The plant is not very showy but is desirable for bog gardens.

This species is found in wet places in neutral to moderately acid soil from New York and Ontario to British Columbia, south to Georgia and Texas. It is occasionally seen in New England.

PROPAGATION   By division in spring.
By seeds gathered in the fall.
By cuttings taken in the summer.

L. Salicaria   Purple Loosestrife

This introduced species is much admired by many gardeners who have not stopped to realize what a pernicious weed it is rapidly becoming. Along riverbanks and in wet meadows the tall spikes of brilliant magenta flowers make waves of color over wide areas, throughout the summer, choking out more choice and interesting native species. The plant is so aggressive that it is truly a menace and should not be planted in any wild garden, whether large or small, for it is liable to take over the entire countryside if allowed to spread.

MELASTOMACEAE
Melastoma Family

This family is represented by small plants with opposite leaves. The showy flowers have four sepals and four petals. The eight stamens, tipped with long golden anthers curving gracefully, are distinctive.

Rhexia virginica   Meadow-beauty

In midsummer the margins of swamps and ponds, in wet sand, become suddenly bright with the magenta-pink flower clusters of rhexia. The petals fall at midday, and the flowers appear from July to September, on a plant growing about 2 feet tall. It is low and bushy with a square stem, the bristly leaves being sharp-toothed, with three conspicuous ribs. This species is a valuable addition to the large or small bog garden, in very acid soil.

The range of this species is from Maine, south to Georgia and Oklahoma and west to Wisconsin and Missouri.

PROPAGATION   By division of old plants in the spring.

By seeds sown in the early spring or fall, collected in October.

Where abundant, the roots of clustered tubers are easily transplanted in spring or summer.

R. Mariana   Maryland Meadow-beauty

A similar hairy species with no root tubers and with paler rose flowers occurs mostly in the damp sands and peats of the Coastal Plain from southern New England to Florida.

PROPAGATION   By division in the spring. By seeds, collected in October.

ONAGRACEAE
Evening-Primrose Family

This family may have simple, opposite or alternate leaves and the flower parts are mostly in fours.

Oenothera biennis   Evening-Primrose

Sooner or later this stout, erect biennial is likely to appear by itself in the summer wild garden, and no effort need be made to acquire it. The large hairy alternate leaves with wavy margins are on stems 2 to 4 feet tall that are often suffused with red. The large fragrant light yellow flowers come in July and August and are in long, erect racemes opening late in the afternoon. They close with the morning sun. The seed pods are prized for flower arrangements.

This species is common along roadsides and in waste places everywhere east of the Rockies.

PROPAGATION   By seeds, only, as the plant is biennial. Shake out the seeds from the spikes in October. Make a new planting yearly.

Epilobium angustifolium
> Fireweed or Great Willow-herb

A showy, tall plant, this species is at its best in boreal America where it is common along roadsides, coming in abundantly after fires. The erect stems have many narrow alternate willow-like leaves and grow to a height of 6 feet or more. The four-petaled magenta-pink flowers are in showy terminal racemes borne throughout the summer. In the fall the velvety curved seed pods open lengthwise and release masses of white silky down which cling to the plants for some time. It is useful only for the large wild garden.

This plant is found in various habitats, and extends south to North Carolina and west to South Dakota and Texas.

PROPAGATION   By seeds sown in the spring or fall.
> By transplanting, in the spring only.

O. fruticosa   Sundrops

Although usually seen in the perennial border, this plant is even better in the summer wild garden where the plants with their bright yellow flowers can be allowed to spread about unchecked. This species makes bushy clumps about 2 feet tall. The sessile alternate, lanceolate leaves are downy to hairy, the plant stems reddish. The large golden yellow flowers open during the day and must have full sun, blossoming in June and July. There are other similar species.

This species is found in dry soil in fields and open ground from Nova Scotia to New York, south to Florida and Alabama.

PROPAGATION   By division in the spring.
> By seeds sown in the spring, from autumn collection.

O. missouriensis   Ozark Sundrops

Splendid for a sunny rock planting, this sprawling plant has gray-downy stems about 1 foot long. The enormous yellow flowers appear in June and July. The plant is perfectly hardy in New England.

This species is found on dry rocky barrens and calcareous soil from Illinois and Missouri to Nebraska, Colorado, and Texas.

PROPAGATION   By seeds sown in the spring.

By division of the crown in the spring.

O. speciosa   White Evening-Primrose

This low, erect plant, to 2 feet tall, inhabits the prairies from Illinois to Georgia, west to Kansas and Texas. The large white flowers are few in number, produced from a long tube in the upper leaf axils, blossoming in June and July.

PROPAGATION   By division in the spring.
The plant spreads rapidly by its roots.

ARALIACEAE   Ginseng Family

Plants in this family have compound, mostly alternate, leaves and tiny five-petaled flowers in umbels.

Aralia racemosa   American Spikenard

This spineless species is very strong-growing, reaching a height of from 2 to 6 feet from stout, deep, aromatic fleshy roots. The large, twice-compound, widely spreading leaves have oval, toothed leaflets. The small whitish flowers are in large terminal panicles, blossoming in June and July. Small dark purple berries follow in August and September.

This species is found in rich woods and thickets in moderately acid soil, from Quebec to Manitoba, south to Georgia and Kansas.

PROPAGATION   By seeds. It transplants with difficulty. Gather the berries in Septimber, allow to dry, then break and sow in spring.

A. *hispida*   Bristly Sarsaparilla

This species makes strong colonies in dry woods and sterile sandy soil and may grow 3 feet tall. The leaves are twice-pinnate and the bristly leafy stems terminate in a peduncle bearing several umbels of small whitish flowers. These appear in June and July followed by blue berries.

This species is found from Quebec to Minnesota, north to Hudson Bay and south to New Jersey, West Virginia, and Indiana.

PROPAGATION   By seeds as for A. *racemosa*

A. *nudicaulis*   Wild Sarsaparilla

This woodland ground cover, about 1 foot tall, may crowd out more delicate species. It grows from creeping horizontal stems below ground, sending up one long-stalked compound leaf each year and one shorter leafless stem with a round terminal umbel of green flowers followed by clusters of black berries. The plant is often a pest, but it is an almost inseparable part of the leafy growth on the forest floor, in moderately acid soil, and belongs in the large woodland wild garden.

This species is found in moist woodlands from Maine to North Carolina along the mountains, and west to Minnesota, South Dakota, and Missouri.

PROPAGATION   By seeds, if rare locally; usually it can be dug and divided in spring.

Panax quinquefolius   Ginseng

A much less common plant than aralia, ginseng may be recognized by the large palmately-compound, long-stalked leaves of five leaflets arranged in a solitary whorl of three around the erect simple stems. A single peduncle above the leaves bears a terminal umbel of small whitish flowers in June and July. The fruits are flat red berries. The plant grows from a large tuber-like aromatic root once sought for medicinal purposes.

This species is found in rich cool woods in quite acid soil from Quebec and Manitoba, south to Georgia, Louisiana, and Oklahoma, and is now very rare.

PROPAGATION   By seeds separated from the pulp and sown in the fall.

By stem cuttings taken in the summer.

By short upright root cuttings taken in the spring.

By suckers which grow after the top of the plant has been cut back.

P. trifolius   Dwarf Ginseng

A tiny species, not over 6 inches tall, this panax grows from a black globular tuber very deep in the ground. The whorl of three leaflets is close to the stem. The berries are yellow.

This species prefers damp clearings and rich woods in neutral to moderately acid soil from Quebec south to Georgia and Nebraska.

PROPAGATION   By seeds. Do not attempt to transplant ginseng.

UMBELLIFERAE   Parsley Family

The Parsley Family is easily identified by the compound flat clusters (umbels) of small yellow or white flowers. The leaves are chiefly alternate and usually compound, divided, or deeply lobed. The stems are hollow with few exceptions. Most members of the family have tap-roots that make them impossible to transplant. Many of them are biennial. There is great similarity between the members of the family, however, often making identification of species quite difficult.

Eryngium yuccifolium   Rattlesnake-master

Long used in the perennial border because of their curious, spiny foliage and stiff, gray-blue flowers, the eryngiums, *E. amethystinum* in particular, are also popular in dried flower arrangements. Not quite so decorative, however, is this species. The stiff, coarse stem, about 3 feet high, rises from a cluster of deciduous yucca-like leaves. The stem leaves are similar, but smaller. The little white flowers, appearing in July and August, are in a conical head, resembling a thistle, with a ring of short, narrow false leaves just below the head. This is a strange-looking species to belong to the Parsley Family.

This plant grows in moist or dry sandy soil and open woods from Minnesota and Kansas, south through the southern states. It has also been found in New Jersey and southern Connecticut.

PROPAGATION   From seeds sown while fresh in the autumn.

Old plants should be left undisturbed.

Angelica atropurpurea
                    Alexanders or Angelica

In swamps and wet woods the lush growth of angelica makes it a very noticeable plant throughout the summer. A large relative of wild carrot, it sends up stout, purple-stained stems to a height of 6 feet, topped with large umbels of tiny, greenish-white flowers. The big leaves have long petioles with swollen bases and are two or three times pinnately or ternately compound. The upper leaves are progressively reduced so that the uppermost are almost bladeless. This is an excellent species for a large stream-side wild garden.

This plant is found from eastern Canada to Minnesota, south to Delaware, West Virginia, and Illinois.

PROPAGATION   By seeds only sown outdoors in the fall.

Poison Angelica. (*A. venenosa*), *not* recommended for the wild garden, is a more slender plant found in drier woods and grows only 2 feet high.

Heracleum maximum   Cow-parsnip

For a large wild garden in wet ground this is perhaps the tallest perennial to be included, since it may reach a height of 8 feet. The plant has very stout woolly grooved stems and huge thrice-divided lobed and toothed leaves. The small white flowers are in immense umbels blossoming in June and July.

This plant is found in large colonies from Labrador to Alaska, south to Georgia and Arizona.

PROPAGATION   By seeds sown when fresh in the autumn.

Zizia aurea   Golden Alexanders

Although a rather weedy plant, as are many members of the Parsley Family, this species has a place in the large moist wild garden. It is a smooth perennial, 1 to 2 feet tall, with thrice-divided light green leaves, the leaflets numbering from six to nine. They are thin and sharply toothed. The tiny greenish-yellow flowers are in many small umbels, each widely separated from the others but radiating from the same point on the stem, blossoming in May and June. A colony of these plants along a shaded roadside or on the edge of a meadow is a pleasing sight.

This plant grows from Quebec and Maine to Saskatchewan, south to Florida and Texas.

PROPAGATION   From seeds sown when fresh.

By division in the spring.

CORNACEAE   Dogwood Family

This family contains trees, shrubs, and herbs with simple opposite leaves (except one species) and mostly small four-parted flowers in cymose clusters. The fruit is a two-seeded drupe.

Cornus canadensis   Bunchberry

This distinctive wild flower is at its best in damp cold northern woods in strongly acid soil, where it makes an unexcelled ground cover. Bunchberry will persist in a warmer climate but without the wealth of flowers and berries found in the North. It sends out horizontal rhizomes that form large colonies. The plant stems are about 4 inches high, bearing a cluster of four to six leaves at the top. The leaves have prominent lateral veins arising from the midvein below the middle. The tiny flowers are in small yellow clusters sur-

rounded by four white petal-like bracts. They blossom from May to July, followed by erect clusters of bright red berries in late summer.

This plant is found from Greenland to Alaska, south to New Jersey and Pennsylvania, in the mountains to West Virginia, west to Indiana, Minnesota, and California.

PROPAGATION   By seeds, separated from the pulp, sown outside, ¾-inch deep, as soon as possible after ripening.

By large divisions.

By transplanting sods, where abundant.

PYROLACEAE   Wintergreen Family

The plants in this family are mostly low evergreens with slender running underground stems. The small nodding white or pinkish flowers have five petals.

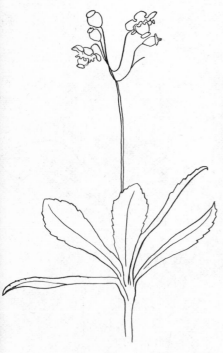

Chimaphila umbellata

Pipsissewa or Prince's Pine

This erect little evergreen, from 4 to 10 inches high, has shining thick denticulate leaves, somewhat whorled around the stems, and small pinkish-white flowers in a few-flowered terminal cluster, blossoming in summer. The plant spreads from creeping subterranean shoots and makes a sparse ground cover in dry woods, in acid leaf mold.

This species is found from Maine to Georgia, west to Colorado.

Striped pipsissewa, *C. maculata,* with mottled leaves, is another sparse ground cover in dry, strongly to moderately acid woods. It has a wide range, but is less abundant.

PROPAGATION   By cuttings in the late fall in sand and peat. Keep shaded.

Pyrola elliptica Shinleaf

This tufted plant sends up a flower stalk only a few inches high. The nodding bilateral white flowers are in a loose wand-like cluster, blossoming in summer. The basal short-stalked elliptic leaves are in a rosette. This is probably the most common of the pyrolas. There are many similar species.

This species is found in dry woods in moderately acid soil, from Newfoundland and Quebec to Minnesota and British Columbia, south to West Virginia, Indiana, and Iowa.

PROPAGATION By division of underground runners in sand and peat in a shaded frame.

All members of this family are difficult to propagate or to transplant. Seed germinates poorly; treat as an alpine heath.

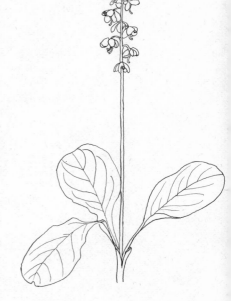

ERICACEAE Heath Family

Most members of the Heath Family are woody plants and require an acid soil. These include many choice broadleaf evergreens.

Arctostaphylos Uva-ursi Bearberry

A remarkably attractive ground cover, bearberry is a creeping evergreen woody plant forming great mats only a few inches high. With its shining leathery alternate leaves it is the best ground cover for sunny sandy slopes in strongly acid soil and it can withstand dry summer heat, bitter winter cold, and salt spray. The little white flowers, tinged pink, are vase-shaped and are borne, in May, in short few-flowered terminal racemes. Mealy red berries remain on the plant all winter.

This plant is found from Maine to New Jersey, west to Minnesota, South Dakota and Colorado, northward and westward.

PROPAGATION   By softwood cuttings, 2 inches long, in July, in sand or peat and sand. By long cuttings in the late fall.

By layering in the summer.

By seeds removed from pulp and sown outdoors in the fall, ¾-inch deep.

Epigaea repens   Trailing Arbutus

The best beloved of all spring wild flowers, at least in Massachusetts, this low evergreen woody plant makes mats of ovate, leathery, alternate hairy leaves bristly on the edges. The intensely fragrant tubular pink and white flowers, in terminal clusters, blossom in April and May. The fruit is a small white berry soon eaten by ants and birds. The plant requires a light acid, rather poor soil and may even grow in sand. It does not succeed in complete shade, needing some sun to flower well. A yearly mulch of very old manure, rotten wood, or acid leaf mold is beneficial.

This plant ranges from Newfoundland to Saskatchewan, south to Florida, Alabama, Kentucky, and Iowa.

PROPAGATION   By layering. This is a good method for those not having greenhouse facilities. In June, remove the soil from beneath some of the runners. Scrape the underside of the stem just below a joint for an inch or so in several places, treat the scraped portions with a rooting hormone, cover the layers with a mound of soil made up of equal parts of loam, peat, leaf mold, and sand, and lay a stone on the mound to keep it moist and in place. The layers may be removed the following year but should spend the next winter thereafter in a frame.

By cuttings. Take cuttings of the current season's growth in late August or early September, insert in peat moss, and keep moist and shaded in a frame or greenhouse. They will need the protection of cold frames for two years at least. One part perlite and two of coarse sand is another recommended medium for inserting cuttings.

By seeds. It is difficult to gather the seeds before they are eaten by ants and birds. Separate the seeds by rubbing between the fingers and sow them at once, but do not cover. They should be kept in a shaded cold frame or greenhouse. This is a slow process, for it takes about three years of greenhouse culture to obtain flowering plants. If grown in frames, a still longer time is required.

By transplanting. In areas where the plants face certain extermination they should be removed in as large sods as can be handled. This should be done in early spring or fall. The plants should be mulched with oak leaves and pine needles, lightly covering the plants from view. They must not be allowed to dry out. Protect from rodents.

Gaultheria procumbens
Wintergreen or Checkerberry

A good ground cover for open woodlands or clearings, in acid soil, this low creeping evergreen has oblong leathery leaves, crowded near the top of stems, 2 to 6 inches tall. The little white urn-shaped flowers are solitary or in small racemes in the leaf axils, blossoming in early summer. The leaves turn bronzy in winter, and the new leaf shoots, in spring, are very red. The aromatic red berries have a fleshy calyx much enjoyed by birds.

This plant grows from Newfoundland to

Manitoba and Minnesota, south to Virginia, Kentucky, and in the mountains to Georgia.

PROPAGATION   By division of the stolons set in moist sand and peat.

Sods can be easily transplanted.

DIAPENSIACEAE   Diapensia Family

This small family of evergreen shrubs or herbs has alternate, opposite, or basal leaves and small pink or white flowers. It is closely related to the Heath Family.

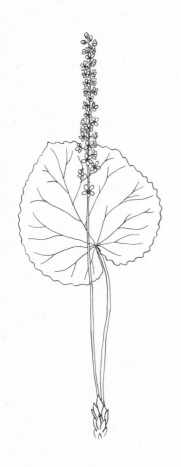

Galax aphylla   Galax

Growing wild only in moist acid mountain woods from Virginia to Georgia and Alabama, this creeping ground cover with handsome large round long-petioled evergreen leaves is, nevertheless, an invaluable addition to the shady wild garden in the North. The leaves are leathery, sharply toothed and shining, and turn red to bronze in winter. In summer the plant sends up leafless stalks from 8 to 18 inches tall, bearing a long spike-like raceme of many tiny white flowers.

PROPAGATION   By division of the matted roots, each with a bud, in the spring or fall.

By seeds sown in peaty soil in the fall or late winter.

Shortia galacifolia   Oconee-bells

Although extremely rare in nature, being found naturally only in the moist acid woods of the North Carolina mountains, shortia is now extensively cultivated in wild gardens even in subzero climates.

The low plant forms loose rosettes of shining round basal leaves about 1 inch across, like a small galax leaf. They are also sharply toothed, evergreen and leathery. The solitary nodding bell-like flowers are on stems only a few inches tall. They have five petals, each one with five lobes, and are white or faintly pinkish; they bloom in May.

PROPAGATION   By division after flowering.

By cuttings in sand and peat in August or September.

Seeds might be tried, treated as a heath.

P R I M U L A C E A E   Primrose Family

The Primrose Family contains genera which differ greatly from one another in general aspect, but they are mostly very desirable for various types of wild gardens.

Dodecatheon Meadia   Shooting-star

An unusually interesting native plant, shooting-star often does surprisingly well in moist spots in the wild garden, in slightly acid to neutral soil, and in places where it receives some sun. If the shade is too heavy it will live but may not blossom. In spring the plant makes a rosette of oblong leaves, often reddish in color. In May and June the leafless flower stalk, about 1 foot tall, bears a cluster of rosy lilac flowers at its summit, each flower having five sharply reflexed petals. The foliage disappears in summer.

This species is found in open woods and on moist slopes and prairies from Pennsylvania to Wisconsin, south to Louisiana and Texas.

PROPAGATION   By division in early
spring or before the plants go dormant.

By seeds sown in late winter, gathered
in autumn.

By upright root cuttings in fall.

Trientalis borealis   Star-flower

One of the most interesting ground covers
for moist woods and peaty slopes, this little
plant, creeping by slender rhizomes, sends up
single stems from 3 to 8 inches high with a
whorl of five to nine narrow leaves at the
summit. The one or two fragile white star-
shaped flowers are on thread-like stalks in the
leaf axils standing well above the whorl of
leaves. They have six or seven pointed petals,
and blossom in May and June.

The plant grows in strongly to moderately
acid soil in rich woods and bogs throughout
the northeastern half of North America.

PROPAGATION   By seeds sown when
fresh on loose leaf mold.

May be transplanted if sufficient soil is
taken, and if abundant.

Lysimachia ciliata   Fringed Loosestrife

This handsome perennial forms large
groups in marshy land and along stream
banks in full sun. The plant grows about three
feet tall and has broad opposite leaves with
hairy petioles. The pretty nodding yellow
flowers with five notched petals are in whorls
on stalks from the leaf axils, blossoming from
June to August. An easily grown plant, it is
desirable for the late spring wild garden. It
will grow in a variety of soils.

This species is found throughout northern North America.

PROPAGATION   By division in the spring.

L. Nummularia   Moneywort

This flat creeping species is a splendid ground cover for sun or shade, but flowers well only in the sun. It was introduced from Europe. The round leaves are in pairs, and the large solitary golden yellow flowers are borne on stalks in the leaf axils from June to August. This plant prefers moist ground and must be kept under control, as it spreads rapidly.

PROPAGATION   By division in the spring.

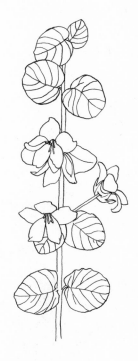

L. quadrifolia   Whorled Loosestrife

Large patches of this species are often seen in open woods where the plants form an excellent but tall ground cover. The leaves are in whorls of three to six, generally four, the young foliage being very red in May. The axillary flowers are on long stalks and have five yellow petals with dark red lines, blossoming in June and July. This species is taller and has larger flowers and leaves than the preceding. It grows in both wet and dry soils.

This species is found from Maine to Wisconsin, south to South Carolina, Kentucky, and Illinois.

PROPAGATION   Easily transplanted in spring, and the rootstock divided.

L. terrestris   Swamp-candles

This loosestrife is especially attractive when, in midsummer, countless yellow "candles" glow in the sunny lowlands. An erect plant, from 1 to 3 feet tall, it has opposite narrow leaves and long spires of small yellow flowers, the five petals marked with purple lines. The plant will form large colonies in wet fields in moderately acid soil. It occurs over the eastern half of North America except in the far south. Often there are bulblets on the stems.

PROPAGATION   Easily transplanted and spreads rapidly, often too readily.

PLUMBAGINACEAE
Leadwort Family

This family comprises seaside plants. They have small regular flowers with five parts.

Limonium carolinianum   Sea-Lavender

Only in seaside wild gardens and in salt marshes by the ocean can a suitable home be made for sea-lavender. The plant has a basal rosette of large leaves and the leafless flower stalk, branching at the top, produces a huge panicle of many tiny lavender flowers. They blossom in July and August.

This species is found near the coast from New England to Texas.

PROPAGATION   By seeds sown in early spring or fall.

GENTIANACEAE   Gentian Family

This family includes smooth herbs with generally opposite leaves, toothless and without petioles. The flowers have petals of varying numbers.

Subfamily Gentianoideae

Gentiana Andrewsii   Closed Gentian

This beautiful wild flower prefers wet ground in sun or part shade. The plant is a long-lived perennial in neutral or slightly acid soil and makes handsome clumps in the fall wild garden. It grows about 1 foot in height with pale green sessile leaves on the slender stems. Tubular dark violet-blue flowers that never open are clustered in the upper leaf axils and are showy in late August and September. There are several similar species much more difficult to grow.

The plant is found in wet meadows and thickets from Quebec to Manitoba, south to New England, New Jersey, Kentucky, Missouri, and Nebraska and in the mountains to North Carolina.

PROPAGATION   By division in the spring. By seeds.

G. crinita   Fringed Gentian

Because this beautiful species is biennial, constant attention is necessary to perpetuate it from season to season. The plant grows from 1 to 2 feet tall with many short erect side branches, each bearing a terminal flower. The deep blue vase-shaped blossoms, appearing in September and October, have four petals, the lobes deeply fringed and opening wide only in sunshine. The opposite leaves are yellow-green.

This gentian is found in neutral to moderately acid soil in wet meadows, low woods, and by brooks from Maine to Ontario, Michigan, and Minnesota, south to Pennsylvania, Illinois, and Iowa, and locally along the mountains to Georgia. Any one with a wet meadow should help to preserve this vanishing species by trying to establish it.

PROPAGATION   By seeds.

Menyanthes Subfamily

Menyanthes trifoliata   Bogbean

This interesting plant must have the permanent shallow water of marshes and bogs, conditions difficult to simulate in an artificial water garden. It has thick, scaly stems that creep in wet peat in acid to neutral soil. The five-parted white flowers are in short racemes above the foliage, blossoming in May and June. The basal leaves on long stalks are divided into three leaflets somewhat resembling those of beans.

This plant prefers cool climates and is found in boreal North America, south to New Jersey, Virginia, Indiana, and Missouri.

PROPAGATION   By division in the spring.

Nymphoides cordata   White Floating-heart

For small pools in the water garden this summer-flowering tiny aquatic is most appropriate. It has small rounded leaves that float in a cluster from long slender stalks, the roots being in water from 2 to 4 feet deep. From July to September, the small five-petaled white flowers are borne in an umbel just above the water, often with a cluster of short and spur-like roots.

This plant inhabits quiet water from Newfoundland and Quebec to Ontario, south to Connecticut and New York and along the Coastal Plain to South Carolina and Louisiana.

PROPAGATION   Gather clumps of spur-roots in September and plant in the mud of the pool.

N. aquaticum is similar but larger. It occurs from New Jersey to Florida and Texas.

APOCYNACEAE   Dogbane Family

This family is closely related to the milk-weeds. The species have milky acrid juice, opposite leaves, and five-parted funnel-shaped flowers. The fruits are long, tubular, many-seeded follicles.

Amsonia Tabernaemontana   Willow Amsonia

Amsonia has long been a favorite plant in the perennial border. It is equally suitable for the large spring wild garden. The plants make strong clumps about 3 feet high with numerous narrow oblong alternate leaves on the slender stems. Clusters of lovely small pale blue flowers with five narrow lobes are borne at the tips of the stems, in May, but are eventually hidden from sight as the stems continue to elongate. The plants are hardy and long-lived and will grow almost anywhere in full sun or part shade.

This plant is found in moist or wet woods on the Coastal Plain from New Jersey to Virginia, west to Oklahoma and Texas.

PROPAGATION   By division in the spring. The plant self-sows freely. Collect seeds in October.

Apocynum androsaemifolium
Spreading Dogbane

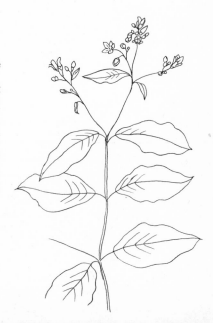

Colonies of this somewhat weedy plant are common along roadsides in June and July. It is useful only in large wild gardens. The leafy forking stems are from 2 to 3 feet tall, the opposite leaves being ovate and dark green. The nodding bell-like pale pink flowers, marked red within, are in small terminal cymes and also in the leaf axils.

This plant is found from Newfoundland to British Columbia, south to Georgia, Texas and Arizona.

PROPAGATION   By division. It transplants readily in spring.

ASCLEPIADACEAE
Milkweed Family

The members of this family are mostly milky-juiced plants with large opposite, alternate, or whorled entire leaves. The small but numerous flowers are in five parts. The five-lobed corolla is deeply reflexed at time of bloom with the five hoods which form the corona being the most conspicuous part of the flower.

Asclepias quadrifolia   Four-leaved Milkweed

This plant, about 1 foot high, has two small opposite leaves near the stem base, another pair near the tip, and a whorl of four near the middle of the stem. The pale pink flowers are in umbels, and blossom in May and June. This species does not spread and is an interesting addition to the wild garden in moderately acid soil.

This species is found in dry upland woods from New England to Minnesota, south to North Carolina and Arkansas.

PROPAGATION   By division in the spring. By seeds, collected in autumn and sown in the fall or spring.

A. incarnata   Swamp Milkweed

A desirable plant for the moist summer wild garden, this species grows about 3 feet high. The smooth opposite leaves are on stems branched near the top. The rose-purple flowers

P. bifida   Cleft Phlox

The pale blue petals of this beautiful phlox are deeply cut, almost as if the flowers had ten petals. The narrow, finely downy leaves are in pairs on slender stems which form broad mounds, in moderately acid to neutral soil on sand dunes, dry cliffs, and rock ledges, in sun, from Michigan to Iowa, south to Tennessee and Oklahoma.

This species is especially good for a rock planting in the wild garden. It flowers in April and May.

PROPAGATION   By seeds sown in the
    early spring. The plant self-sows widely.
        By cuttings inserted in sand after
    blooming.
        The clumps are not readily divided, un-
    less they are very old plants.

P. maculata   Meadow Phlox

The purple to white flowers of this phlox are borne in a cylindric cluster. The leaves are narrow but broader toward the base. The plant grows 2 to 3 feet tall, and the stems are often mottled purple. It flowers from late May to August.

This species is found in wet meadows in moderately acid soil and is suitable for the moist wild garden. Its range is from Quebec to Ohio and North Carolina and from Minnesota to Missouri.

PROPAGATION   Same as for *P. glaber-
    rima.*

The summer phlox *P. paniculata,* the standby of the summer perennial border, is native in its magenta-colored form in rich moist soil from New York to Indiana and Kansas, south to Georgia and Arkansas. Its color might not make it too popular in the wild garden.

P. glaberrima   Smooth Phlox

The white cultivated phlox, "Miss Lingard," is a named variety of this species. The plant has smooth, shining narrow leaves and grows 2 to 3 feet tall. The reddish-purple flowers are grouped in cymes, both terminal and from the upper pairs of leaves, blossoming in May and June.

This species is found in swampy woods and thickets from Ohio and Kentucky south to Georgia and west to Texas.

PROPAGATION   By division in the spring.
By softwood cuttings taken in the summer.

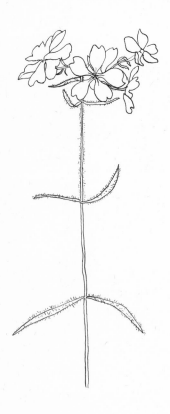

P. divaricata   Blue Phlox

One of the most desirable and attractive plants for the spring wild garden is blue phlox. It is a low, erect species, the flowering stems being 6 to 18 inches tall; the sterile shoots are often prostrate; the opposite leaves are oblong and nearly smooth. The lovely pale blue-purple flowers with notched petal lobes are in loosely branched flat terminal clusters and blossom in April and May. They make quite large clumps under favorable conditions.

This species is found in neutral soil in rich moist open woods and on rocky slopes from southwestern Quebec and New York to Michigan and Illinois, south to South Carolina and Alabama.

PROPAGATION   By division in the spring.
By softwood cuttings of nonflowering shoots in May and June.

P. divaricata Laphami has unnotched petal lobes and is deeper blue in color.

P. pilosa   Downy Phlox

A more southern and western species very similar to *P. divaricata,* this phlox is more slender with very hairy stems and no basal runners. The red-purple flowers are smaller with rounded petals and open in May and June.

This species inhabits dry upland woods and prairies in moderately acid soil from Connecticut and New Jersey, south and west to Texas and South Dakota.

PROPAGATION   Same as for *P. glaberrima.*

P. stolonifera   Creeping Phlox

Unexcelled as a ground cover for the spring wild garden in a woodsy, partly shaded area, in or out of flower, this low phlox has widely creeping runners with nearly round opposite leaves and evergreen basal rosettes. In May and June, loose small clusters of large pinkish or blue-purple flowers are borne on 6-inch stems. In the wild the flowers are usually red-purple and much less attractive.

This species is found in moist woods and bottoms in moderately acid soil from Pennsylvania and Ohio, south to South Carolina and Georgia. It cannot survive long summer drought.

PROPAGATION   By division of the rooted runners.

P. subulata   Moss Phlox

A common dwarf plant universally grown in rock gardens, in full sun, the magenta or white moss phlox is found, in nature, on dry, sandy, gravelly, and rocky soil from Long Island to Michigan, south to North Carolina and Tennessee. It has become naturalized in many areas, including New England.

The plant has harsh, needle-like foliage on stems making large prostrate moss-like mats. The few-flowered clusters of purplish-pink blossoms are on short stems, 2 to 5 inches high, which completely hide the foliage in early spring.

P. nivalis is a similar species, more common in the South, which is larger in general habit of growth. It flowers in May.

PROPAGATION   By layering and by division after blooming.

By cuttings in October or November in sand in a cold frame.

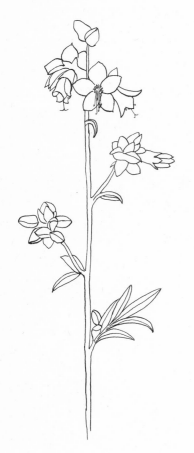

Polemonium Van-Bruntiae   Jacob's-ladder

This handsome plant resembles the upright blue polemonium found in cultivated gardens. It may grow 3 feet tall. The alternate pinnately-divided leaves have 15 to 21 leaflets. The blue-purple flowers are in terminal compact few-flowered panicles, and blossom from mid-June through July.

A somewhat rare species, the plant grows in wooded swamps and mossy glades from Vermont and New York to Maryland and West Virginia. All the polemoniums are suitable for the wild garden.

PROPAGATION   By division in the spring.

By seeds, though they are rarely offered by dealers.

P. reptans   Jacob's-ladder

Although a low-branching plant, about 1 foot high, this species does not creep. The leaves have 5 to 15 leaflets, and the nodding blue flowers appear in May. It is an easy and desirable plant for the wild garden.

This species grows wild in open woods and on the margins of meadows in neutral to moderately acid soil from New York westward and southward. It is abundant in moist open fields in the Great Lakes region.

PROPAGATION   By division after flowering.

By seeds. The plant self-sows readily.

HYDROPHYLLACEAE
Waterleaf Family

Plants in this family have alternate entire to compound leaves and small to medium-sized five-parted white to blue or purple flowers, the inflorescence somewhat spiraled.

Hydrophyllum virginianum
Virginia Waterleaf

This erect leafy plant grows 1 to 2 feet tall and has leaves pinnately divided into five, six, or seven cut-toothed leaflets. The white to rose-purple tubular flowers are in curved cymes, borne well above the leaves, blossoming in June. The plant is excellent for the woodland garden. There are several similar species.

This plant prefers neutral or slightly acid soil and is found in wet woods and open wet places from Quebec to North Dakota, south to Virginia, Kentucky, Arkansas, and Kansas.

PROPAGATION   By seeds, gathered as soon as ripe and sown in the fall or spring.

By division in the spring.

BORAGINACEAE   Borage Family

This family is distinguished by the spiraled arrangement of its flower clusters. The individual flowers are mostly on one side of the inflorescence, simulating a raceme or spike which is rolled up from the end, straightening as the flowers unfold. They have five petals. The leaves are alternate, entire, or shallowly toothed.

Mertensia virginica   Virginia Bluebells

A favorite plant both in the cultivated border and in the wild garden, this species is one of the gardener's standbys. It sends up smooth stems 2 feet tall with glaucous oblong leaves, mostly basal, which are reddish when they emerge from the fleshy tubers. The clusters of nodding bell-like flowers, pale blue in color, are pink in the bud and blossom in late April and May. The plants disappear in summer.

This plant prefers some moisture and partial shade and grows in rich, usually neutral soil from New York and Ontario to Minnesota, south to South Carolina, Alabama, and Arkansas.

PROPAGATION   By division of the tuberous roots in midsummer.

By seeds sown in February. The plant self-sows freely.

By transplanting self-sown seedlings in the spring.

Lithospermum canescens
Puccoon or Golden Gromwell

A densely white-downy plant, 8 inches or more in height, this species has crowded curved clusters of golden yellow tubular flowers in June. It grows from a large woody red root. It is a difficult plant to naturalize and is probably not long-lived.

This plant is found in dry sunny ground or in gravelly clayey, poorly drained soil that is neutral to slightly acid, from Georgia to Texas and northward.

PROPAGATION From seeds sown in peaty soil in early spring.

Myosotis laxa   Forget-me-not

This species with pale blue flowers and a yellow eye often chokes brooks and the borders of small streams, blossoming through much of the summer. The plant has pale green oblong leaves and floats out over the water on 6-inch stems.

This species is found in muddy ground from Newfoundland and Quebec to Minnesota, south to Georgia and Indiana; also from British Columbia to California.

PROPAGATION   By division in the spring.
By seeds sown at any time on moist soil.

M. scorpioides came from Europe and has escaped from gardens. It is a larger, more hairy plant than the preceding and produces quantities of bright blue flowers in the spring and summer. It enjoys a somewhat moist soil.

There are also annual species for the spring garden which self-sow freely.

PROPAGATION By cuttings in sand.
By cuttings inserted where they are to grow.
By seeds sown any day on wet soil.

Echium vulgare Viper's Bugloss or Blue Devil

Introduced from Europe, this coarse rough hairy biennial is very showy with its curving dense cymes of deep-blue two-lipped flowers produced in great abundance throughout the summer on stems 1 to 2 feet tall.

Although quite handsome seen at a distance in dry waste places and along roadsides, it must not be planted in the wild garden unless it can be kept under control.

PROPAGATION By seeds only.

VERBENACEAE   Vervain Family

The plants of the Vervain Family have opposite leaves and more or less irregular corollas of four or five petals united below. The stamens are a distinguishing feature, being in two pairs of unequal length.

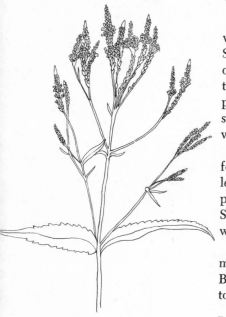

Verbena hastata   Blue Vervain

When growing in large colonies, blue vervain casts a violet mist over the landscape. Single specimens are not so effective since only a few flowers are out at one time. This, the tallest of the verbenas, is of value in a planting of wild flowers in a moist area with such robust companions as boneset, Joe-Pye-weed, and ironweed.

An erect leafy plant, which may grow to 7 feet high, it has stiff stems, ovate, toothed leaves, and many long terminal spikes of tiny purple flowers. They blossom from July to September. There are less desirable species with white or pale-colored flowers.

This species is found in moist places in moderately acid soil from Nova Scotia to British Columbia, south to Florida, and west to Nebraska and Arizona.

PROPAGATION   By division in the spring.
The plant self-sows freely.
By cuttings taken in the summer.

V. canadensis   Rose-Verbena

The most showy of the verbenas, this low, spreading perennial has stems reaching a length of about 1 foot. The broad, coarsely toothed leaves are cut into three lobed divisions. Elongated heads of rose-purple flowers with five small petals, notched at the tip, blossom over a long period in late spring and summer. The plant is easily grown in wild gardens, but in good soil it usually dies in a few years. It may be carried on indefinitely, however, by starting new plants from the self-rooting stems.

This species grows in sandy, rocky, neutral to moderately acid soils from Florida to Texas, north to Virginia, Illinois, and Colorado.

PROPAGATION   By division in the spring.
By seeds sown in the spring or fall.
By cuttings taken in the summer.

LABIATAE   Mint Family

The Mint Family is characterized by plants having simple opposite leaves and square stems. The two-lipped flowers are in small, usually dense cymes in the axils of the foliage leaves, often surrounding the stem and thus forming a verticil. When the foliage leaves below the verticils are greatly reduced and bract-like, the inflorescence forms a terminal, continuous, or interrupted spike. Sometimes there is only one verticil forming a terminal head, or there may be a few terminal and subterminal ones. These characteristics are useful in identification. Many mints secrete oils which have a strong odor and taste.

Agastache Foeniculum   Blue Giant Hyssop

The dry upland woods and prairies of the Midwest are the natural habitat of this handsome mint. It is found from Ontario and Manitoba to Iowa, west to Colorado and Washington. It has also escaped to New England and Delaware.

This species is a stout perennial making an upright clump from nonspreading roots, and grows 3 feet tall. The square stem is smooth, and the petioled, toothed leaves are white below. Deep blue-purple flowers are borne in dense interrupted terminal spikes in June and July. The whole plant is anise-scented.

PROPAGATION   By division in spring. It does not spread from the roots.

By seeds. It self-sows widely. Gather seeds in autumn from the dried flower heads.

A. nepetoides   Yellow Giant Hyssop

A hyssop with yellow flowers, this plant has smooth, coarsely toothed leaves and is found from eastern Canada to South Dakota, south to North Carolina and Kansas.

PROPAGATION   Same as for *A. Foeniculum.*

A. scrophulariaefolia   Purple Giant Hyssop

This species has deep purple flowers in dense continuous spikes sometimes interrupted at the base. The leaves are slightly pubescent, and green below. The plant occurs in rich thickets and slightly acid upland woods from Vermont and New York to Ontario, south to North Carolina and Kansas.

PROPAGATION   Same as for *A. Foeniculum.*

Blephilia ciliata   Downy Wood-Mint

This species grows in a clump about 2 feet tall. The oblong, toothed leaves are whitish below. The pale blue flowers are spotted with purple and crowded into a continuous terminal spike, 2 to 5 inches long, and blossoming from June to August.

This species is found in moist or dry woods from New England to Wisconsin, south to Georgia and Arkansas.

PROPAGATION   By division in the spring. By seeds as for other mints.

B. hirsuta   Wood-Mint

This is a taller species than the above, and very hairy throughout. The flowers are similar, and blossom from June to September.

This species grows in moist shady places from Quebec and Vermont to Minnesota, south to Georgia and Texas.

PROPAGATION   Same as for *B. ciliata.*

Collinsia canadensis   Horse-Balm

This lemon-scented perennial grows from thick woody rhizomes to a height of about 3 feet. The large ovate leaves are toothed. The yellowish flowers are in pairs on slender pedicels arranged in loose terminal panicles, blossoming from July to September.

This plant grows in rich moist, slightly acid or neutral woods from New England to Wisconsin, south to Florida and Arkansas.

PROPAGATION   By division in the spring. By seeds. Plants self-sow readily.

Cunila origanoides   Common Dittany

This tufted, somewhat woody, much-branched plant, about 1 foot tall, has small ovate, toothed leaves close to the stem. The rose-purple to white flowers are in small clusters in the upper leaf axils at the branch tips, blossoming from July to October, and are strongly fragrant.

This plant frequents dry or rocky acid woods and clearings in acid soil from New York and Pennsylvania to Indiana and Missouri, south to South Carolina and Oklahoma.

PROPAGATION   By division in spring only.

By seeds sown at any time.

Hedeoma pulegioides   American Pennyroyal

A neat, bushy annual, about 1 foot tall, this species is suitable for naturalizing in very poor, dry stony soil. It has small narrow leaves and tiny pale lavender flowers in whorls in the axils of the upper leaves, blossoming from July to September. All parts of the plant have the strong fragrance of pennyroyal, very noticeable in the heat of a warm summer day.

This plant is found from Quebec and Nova Scotia to Michigan and South Dakota, south to Alabama, Arkansas, and Kansas.

PROPAGATION   By seeds sown in the spring or fall.

Mentha arvensis   Field Mint

Although most of the true mints are not native, the field mint is an exception. It is a leafy, much-branched rapid spreader about 2 feet high. The small lilac-pink flowers are in tiny axillary clusters, and blossom in July and August.

The mints soon form large colonies in moist soil throughout northern North America, south to Virginia and Missouri, west to California. They hybridize freely. All are strongly fragrant.

PROPAGATION   By division of the roots in spring.

Glechoma hederacea Gill-over-the-ground

This creeping round-leaved perennial is a good ground cover for damp, shady places. The small purplish-blue flowers are borne usually three in each leaf axil. Although an introduced plant, it is now widely naturalized. It has a strong odor of catnip. The flowers appear from July to September. It often becomes a pest.

PROPAGATION By division in the spring.

Monarda didyma Oswego-tea or Bee-balm

This plant has long been common in perennial borders and is invaluable for the summer wild garden, flowering much of the season. The erect clumps grow up to 4 feet tall with broad, coarse-toothed leaves. The red flowers are in two to three large heads borne well above the foliage. The bracts between the flowers are also red.

This species grows in moist soil in moderately acid woods or part shade from New York to Michigan, south to New Jersey, West Virginia, and Ohio.

PROPAGATION By division in the spring only.

By seeds gathered in October and sown at any time.

By cuttings in the summer, in a moist medium.

M. fistulosa Wild Bergamot

In size and habit of growth this species resembles Oswego-tea. The pale lilac-pink flowers are in two to three large, dense terminal whorls carried well above the hairy gray-green leaves. The upper lip of the downy blossom is noticeably bearded, and the bracts below the flower clusters are pink-tinged. This monarda belongs with such plants as yellow bedstraw, crown-vetch, and black-eyed Susan in dry, sunny fields.

This species is found in dry, slightly to moderately acid fields and clearings from Quebec to British Columbia, south to Georgia, Texas, and Arizona.

PROPAGATION   Same as for *M. didyma.*

M. punctata   Spotted Monarda

The flowers of this species are creamy in color, with purple spots, and are borne in interrupted spikes of two to five whorls. The bracts below each flower cluster are purple to white, and bloom over a long season from late July.

This species grows in acid sandy soil from Long Island to Florida and Texas along the Coastal Plain.

PROPAGATION   Same as for *M. didyma.*

Physostegia virginiana
False Dragonhead or Obedient-plant

This smooth, easily grown, and dependable plant has leafy stems 3 feet tall, the leaves narrow and sharply toothed. The rose-colored flowers, quite close together in terminal spikes, are usually in two rows and can be pushed out of line with the fingers, hence the common name of obedient-plant. The species flowers all summer, a white form being especially attractive as well as a less rampant grower. It is common in cultivation and is suitable for the large wild garden with other strong-growing spreaders.

This plant is found in moist sunny thickets

in slightly acid soil from Vermont to Minnesota and Illinois, south to South Carolina and Texas.

PROPAGATION   By division of the creeping stolons in the spring.

Prunella vulgaris   Selfheal

The basal rosettes of oval leaves and the much-branched, closely matted stems, only a few inches high, make this perennial a valuable ground cover for moist areas that are frequently walked upon. The medium-sized purple flowers are in three-flowered clusters in the axils of round bract-like floral leaves forming a dense terminal head, blossoming from May to September.

This plant is found throughout the Northern Hemisphere.

PROPAGATION   By division in the spring. It self-sows.

Pycnanthemum virginianum   Mountain-Mint

Although not showy, this stiff upright, perennial herb is desirable for dry or wet spots, in sun, even in the small wild garden. The bushy much-branched clumps grow about 2 feet tall with many narrow leaves and small white flowers borne in close, rather flat-topped head-like cymes terminating the branches. These are nearly hidden by the green bracts below them, and they blossom in August. The plants have a pleasant thyme-like odor.

This species occurs from Maine to North Dakota, south to Georgia and Oklahoma.

PROPAGATION   By division in the spring. By seeds, collected in October and sown at any time.

There are several very similar species. A very familiar one is *P. flexuosum,* with smooth linear bright green, sharp-pointed leaves and tiny white or lavender flowers in summer. It prefers moderately acid soil.

Salvia azurea   Blue Sage

This attractive salvia is also known as S. *Pitcheri,* the pale blue form. It is an erect perennial about 5 feet tall with many narrow dark green, toothed leaves. The large clear blue flowers are in dense spike-like racemes at the ends of the main stems and adjacent short lateral branches, blooming in late summer. They are reminiscent of the flowers of the popular annual blue salvia, S. *farinacea.* The plant requires staking in the cultivated garden, but its floppy habit would, perhaps, be less objectionable in the wild garden.

This species is found on dry plains and prairies from Missouri and Arkansas to Nebraska and Texas. It has also escaped from cultivation into New England.

PROPAGATION   By seeds sown in the spring or fall.

By cuttings taken in the summer.

S. lyrata   Lyre-leaved Sage

A salvia less frequently seen than the preceding species, it is a hairy perennial with a basal rosette of deeply lobed leaves. The violet flowers are in a few widely separated whorls on stems about 2 feet tall, blossoming in May and June.

This species is found in sandy, moderately acid open woods and thickets from Connecticut to Pennsylvania, south to Florida and

Texas. The salvias from the South would not find it easy to survive northern winters.

PROPAGATION   Same as for *S. azurea.*

Scutellaria integrifolia   Hyssop Skullcap

Because of the clear violet-blue color of the flowers, the skullcaps should be better known. They receive their name from the peculiar "hump" on the top section of the green calyx resembling a skullcap. Although bitter herbs, these perennials are not aromatic.

This species has narrow, entire leaves and solitary blue-purple flowers about an inch long in each upper leaf axil, forming handsome terminal clusters. They blossom in June and July on plants from 6 to 18 inches in height.

This species is found on the borders of woods and thickets from New England to Florida and Texas. It is most abundant on the Coastal Plain but also ranges inland to southern Ohio and Tennessee.

PROPAGATION   From seeds sown at any time. It self-sows.

From cuttings in early summer.

By division in early spring.

S. serrata   Showy Skullcap

This species has bright green ovate leaves and large blue-purple flowers in pairs near the branch tips, blooming in late spring. It grows to 2 feet tall, forming small dense clumps in open woods in slightly acid soil.

It is found from South Carolina to Alabama, north to New York and Illinois.

PROPAGATION   Same as for *S. integrifolia.*

Stachys hyssopifolia   Hedge-Nettle

This widely creeping plant with slender stems 2 feet tall is a subject for wet sands and peat bogs. The entire, pale green leaves are very narrow, and the pink flowers, mottled purple, are in widely separated whorls, blossoming from June to October. The plant has a strong musky odor.

Preferring to grow near the coast, this plant is found from Massachusetts to Georgia and also near Lake Michigan.

PROPAGATION   By division in the spring. By seeds or cuttings.

Teucrium canadense
                    American Germander or Wood-Sage

This stiff, bushy plant may grow 3 feet tall. It has thick narrow, toothed leaves which are white below. The small pink, purple, or dull white flowers are in close whorls on a long spike, and bloom from July to September.

This species prefers to grow in moist or wet soil near the coast and is found from Maine to Florida. It should do well in the seaside garden.

PROPAGATION   By division in the spring. By seeds sown in spring.

Thymus Serpyllum
                    Creeping Thyme or Wild Thyme

Very well known is this little creeper which was introduced from Europe and which has escaped from gardens. It forms large mats in dry fields and lawns in full sun. The plant is evergreen and aromatic with small dark green leaves. The little purplish

flowers appear from June to September and are crowded in small erect racemes at the ends of the wiry stems. The plant is an excellent ground cover for the summer wild garden.

PROPAGATION   By division in the spring. By seeds sown in May.

SOLANACEAE   Nightshade Family

This family includes plants with alternate leaves and five-parted flowers, the petals united to a starry or funnel-shaped corolla.

Solanum Dulcamara   Bitter Nightshade

This woody climber is common in moist waste places, having been introduced from Europe. The alternate, ovate leaves are usually roundly lobed. Deep purple flowers are produced in both terminal and axillary clusters from May to September. The small ovoid bright red fruits are quite showy and are well liked by birds. They are poisonous to humans. The plant is decorative for large wild gardens. The flowers, shaped like those on potato plants, and the berries are borne at the same time and will add interest to areas too overrun for more choice species.

PROPAGATION   The basal shoots are readily transplanted in the spring. By seeds. The plant self-sows freely.

SCROPHULARIACEAE
Figwort Family

The flowers of the Figwort Family are two-lipped, the petals more or less united, and vary in shape from tubular to nearly round. Snapdragon and foxglove are familiar examples.

Chelone glabra   White Turtlehead

The turtleheads are very useful for moist spots in the wild garden, and bloom in August when color is much needed. Although tall, they are not weedy and are suitable for fairly small areas. This species is a slender, smooth erect plant about 3 feet tall. The large serrate opposite leaves are always attractive, and the tubular white flowers, shaped like a turtle's head, are in dense spikes at the ends of the stems.

This species grows on low ground and along streams, in moderately acid soil, from Newfoundland to Ontario and Minnesota, south to Georgia and Missouri.

PROPAGATION   By seeds. It self-sows readily.

By division in the spring.

By cuttings taken in the summer.

Transplants easily in the spring, where abundant.

C. Lyoni   Pink Turtlehead

This species has broader leaves which are handsome all summer. It should be used with the white turtlehead. The flowers are deep rose, the lower lip with a deep yellow beard and bright purple lines. This species is cultivated and has escaped from gardens in New England, although native in the Carolina mountains, where it grows in quite acid soil. It flowers in September and October. It does well in tiny city gardens.

PROPAGATION   Same as for *C. glabra*.

C. obliqua is similar, with narrower leaves and purple flowers with a pale yellow beard. It grows in wet woods and cypress swamps from Maryland and Tennessee to Florida and Mississippi, flowering in late August to October.

Gratiola aurea   Golden Hedge-hyssop

This is a delightful small bog plant for summer flowering, in full sun, with its small two-lipped bright yellow flowers in flat clusters. It grows 1 foot tall in a close clump and has four-sided stems with smooth narrow clasping leaves.

This plant is found on wet sands or acid peat mostly near the coast from Newfoundland and Quebec to Florida. It also grows at numerous inland stations from New York and Ontario to North Dakota and Illinois.

PROPAGATION   By division at any time in the summer.

By transplanting at any time, where abundant.

Linaria vulgaris   Butter-and-eggs

This introduced wild flower needs little description. In fields and waste places, from spring to fall, the plants make large mats of narrow blue-green leaves with tubular yellow flowers with orange throats blooming in terminal racemes. They are like small snapdragon flowers with the addition of a long rear spur.

PROPAGATION   By seeds, gathered in October and sown at any time.

Large sods may be transplanted, where abundant.

There are various other species, some annual, some perennial.

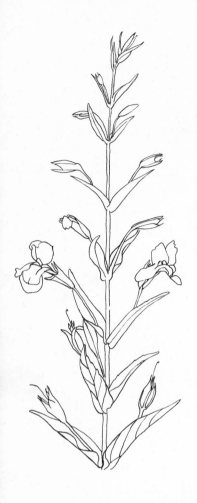

Mimulus alatus   Monkey-flower

There are two species of monkey-flower very similar in appearance, varying mostly in their range, which are desirable for the moist summer wild garden.

This species has stems with thin wing-angles, and grows from 2 to 3 feet tall. The opposite oblong, toothed leaves are petioled. The solitary tubular lavender flowers in the upper leaf axils are on short stalks. The two petals forming the upper lip, and the three the lower, remotely suggest a monkey's face, hence the name. It flowers from June to September.

This species is found in wet neutral or slightly acid soil from Connecticut to Ontario, Michigan and Iowa, south to Florida and Texas.

M. ringens differs in having square stems and sessile leaves. It is found from Nova Scotia and Quebec to Saskatchewan, south to Georgia, Louisiana, and Oklahoma.

PROPAGATION   By seeds sown in March. It should flower the same year.

By division in the spring.

By cuttings taken in the summer.

By transplanting, where abundant.

There are handsome species of *Mimulus* in the West with red, pink, or yellow flowers.

Penstemon   Beard-tongue

There are many beautiful species of Penstemon, growing mostly in the western part of the country, which are difficult to make happy in eastern gardens. The majority are short-lived plants, especially under cultivation. Several of the taller-growing, more reliable species, only, are included here.

P. Cobaea   Cobaea Penstemon

This is another downy species about 2 feet tall. The large purple flowers have swollen throats, blossoming in May and June. The plant is frequently cultivated and has escaped into eastern areas. Its range is in calcareous rich soil from Nebraska to Arkansas and Texas.

PROPAGATION   By seeds sown in the fall or spring.

P. grandiflorus   Large-flowered Penstemon

This is a striking and unmistakable species. The plant is smooth throughout, covered with a bluish-white bloom, and may grow 4 feet tall. The thick rounded leaves clasp the stem in pairs, and there is little basal foliage. The large pinkish-lavender flowers are borne well above the top pair of leaves in June and July. The plant is desirable for any type of garden but is very short-lived.

This species is found on dry prairies and barrens from Wisconsin to North Dakota and Wyoming, south to Missouri and Texas.

PROPAGATION   Plant seeds yearly for best results. Treat as a biennial.

P. hirsutus   Eastern Penstemon

A relatively low plant, growing not over 2 feet tall, this is an easy and useful species for dry and rocky situations in neutral or slightly acid soil. The plant is covered with small white hairs, and the many narrow dull purple flowers with a white lip are not very showy. They appear from May to July.

This species is found in dry woods and fields from Quebec and Maine, Michigan and Wisconsin, south to Virginia and Kentucky.

PROPAGATION   Transplant new seedlings, which self-sow readily.

By seeds sown in the spring.

By short cuttings from July to September.

By division in the spring.

P. Digitalis   Smooth White Penstemon

This very smooth plant grows from 3 to 4 feet tall. It has opposite ovate, toothed leaves close to the stem, and many basal ones in a permanent rosette. The flowers are borne in compound groups, blossoming in June and July. The corolla-tube of the white flowers, faintly marked with purple lines, swells abruptly near the middle into a wide throat.

This species is found in open woods, meadows and prairies from Maine and Quebec to South Dakota, south to Virginia, Louisiana, and Texas.

PROPAGATION   By seeds sown in March or in the fall.

By division in the spring.

There are several similar white-flowered species.

Veronicastrum virginicum   Culver's-root

One of the tallest plants for the wild garden, this stout perennial often grows 6 feet tall. It has leafy stems, the narrow dark green, sharply-toothed leaves being arranged in whorls around the stem. The small white flowers blossom from July to September in long, erect branched spikes like a huge veronica. It is a splendid background plant for the wild garden in sun or part shade.

This plant is found from New England, Ontario, and Manitoba south to Georgia and Louisiana in moderately acid soil.

PROPAGATION   By division in the spring. The clumps thicken rapidly.

By seeds sown at any time.

By cuttings taken in the summer.

ACANTHACEAE   Acanthus Family

This family has simple opposite leaves and usually five-parted, brilliantly colored, handsome flowers.

Ruellia caroliniensis
          Wild Petunia or Carolina Ruellia

Seldom seen in northern gardens, this plant is more common from New Jersey southward and west to Indiana and Texas where it is found in sandy woods, flowering from June to August.

The erect plants with simple or branching stems from 1 to 3 feet tall, are very hairy or downy. The leaves are oval, and the beautiful tubular lavender flowers with five petals are borne singly in the leaf axils. The plants are very desirable for the wild garden. They are worth trying north of their natural range.

PROPAGATION   By division in the spring. By seeds, sown in the spring.

RUBIACEAE   Madder Family

Members of the Madder Family included here are rather small plants with opposite or whorled leaves. The regular flower parts are mostly in fours, united at the base.

Galium boreale   Northern Bedstraw

Although somewhat weedy, the bedstraws, of which there are many species, have a place in the summer wild garden.

This species has leaves in fours and compact axillary clusters of tiny white flowers at the top of stems growing 1 to 2 feet tall. It frequents meadows, gravelly banks and shores from Maine and New York to New Jersey and from Minnesota and Nebraska westward, flowering from June to August. It prefers neutral or slightly acid soil.

PROPAGATION   By division in the spring or by seeds sown in the spring.

G. triflorum   Sweet-scented Bedstraw

A slender perennial with weak stems about 3 feet long, this species has narrow leaves in whorls of six and small greenish-white flowers with four petals. These are on peduncles in terminal groups of three and also in the leaf axils, blossoming from June to August. When dried, this species is usually fragant.

This galium is found in open woods and thickets throughout the northern states and Canada and, sparingly, south to Louisiana and Texas.

PROPAGATION   Same as for *G. boreale.*

G. verum   Yellow Bedstraw

Since this species succeeds in dry soil, it can be very useful where many other wild flowers would not grow. It makes large clumps and would become a pest if well treated.

The narrow leaves are mostly in whorls of eight on upright stems growing 3 feet long. The tiny yellow blossoms are in many-flowered compact clusters from the upper leaf axils.

This species was introduced from Europe and has become naturalized in fields and along roadsides.

PROPAGATION   Same as for *G. boreale,* but spring division is sufficient.

Houstonia caerulea   Bluets or Quaker-ladies

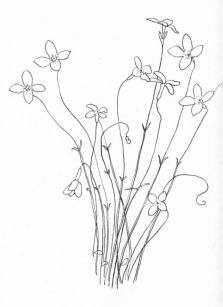

It is a sure sign that spring has arrived when this little plant, only 3 to 6 inches high, carpets moist meadows and sunny fields with its little pale blue flowers during April and May. The solitary blossoms have four petals and a bright yellow center. They are of two kinds; some have styles extending above the anthers; others have anthers standing above the styles, they being dependent upon long-tongued insects for cross-pollination. Dense tufts of minute opposite leaves lie close to the ground.

Although bluets are considered easy to introduce into wild gardens, they sometimes refuse to take hold in spite of the gardener's most determined efforts. The reason for this is not understood.

This species is found in moderately to very acid soils from Nova Scotia and Quebec to Wisconsin, south to Georgia and Arkansas.

PROPAGATION   By division in the spring or after flowering. Pot the divisions in leafy soil and winter in a cold frame.

By seeds sown in March or in the fall.

By cuttings, after flowering, rooted in sand and peat in a shaded frame.

H. purpurea   Purple Bluets

This is a taller, southern species found from Delaware to Georgia and Alabama, west to Arkansas. It prefers open sandy woods or rocky slopes.

The erect plant may grow 20 inches tall. It has many opposite pale green ovate leaves and small clusters of purple long-tubed flowers blossoming from May to July.

PROPAGATION   By division in the spring.

By seeds sown in the spring or fall.

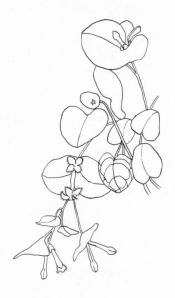

Mitchella repens   Partridge-berry

Very popular at Christmas time is this low creeping evergreen which makes large mats in acid soil in shade or part shade. The plant has shining, opposite leaves and small, very fragrant white flowers in pairs. These join together and form one red berry with two "eyes" in the leaf axil. The berries last all winter if not eaten by birds. The blossoms appear in June and July.

This splendid ground cover is widespread from Nova Scotia to Ontario and Minnesota, south to Florida and Texas.

PROPAGATION   By division in spring.

By softwood cuttings in August in a shaded frame in sand and acid peat. The new plants should be potted and plunged in peat in a shaded frame through the next winter or longer.

If transplanting from the wild, large sods should be carefully lifted. Take only from areas where abundant.

The berries may be planted (whole or broken) in a moist acid medium in the fall.

CAPRIFOLIACEAE
Honeysuckle Family

This family is much like the Madder Family, although the flower petals often number five and may be bilateral. The plants are mostly woody.

Triosteum perfoliatum   Horse-gentian

This coarse perennial has stout downy stems, 3 to 4 feet tall, and opposite oval sessile leaves. In May and June, three or four small tubular dull greenish or reddish flowers are borne in the leaf axils. Dull orange berry-like fruits appear in September.

This plant occurs in thickets in sun or part shade in neutral or moderately acid soil from Massachusetts to Ontario and Minnesota, south to South Carolina, Missouri, and Nebraska. It would be an interesting addition to the wild garden.

PROPAGATION   Small plants may be collected if abundant.

Old plants are not readily divided, and seeds germinate poorly.

Linnaea borealis var. *americana*   Twinflower

In cold mossy wet woods and swamps, in strongly acid soil, this rather woody evergreen creeper grows to perfection, having trailing stems up to 20 inches long. It is difficult to naturalize in the average wild garden and should not be attempted.

The plant has small roundish leaves and sends up thread-like flower stalks, 3 to 4 inches high, from the branch tips, bearing, in summer, a pair of nodding, fragrant pink bell-shaped flowers only ⅓ of an inch long. The plant is delightful in every way.

This species is found throughout northern North America, south through the mountains.

PROPAGATION   By division in the summer. Plant in peaty soil.

By cuttings in May taken with a heel inserted in sand and acid peat in a shaded frame.

CUCURBITACEAE   Gourd Family

This is a family of climbing vines, generally with tendrils and with simple, often lobed, alternate leaves and small to large white or yellow or greenish flowers.

Echinocystis lobata   Wild Cucumber

This annual vine may grow 20 feet long and must be kept under control. It is not suited to a small wild garden unless confined to a trellis. The leaves are deeply five-lobed and rough on both sides. The flowers are of two sexes; the greenish-white male ones are small and are borne in erect racemes above the foliage in the leaf axils; the female flowers are few and prickly, hidden in the same leaf axils and followed by prickly, bladdery fruit. The flowers appear from June to September.

This plant is found in wet waste places from New Brunswick to Saskatchewan, south to Florida and Texas.

PROPAGATION By seeds sown in the fall, and it self-sows easily. Or seeds may be dried (from the watery capsules), saved dry all winter and sown in place in March. Germination is rapid.

CAMPANULACEAE Bluebell Family

Members of this family are delicate plants with milky juice. The leaves are alternate, and the radial or irregular flowers have their outer parts in fives.

Bluebell Subfamily

Campanula rotundifolia

Harebell or Bluebell

Among the daintiest of summer wild flowers, harebells can be made to thrive in a variety of situations in the wild garden. They will grow in sun or part shade, on rocky ledges or in moist meadows. They are at their best in a cold climate. The plant sends up wiry stems from 6 to 12 inches long from clumps of round basal leaves. The alternate stem leaves are very narrow, and the nodding lavender-blue bell-shaped flowers are borne throughout the summer. They are solitary or in small groups. A space for this delightful little bell-flower should be found in every wild garden.

This plant extends through boreal America, south to Connecticut, New Jersey, Indiana, and Iowa, being found in neutral to moderately acid soil, often on high cliffs. There is a meadow by the ocean on Mount Desert Island literally filled with harebells and yellow bedstraw, a truly remarkable sight when they are in flower.

PROPAGATION   By seeds sown in early spring or in the fall.

By division in the spring.

By stem cuttings in the summer; by root cuttings in the fall.

Lobelia Subfamily

Lobelia Cardinalis   Cardinal-flower ✗

This favorite wild flower is found, in nature, in moist thickets and along stream banks, often in part shade. It is an erect plant from 2 to 3 feet tall, with unbranched leafy stems, the toothed leaves often a bronzy green. The tubular, irregular two-lipped clear red flowers in long terminal racemes, borne from July to September, are extremely handsome. The plant has a very shallow root system and is frequently winter-killed unless lightly mulched or submerged in water in winter. It self-sows in all sorts of places, however, even in the dry sunny rock garden. New basal rosettes of leaves are formed as offshoots beside the old flowering stems and these continue the plant on to the next season. It is really a short-lived perennial, and new seedlings and offshoots are needed to maintain a good stand.

This species is found in moderately acid soil in wet ground from New Brunswick to Michigan and Minnesota, south to the Gulf of Mexico.

PROPAGATION   By offsets in the spring. By division of the roots.

By stem cuttings in midsummer.

By seeds sown in the early spring or fall. The plants set a tremendous number of seeds.

L. siphilitica   Great Blue Lobelia

Although a coarser plant than cardinal-flower, this species is valuable for summer flowering in the moist wild garden or in the perennial border in sun or part shade. It self-sows freely everywhere and is decorative. The plants are 2 to 3 feet tall with stout, very leafy stems. The alternate thin light green ovate leaves are slightly toothed. The two-lipped blue flowers blossom in crowded termi-nal racemes in the axils of leafy bracts. They come in late summer and fall. There is a pretty white form.

This species is found in wet, neutral to slightly acid soil from New England to Min-nesota, South Dakota, and south to North Carolina and Kansas.

PROPAGATION   Same as for *L. Cardi-nalis,* but easily grown from seed.

COMPOSITAE   Composite Family

The flowers of this very large family are in a close head on a common receptacle sur-rounded by an involucre. There is usually a central disk composed of tiny tubular flowers surrounded by brightly colored ray flowers. The individual flowers are found in various combinations of perfect, polygamous, pistillate and staminate blossoms on the same or on different plants. The species comprise annual, biennial, and perennial herbs diverse in foliage and inflorescence.

Anaphalis margaritacea   Pearly Everlasting

A silvery plant about 2 feet tall, this species makes leafy clumps in dry sunny fields and open woods. The narrow leaves are silvery on both sides, and the dry flower heads are also silvery, being much used in dried flower arrangements. They blossom from June to September.

This plant is found in gravelly or sandy soils from Newfoundland to Alaska, south and west to New England, New York, Minnesota, South Dakota, and California.

PROPAGATION   By division in the spring only.

By seeds; shake the tiny seeds from the dried flower heads in October.

Other everlastings are mostly annual, found under *Gnaphalium*.

Achillea Millefolium   Common Yarrow

This weedy perennial, introduced from Europe, is welcome in the sunny wild garden because of its attractive fern-like leaves. The plant may grow 3 feet tall, and spreads by creeping roots. The heads of five small white ray flowers and yellow disks blossom from June to September. Sometimes the ray flowers are bright pink, and these forms can be collected. The color fades badly, however, as the flowers age.

This plant occurs in fields and waste places everywhere.

PROPAGATION   By division, sure to flourish.

By seeds, as it self-sows.

Actinomeris alternifolia   Wing-stem

A tall, strong hairy plant growing 6 feet tall, it has opposite oblong feather-veined leaves, the upper ones alternate, the petiole running down the stem to make it winged above. The yellow flowers resemble sunflowers, and blossom in August and September.

This plant is found in rich thickets from Florida to Louisiana, north to New York, Iowa, and Ontario.

PROPAGATION   By seeds, in the fall or spring.

Antennaria plantaginifolia
Pussy's-toes or Ladies'-tobacco

A good ground cover and an early bloomer for dry sunny places, this plant makes large flat silvery patches, a few inches high, increasing from runners. It has small silvery-downy, paddle-shaped leaves and little heads of whitish tubular flowers with dry papery bracts around each head, blossoming from April to June. The sexes are on separate plants.

This species is found in dry pastures and rocky banks from Maine to Minnesota, south to Georgia and Missouri.

PROPAGATION   By division in the spring.

By cuttings, in sand, in August.

Artemisia Stelleriana   Beach Wormwood

Known for its beautiful silvery foliage, this species was introduced from Japan, has escaped from cultivation and is now found on sandy beaches from Quebec to Virginia and inland on lake shores to Minnesota. Although particularly suited to beach planting, it will grow in any sandy soil, in sun, reaching a height of about 2 feet.

The silvery white leaves are roundly, deeply lobed and the tiny greenish-white flowers are in erect leafy spikes, in summer.

PROPAGATION From seeds. Dry the stalks in a paper bag in October.
Division is easy.

Aster　　　　　　　　　　　Aster

There are about sixty-five species of native asters found between the Atlantic Ocean and the Mississippi River. A few are biennial or annual, but most are perennial. A few characteristic species are described here.

Plants of asters to be transplanted to the garden should be marked when in flower and collected the following spring. A stake put close to the crown will mark the spot.

A. cordifolius　　　　Blue Wood Aster

The large leaves with heart-shaped bases help to identify this aster. They are on long petioles, and coarsely toothed. The numerous pale violet heads are small in loose panicles and blossom in August and September. The plant grows about 4 feet tall.

This is the common blue aster of woodlands, and is found from Quebec to Wisconsin southward to Georgia and Missouri. It is very useful in the wild garden.

PROPAGATION By division in the spring.
Transplants readily.

A. *divaricatus*   White Wood Aster

A splendid ground cover for dry places in open woods, this plant spreads from creeping rhizomes. It is usually about 1 foot tall but may reach a height of 3 feet. The basal foliage is in a rosette, and the smooth ovate leaves are sharply toothed, the upper ones on long petioles. The flowers with white rays and purplish disks are in flat corymbs and blossom in August and September. Although a common plant, the white flowers in large colonies are very attractive beneath the woodland trees.

This species is found from New Hampshire and New York to Georgia and Ohio.

PROPAGATION   The compact, shallow roots are easily divided in the spring.

The plant self-sows freely on disturbed soils.

A. *ericoides*   Wreath Aster

A bushy plant with stiff branches, which may grow 3 feet tall, it is found in dry sunny places. The leaves are small, narrow, and stiff, and the little white flower heads with dark disks are in one-sided racemes blossoming in July and August.

This species is found from Maine to British Columbia and southward to Georgia, Texas, and Arizona.

PROPAGATION   The slender creeping roots are easily dug in spring.

A. *laevis*   Smooth Aster

This slender unbranched aster grows in dry soils from 1 to 3 feet tall. The broad basal leaves are thick and very smooth. The stem leaves are long—oblong and clasping. The flower heads are in loose panicles, the ray flowers being bright violet in color and appearing in August and September. The plant is not a heavy bloomer and is inclined to be short-lived.

This species is found from Maine to Saskatchewan and southward to Georgia, Louisiana, and Kansas.

PROPAGATION   By division in the spring only.

A. linariifolius   Savory-leaved Aster

A dwarf species, splendid for the dry sunny rock garden, this aster is very desirable for fall bloom when there may be little else in flower. The plant makes close clumps about 1 foot high with many wiry, leafy stems and stiff, narrow foliage. The flower heads are in loose clusters at the top of the stems with lavender-blue ray flowers and yellow disk flowers blossoming from August to October.

This aster is abundant in dry soils from New Brunswick to Minnesota southward to Florida and Texas.

PROPAGATION   By division, preferably in the spring; but also may be lifted in full bloom.

It self-sows freely.

A. novae-angliae   New England Aster

A very tall perennial often seen under cultivation, this aster prefers moist meadows where it may grow 6 feet tall. The plant has many narrow downy leaves clasping the stem and showy flower heads with numerous purple, reddish-purple, or white ray flowers appearing in September and October. A very durable, disease-free species, it is valuable for the moist sunny wild garden.

This aster is found from New England to Alabama and westward to North Dakota and Wyoming. Easily transplanted at any time of year, even in full bloom.

PROPAGATION   By division in the spring or fall.

It self-sows freely.

A. *novi-belgii*   New York Aster

The parent of the garden Michaelmas-daisies, this bushy aster grows 3 to 4 feet tall and spreads rapidly from widely creeping roots. The many smooth leaves are narrow and toothed, the upper ones clasping the stem. The flower heads are also numerous, in dense panicles, the ray flowers being purple, violet, rose, or white, blooming from August to October.

This aster is subject to disease and to insect pests and should be divided every few years, in the spring, to flower at its best.

This highly variable species is found, mostly near the coast, from Newfoundland to Georgia.

PROPAGATION   By division in the spring only.

It may not come true to color from seeds.

A. *puniceus*   Swamp Aster

This tall leafy, weedy aster forms close clumps and spreads rapidly in wet meadows and ditches. Although it makes large colonies, the plant is not very showy because of the washed-out pale violet color of the ray flowers. The narrow oblong, coarsely toothed hairy leaves clasp the stems, which branch only at the top. This swamp species may grow 6 feet tall, or higher, and flowers from August to November. It will probably appear in the moist sunny wild garden without being invited.

This species is found from Newfoundland to Georgia and Alabama, westward to Illinois and North Dakota.

PROPAGATION   The plant grows and self-sows readily without help.

A. ptarmicoides   White Upland Aster

An erect, slender leafy plant, this aster grows in clumps, which do not spread, to a height of 1 to 2 feet. The many long narrow stiff leaves are without petioles, mostly on the upper part of the stem. The flower heads are in compact flat-topped corymbs, the rays pure white, flowering from June to August. The plant grows in dry sunny spots and prefers an alkaline soil. A related species, *A. lutescens*, with pale yellow ray flowers is desirable in the perennial border as well as in the wild garden. It is not a hybrid with goldenrod as is often claimed.

The white upland aster is found in prairies and other open dry places from Vermont and western Quebec to Saskatchewan and Wyoming, southward to Georgia and Arkansas.

PROPAGATION   By division in the spring. By seeds sown in the spring.

A. spectabilis   Seaside Aster

A charming species making large clumps in dry sunny fields, this bushy, much-branched aster grows 2 to 3 feet tall, often in very poor soil. The broadly ovate leaves are sharply toothed with definite petioles. The large flower heads have handsome bright violet ray flowers, the bracts below in about six rows, their tips leafy and recurved, blossoming from August to October.

This species often comes in on disturbed soil and is very beautiful along new highways, in full sun. It is very desirable in every way for the sunny wild garden. When the clumps become crowded they must be divided to ensure continued bloom.

This aster is found near the coast from Massachusetts to South Carolina and in the mountains of North Carolina.

PROPAGATION   From seeds sown in the spring.

From division or transplanting in spring only.

A. umbellatus   Flat-topped Aster

This tall white aster, sometimes 10 feet high, prefers moist fields in sun or part shade. The leafy stems are unbranched, the long ovate leaves being smooth and very numerous. The small flower heads are in large flattened white corymbs blossoming in August and September. This is an excellent species for the moist wild garden, associating well with Joe-Pye-weed and other robust summer bloomers.

This species occurs in moist low places from Newfoundland to Georgia and westward to Minnesota and Illinois.

PROPAGATION   It transplants readily, even in flower.

It self-sows readily.

Bidens coronata   Tickseed-Sunflower

Although one of the stick-tights, this showy and attractive annual is very noticeable in wet ground and shallow water in late summer and fall. The tall, slender, much-branched plant has large opposite, deeply thrice-divided leaves. The large flower heads have long yellow ray flowers with a bristly cone in the center. The plant would certainly add color to the moist fall wild garden if not allowed to self-sow too freely. Some of the superfluous plants can be pulled up before they go to seed.

This plant is found in wet places from Massachusetts to Florida, west to Kansas.

PROPAGATION By seeds gathered in October and sown in place.

A flowering plant can be transplanted to self-sow.

Boltonia asteroides   White Boltonia

A familiar tall plant of the perennial border, very like a white aster, this robust smooth species has many narrow blue-green leaves on stems from 6 to 10 feet tall. The many rather small flower heads have white ray flowers and yellow disks, and appear from July to September.

This species prefers moist soil and is found in the coastal states from New Jersey to Louisiana. It is hardy in northern gardens.

PROPAGATION By division of the rosettes in the spring.

The plant self-sows.

B. latisquama   Violet Boltonia

This species is less tall, in eastern gardens, than the above, and the ray flowers are lavender-pink. It is a desirable plant for the wild garden but less robust than the white one. Also, it is not so hardy. When the plant is native, the reverse is true.

This species is found on the prairies and along stream banks from Missouri and Kansas to Oklahoma.

PROPAGATION   By division in the spring.

Chrysanthemum Leucanthemum
White or Ox-eye-Daisy

Every large summer wild garden will contain the common field daisy, so beloved by children. It is too well known to describe here.

Chrysogonum virginianum   Golden-star

A low tufted plant, eventually elongating to 2 feet high, this species has opposite hairy leaves and rather small flower heads with about five broad yellow ray flowers around the disk, blossoming in April and May. It is an excellent plant for the moist rock garden but is not reliably hardy in northern gardens except in sheltered areas.

This plant is found in rich woods and among shaded rocks from Pennsylvania and West Virginia to Florida and Louisiana.

PROPAGATION   By seeds sown in the spring.
By division in the spring only.

Chrysopsis falcata   Golden Aster

A splendid plant for dry sandy soil in full sun, it makes a low compact mat only 6 to 8 inches high. The wiry leaves are very narrow and curved, and the small flower heads, in loose panicles, have both ray and disk flowers of yellow, blossoming in July and August.

This species occurs along the Coastal Plain from Massachusetts to New Jersey.

PROPAGATION   By division in the spring.
Self-sows freely.
By seeds sown in spring or fall.

C. mariana   Maryland Golden Aster

This is taller and larger than the preceding. It is found from New Jersey to Texas.

Coreopsis auriculata   Eared Coreopsis

A very desirable plant for wild or cultivated gardens, this is a low species with ovate leaves, often with a pair of small lateral lobes at the base, growing only 1 foot tall. The golden-yellow flowers are on long naked stalks. The form *nana* is popular for rock gardens.

This coreopsis is found in woodlands from Virginia and Kentucky to Florida and Louisiana, but it is hardy in New England.

PROPAGATION   By division in the spring.
By seeds sown in the spring.

C. lanceolata   Lance Coreopsis

This has been popular in perennial borders for years and is an indestructible species. When allowed to spread through a dry sunny field, it makes a brilliant display from June to August. It will grow well in seaside gardens also. It is a smooth plant with branching stems and narrow shining green leaves mostly at the base of the plant. The large flower head has bright yellow ray and disk flowers on long stalks, the ray flowers being three-lobed.

This species is found in dry sandy or rocky soils from southern New England and Michigan south to Florida and Texas.

PROPAGATION   By division in the spring, as it is a true perennial.
By seeds sown in the spring.

C. grandiflora is the common large-flowered "wild" species in our fields. It is truly biennial and self-sows freely.

C. rosea   Rose Coreopsis

This slender branched plant makes widely creeping mats in sandy swamps. The opposite leaves are very narrow, and the many small flower heads have pale rose-colored ray flowers and yellow disks. It flowers in July and August and is not very showy. It may grow 2 feet tall.

This species is found in wet sandy or acid soil from Nova Scotia to Georgia.

PROPAGATION   By division in the spring. Spreads rapidly by creeping roots.

C. verticillata   Thread-leaved Coreopsis

Several species of coreopsis have palmately divided leaves. They all spread rapidly from the roots, and should not be given choice locations in the garden.

This species grows 1 to 2 feet tall with delicate gray-green leaves and pale yellow flowers very like a yellow cosmos. It spreads by creeping roots but can be kept under control.

This plant is found in dry open woods from Maryland to Alabama and Arkansas. It is hardy in northern gardens.

PROPAGATION   By division in the spring only.

Echinacea purpurea   Purple Coneflower

Often planted in the garden border, this stiff perennial grows from 3 to 4 feet tall. The rough toothed leaves are alternate with five veins. The stiff, solitary terminal flower head has drooping dull purple ray flowers and a harsh dark cone and blossoms from June to

October. This interesting plant would be a welcome addition to the dry summer wild garden.

The coneflower is found in open woodlands and prairies from Ohio to Iowa and southward to Georgia and Oklahoma.

PROPAGATION By seeds sown in the spring or fall.

By division in the spring.

There are various species in the West.

Erigeron pulchellus   Robin's-plantain

This is the earliest of the lavender-flowered aster-like composites, blossoming in early spring. The slender plant produces rooting rosettes from long surface runners, forming large colonies. The stems are soft and hollow and about 1 foot high. The paddle-shaped thin toothed leaves are softly hairy. There are several clustered flower heads, the many narrow rays lavender-blue to white, the disks yellow. This is an excellent species for the spring wild garden in moist soil in full sun or part shade.

This plant is found in moist open woods and meadows from Maine to Ontario and Minnesota and south to Florida and Texas.

PROPAGATION By division in the spring.

By seeds as it self-sows.

Eupatorium album   White Thoroughwort

There are many species of Eupatorium, some of the white-flowered species being called Thoroughwort. These are very similar in appearance, all of the flowers being tubular. The three species listed below need dry sandy soil in full sun.

This species grows 3 feet tall with opposite, oblong coarsely toothed leaves and white flowers in terminal clustered heads. It is like a very slender boneset, flowering from August to October.

This plant is found along the coast from New Jersey to Florida and Louisiana in dry thickets and clearings.

PROPAGATION   By division in the spring only.

By seeds sown in the spring or fall.

E. altissimum   Tall Eupatorium

A very leafy gray-downy plant, this is the eupatorium most frequently seen on the dry open places of the Midwest. It may grow 6 feet tall, and sends up many slender stems from a strong clump. It flowers from August to October.

This species is found in dry woods and calcareous soils from Pennsylvania to Nebraska, southward to North Carolina, Oklahoma, and Texas.

PROPAGATION   Same as for *E. album.*

E. hyssopifolium   Hyssop Thoroughwort

This species, 2 to 3 feet tall, grows in poorest, driest soils in full sun. It differs from other species in the narrow leaves so divided as to appear whorled around the stem.

This plant is found from Massachusetts to Georgia and Texas.

PROPAGATION   Same as for *E. album.*

When trying to identify the white thoroughworts, it is a help to know whether they were growing in wet or dry places. The bonesets like wet places.

E. coelestinum   Mistflower or Blue Boneset

Very much like a tall blue ageratum, this plant has many strong creeping roots that form tight mats. The opposite, triangular leaves are toothed. From August to October the blue-violet flower heads are borne in compact terminal clusters, the plants growing about 2 feet tall. They require moist soil, and will succeed in sun or shade. Since the plant spreads rapidly by underground stolons, it may become a pest unless in a large wild garden. In northern gardens, however, the plants are often partially winter-killed and thus are kept in bounds. They become stunted in dry soil.

The plant is found in low woods and on the borders of streams in the whole Mississippi Basin and from New Jersey southward to Florida and Texas.

PROPAGATION   By division in the spring.

E. perfoliatum   Boneset

Easily recognized by the pairs of very rough, hairy ovate leaves clasping the stem and joined at the base, this tall, rather slender plant grows in swamps and wet fields to a height of 4 feet. The small heads of white flowers are in flat terminal clusters, blossoming from late July to October.

This species is found in wet low ground from Nova Scotia and Quebec to Florida and west to Minnesota, Louisiana, and Oklahoma. It combines well in the large moist wild garden with Joe-Pye-weed and ironweed. There are various similar species

PROPAGATION   The plant moves about in the wild and may be short-lived.

It self-sows freely.

Transplant as early as the plant can be recognized.

E. dubium   Joe-Pye-weed

This is one of four species having large leaves in whorls about the stem. They are much alike and are found in wet meadows. This species may grow 6 feet tall. It has thick firm, ovate leaves in whorls of three or four on rough-downy, purple-speckled stems, very sticky below the flowers. The deep purplish blossoms are in flat clusters blossoming in August and September.

This species occurs in acid soils along the Coastal Plain from Nova Scotia to South Carolina.

PROPAGATION   Same as for *E. album.*

E. fistulosum   Joe-Pye-weed

This is a smooth species with hollow purple stems, the leaves in whorls of four to seven. There are five to eight flower heads, lilac-pink in color, blossoming from mid-July to September.

This species is found in damp thickets from Quebec to Florida and from Iowa to Oklahoma.

PROPAGATION   Same as for *E. album.*

E. maculatum   Spotted Joe-Pye-weed

A very tall, leafy species, the plant has leaves in whorls of fours or fives on solid speckled stems up to 8 feet high. The numerous deep purple flower heads are in flat cymes in August and September.

This species is found in wet meadows in rich or calcareous soils from Newfoundland to British Columbia, southward to Maryland, Ohio, and New Mexico.

PROPAGATION   Same as for *E. album.*

E. purpureum   Sweet Joe-Pye-weed

Another tall species up to 6 feet tall, this plant has long ovate, sharply toothed leaves in whorls of twos to fives. The flower heads are palest lilac, and blossom in August and September. The plant is vanilla-scented.

This species occurs in dry or moist rich calcareous thickets or open woods from New England to Minnesota and Nebraska, south to Florida and Oklahoma. It is easily grown and, with the other three similar species, is desirable for the large moist summer wild garden.

PROPAGATION   Same as for *E. album.*

E. rugosum   White Snakeroot

Often seen under cultivation, this is the best white eupatorium. It is a bushy branched plant growing in clumps from 2 to 5 feet tall. The opposite petioled leaves are coarsely toothed. The small white flowers are in showy terminal clusters blooming in August and September.

This species is found in moist or drier woods from New Brunswick to Saskatchewan, southward to Georgia and Texas.

PROPAGATION   Same as *E. album.*

Helianthus atrorubens   Dark-eyed Sunflower

It would be a large wild garden, indeed, that could accommodate many species of sunflower. Only a few representative ones are given here, the annual ones being omitted entirely. All have yellow ray flowers.

This southern species grows about 5 feet tall. Its oval leaves are mostly near the ground, the upper ones, with winged petioles, alternate. The flower heads are of medium size, the disks dark red-purple, blossoming in August and September.

This species is found in dry or moist woods from Virginia to Florida and from Missouri to Louisiana.

PROPAGATION   By seeds sown in the spring.

By division in the spring.

H. decapetalus   Thin-leaved Sunflower

This species grows 5 feet or more in height and spreads rapidly by underground stolons. There are many small heads at the top of branched stems, flowering from August to October. A double form is sometimes seen in flower borders.

This sunflower is found in open woods and thickets from Maine and Quebec to Wisconsin and south to Georgia and Missouri.

PROPAGATION   Same as for *H. atrorubens,* and is easily divided (spring only).

H. divaricatus   Woodland Sunflower

The smallest of the sunflowers, this is an excellent species for the wild garden. The erect plants grow from 2 to 4 feet high with opposite triangular leaves and terminal flower heads of medium size, few in number, blossoming from July to September.

This species is found in dry thin woods from Maine to Florida, west to Nebraska and Arkansas.

PROPAGATION   Same as for *H. atrorubens.*

H. grosseserratus   Sawtooth Sunflower

Considered the most beautiful of the Midwest sunflowers, this species may reach 10 feet in height and is abundant along roadsides and on moist prairies and plains. The narrow leaves are coarsely toothed, and the many flower heads are yellow-centered. It is an excellent species for the wild garden, blossoming from July to October.

This plant is found in moist ground from Ohio to North Dakota, south to Arkansas and Texas, and has spread eastward.

PROPAGATION. Same as *H. atrorubens,* but it is a compact clump, to be divided with difficulty.

H. Maximiliani   Maximilian Sunflower

This distinctive species is sometimes 12 feet tall. It has very narrow leaves folded lengthwise, like a trough, which are mostly alternate. The flower heads, with yellow centers, on short peduncles in the leaf axils along the upper part of the stem, have the appearance of a coarse raceme, an unusual feature. They blossom from July to September.

This species is found on rocky prairies and waste ground, often in sandy soil, from Minnesota to Missouri and Texas.

PROPAGATION   Same as *H. atrorubens,* but the closely packed crown of roots divides with difficulty.

H. mollis   Ashy Sunflower

In its wild state this is a very beautiful sunflower, growing around 4 feet tall. The opposite, sessile leaves, clasping the stem, are very rough and gray-green in color. The flower heads with yellow disks are few, in short stiff stalks. The plant grows well in poor soils, and loses its charm under cultivation in good soil. It flowers in August and September.

This species is found from New England to Illinois, southward to Georgia and Texas.

PROPAGATION   Same as *H. atrorubens.*

H. salicifolius   Willow-leaved Sunflower

The tall slender stems, from 6 to 10 feet in height, and the very numerous willow-like leaves, giving the plant a shaggy effect, are characteristic of this species. The many small flower heads, in terminal panicles, have yellow rays and purplish-brown disks, blossoming in September and October. This is an excellent background plant for the wild garden, especially in limestone soils.

This species is found in dry soils from Missouri to Kansas and Oklahoma.

PROPAGATION   Same as *H. atrorubens*, but the closely packed crown of roots divides with difficulty.

Heliopsis helianthoides   Ox-eye

A short-lived perennial growing 5 feet tall, this plant has smooth ovate, opposite leaves, the stem being branched at the top and bearing many solitary heads of yellow ray flowers with dark flat disks. They blossom from July to September.

Long grown in the cultivated border, this plant is found in dry open woods and thickets from New York to Minnesota south to North Carolina and Illinois.

PROPAGATION   By division in the spring. By seeds in the spring.

H. tomentosus   Woolly Sunflower

This very hairy, stout species grows 10 feet tall in dry soils. The flower heads have gray disks and blossom in August and September.

It is found from Virginia to Florida in open woods and thickets.

PROPAGATION   By division in the spring.

Tetragonotheca helianthoides
Winged Sunflower

An erect branched plant growing 3 feet tall, this species has opposite, ovate leaves which are coarsely toothed and sticky-downy. The solitary flower heads have three-toothed ray flowers, and yellow disks. They blossom from May to July.

This plant is found in dry soils from Virginia to Florida and from Tennessee to Mississippi.

PROPAGATION   By seeds sown in the spring.
By division in the spring.

Helenium autumnale   Sneezeweed

This tall, leafy plant reaches a height of from 4 to 6 feet. The stems branch only at the top, and the many alternate oblong, toothed leaves are narrowed to a sessile base, running along the stem as wings. The rounded flower heads have yellow disks, and the rays may be brown, red-brown, or yellow. The plants flower from July to September and are often seen in cultivated gardens. They are often short-lived and need to be reset frequently. They need a wetter soil than most perennial borders afford.

This plant is found in wet fields and thickets from Quebec to Florida, west to British Columbia and Arizona.

PROPAGATION   By seeds. It self-sows freely.
Transplant in the spring only.

H. tuberosus   Jerusalem Artichoke

A very common plant in gardens, this species forms strong clumps 6 to 10 feet tall. The potato-like roots increase rapidly. The opposite, ovate, toothed leaves are rough above and downy below. The yellow flower heads, clustered at the top of the stems, are about three inches across and blossom in August and September.

This species is found in moist rich soil from Ontario and Saskatchewan to Georgia and Arkansas.

PROPAGATION   By division in spring, a very easy task.

Hieracium venosum   Rattlesnake-weed

This plant is useful in the wild garden because of its attractive, mostly basal leaves. They are hairy and light green in color, dull magenta on the edges, ribs, and undersides. The heads of ray flowers, only, are light golden yellow, blossoming from May to July, on almost leafless stalks, 1 to 2 feet tall.

This plant is found mostly in dry open woods from New Hampshire and Vermont south to Georgia and Alabama, occasionally westward.

PROPAGATION   By seeds sown in the spring.

By offshoots. Old plants are not readily divided.

Kuhnia eupatorioides   False Boneset

Closely resembling eupatorium, this genus differs in that its alternate leaves vary from narrow to broad ovate. The leafy stems are 2 to 3 feet tall, gland-dotted beneath. The creamy-white disk flowers are in clustered heads, blossoming from August to October.

The plant is found in dry open places, especially in sandy soil, from New Jersey to North Dakota, south to Florida and Texas.

PROPAGATION   By seeds sown in the
     fall or spring.
          By division in the spring.

Inula Helenium   Elecampane

This coarse perennial, introduced from Europe, grows about 5 feet tall. The large ovate, alternate leaves have petioles near the base of the plant and clasp the stem higher up. They are densely velvety beneath. The several large solitary flower heads have very many narrow yellow rays and blossom from July to September.

This plant is found in wet meadows and waste places in cold climates.

PROPAGATION   By seeds sown in the
     spring.
          Young plants may be collected.
          Old plants have enormous mucilaginous
     roots which are very difficult to dig.

Liatris graminifolia Grass-leaved Blazing-star

A very slender plant growing 3 feet tall from small corms, this species has many narrow leaves and narrow spikes of rosy purple flower heads in August. It is excellent for the wild garden.

This species occurs in dry open woods and sandy pinelands on the Coastal Plains from New Jersey to South Carolina.

PROPAGATION   By seeds sown in the
     spring or fall.
          Baby corms can sometimes be removed
     in the spring.
          There are various similar species.

L. scariosa   Button Blazing-star

This stiffly erect plant with a single leafy stem grows in full sun in dry soils to a height of from 2 to 5 feet. The many narrow leaves extend to the tip of the flower stalk. The flower heads of from 25 to 60 purple disk flowers (sometimes white) are well separated in long spikes, blossoming in August. The upper flowers open first.

This species is found in dry open places from Pennsylvania to Georgia, and west to South Dakota and Texas. It is suitable for light soils in the wild garden. It probably needs good drainage to survive the winter.

PROPAGATION   By seeds sown early in the fall.

Difficult from division.

L. spicata   Spiked Gay-feather

A fairly common species found in moist soil, this plant has very dense spikes of 10 to 18 rose-purple disk flowers from July to September. The smooth leaves are linear, and the plant grows about 3 feet tall.

This species is found in moist low ground from New York to Michigan and south to Florida and Louisiana.

PROPAGATION   By seeds planted in the fall.

By division in the spring.

There are various similar species.

Ratibida pinnata   Prairie-Coneflower

This stout perennial grows from deep roots to a height of 6 feet. The hairy stems are grooved and branched at the top. The alternate leaves have three to seven leaflets, pinnately divided. The large flower heads have gray cones and very long, drooping, yellow ray flowers. The whole plant has an anise odor. It blossoms from June to August.

This species is very common on the dry Kansas prairies and its range is from Ontario to Minnesota south to Georgia and Oklahoma. All the coneflowers are good subjects for the wild garden.

PROPAGATION   By seeds sown at any time.

By division, but more difficult.

Mikania scandens   Climbing Hempweed

The only native species of composite that climbs, this species clambers by twining stems to a height of 5 to 10 feet, on bushes, in swampy land. The plant has thin entire, opposite cordate leaves on long petioles. The small flower heads, like a pink-purple ageratum, are in axillary and terminal cymes, with about four small disk-flowers in each head. They blossom in August and September. This is a very valuable vine for the moist wild garden, and should be planted more often.

This plant is found in wet thickets and swamps from Florida and Texas northward to southern New England and New York.

PROPAGATION   By seeds sown in the spring.

By transplanting in the spring.

R. columnifera   Upright Prairie-Coneflower

This species grows only 2 feet tall with upright slender stems, leaves deeply pinnately divided into very narrow segments, and flower heads with short yellow ray flowers and very long, erect gray to purplish-brown disks. The species has long been cultivated in English and European gardens, and flowers from June to August.

This species is found on dry prairies and waste ground from Minnesota to Missouri, west to Montana, and south to Texas and Mexico. It has escaped eastward.

PROPAGATION   By seeds sown at any time.

Rudbeckia fulgida   Orange Coneflower

Usually considered a biennial, this bushy plant grows 2 to 3 feet tall. The narrow oblong leaves are stiff, hairy, and sharply toothed. The numerous rather small flower heads have orange ray flowers and purple-brown cones, blossoming in August and September. This is a very desirable plant for the wild garden, succeeding in a variety of habitats.

This species is found in dry or moist places from Michigan to Pennsylvania, south to Missouri, Florida, and Texas.

PROPAGATION   By seeds. It self-sows readily and should be allowed to remain wherever it chooses to grow.

R. hirta   Black-eyed Susan

Familiar to everyone, this stiff species grows about 2 feet tall. The broad-ovate rough leaves are toothed, and the flat flower heads have deep yellow ray flowers and a large brown cone. The plant blooms over a long period in July and August. It is a biennial or a short-lived perennial.

This species is found in meadows and by roadsides from Nova Scotia to Florida and from Colorado to Texas.

PROPAGATION   By seeds. It self-sows widely.

It cannot be divided.

R. serotina   Black-eyed Susan

This species is similar to the preceding, but its leaves are smaller and not usually toothed. This plant has spread eastward from the Great Plains and has become so prevalent in sunny fields everywhere that it is now regarded as the common "native" species. It is probably a biennial.

PROPAGATION   By seeds. It self-sows freely.

R. laciniata   Cutleaf Coneflower

A tall, robust species growing, sometimes, 7 feet tall, this smooth plant has large alternate leaves divided into five to seven parts. The solitary flower heads have green cones and long yellow rays, blossoming from July to September. This is an excellent plant for the summer wild garden, just as desirable as its double form the popular golden-glow of perennial borders.

This species is found in moist soils from Quebec to Florida, west to Montana and Arizona.

PROPAGATION   By division in the spring. The double form has no seeds.

R. subtomentosa   Sweet Coneflower

This lusty perennial has several erect stiff stems reaching a height of 2 to 6 feet. The plant is downy, the foliage scented like lavender. The stems bear numerous three-parted leaves. The large flower heads, appearing in August and September, have lemon-yellow ray flowers and dull brown disks.

This species requires moist soil to support its vigorous growth. It is a desirable, long-lived plant found in moist woods and thickets and along stream banks from Wisconsin and Indiana south to Louisiana and Texas.

PROPAGATION   By division in the spring. By seeds at any time.

There are many other rudbeckia species in the southern and western parts of our range.

Senecio aureus   Golden Ragwort

This erect, branching plant reaches a height of 1 to 2 feet. The basal leaves are round-ovate and sharply toothed; the stem leaves are linear and variously lobed. The small flower heads, with orange-yellow rays are in a flattened corymb and blossom in May and June. It is unusual to see a composite of this type in blossom in the spring, and the species is especially useful for the moist wild garden. Its feet should be perpetually wet.

This species is found in moist woodlands and swampy places from Labrador to Georgia, west to Minnesota and Arkansas.

PROPAGATION   By division in the spring. By seeds if kept very wet.

S. obovatus   Obovate Ragwort

Very similar to the above, this species does not require a swampy habitat but prefers a less moist one. The plant grows only 18 to 24 inches high. It also flowers in May and June.

This species is found on moist calcareous rocks and slopes and rich wooded banks from

Vermont to Florida, west to Kansas and Texas.
It is rare northward. *S. aureus* is more common northward.

PROPAGATION   Same as for *S. aureus*.

Sericocarpus linifolius   White-topped Aster

Early in the summer, the white flower
heads of this aster-like plant are noticeable
in dry woods and clearings. The species has
very narrow smooth, entire leaves, the plant
growing from a branching woody base. The
little flowers have about five rays and pale
yellow disks borne in flat clusters, well above
the leaves, and blossom from June to August.
The white, winged seeds are more silky than
those of asters.

This plant is found from New England to
Ohio, south to Georgia and Alabama.

PROPAGATION   By division in the spring.
By seeds sown at any time.
S. asteroides is a similar, but perhaps bet-
ter, species. Both are useful in the wild garden.
This species has toothed oblong leaves, and
the silky seed plumes are red-brown.

It is found from Maine to Michigan,
south to Florida and Mississippi.

PROPAGATION   Same as for *S. linifolius*.

Silphium laciniatum   Rosinweed

This tall, stately plant is a conspicuous
feature of the prairie flora of the Midwest. It
is found only where the subsoil is deep and
moist. The rough and bristly stout stems are
often 10 feet tall, the large leaves basal and
deeply pinnately divided. The smaller stem

leaves are alternate and also divided. The sunflower-like flower heads are yellow, and blossom from July to September. The basal leaves are held vertically, supposedly pointing north-south, giving the genus the common name of compass-plant.

This species is found on moist prairies from Michigan and North Dakota south to Oklahoma and Texas. This giant among perennials will also grow well in the Atlantic states.

PROPAGATION   By seeds sown at any time.

The root stock is massive and too bulky to divide.

S. perfoliatum   Cup-plant

A tall, robust perennial, this species forms strong clumps growing to a height of 6 to 8 feet. The plant has square stems, and some of the upper pairs of opposite leaves grow together at their bases, forming cups which can hold rainwater. The yellow flowers blossom from July to September. The plant frequents moist soil and can stand partial shade, making it especially useful in the wild garden.

This plant is found in rich woods and moist prairies from Ontario to South Dakota, south to Georgia and Oklahoma. It has escaped eastward to New England and Pennsylvania.

PROPAGATION   By division of old clumps.

By seeds, sown at any time.

There are other species of silphium, all strong-growing, perhaps the most enormous being *S. terebinthinaceum,* long-lived and huge in every way.

Solidago bicolor

White Goldenrod or Silverrod

There are well over 100 American species of goldenrod, some of which are difficult to identify because they hybridize in nature. Many are weedy but a few are desirable for the wild garden.

This erect, unbranched species grows 1 to 2 feet tall. The paddle-shaped basal leaves are toothed and downy, the upper ones long oblong. The spike-like flower heads have cream-white ray flowers and yellow disk flowers, blossoming in August and September. A good colony of silverrod is attractive but seldom stays long in the same place, since it may be biennial.

This species is found in dry, sterile, quite acid soil in thin woods from Nova Scotia and Quebec to Wisconsin, south to North Carolina and Missouri.

PROPAGATION   By seeds sown in the spring.

By division in the spring.

S. caesia   Blue-stemmed Goldenrod

This graceful plant has slender, wiry arching stems of a purplish color, growing 2 feet tall. The narrow sessile, toothed leaves are very numerous. The light golden-yellow flower heads are in elongate axillary clusters along the stems, blossoming in September. This is a useful goldenrod for the wild garden because it grows in the shade, providing color especially appreciated at that time of year.

This species is found in woodlands from Nova Scotia and Quebec to Wisconsin, south to Florida, Oklahoma, and Texas.

PROPAGATION   Same as for *S. bicolor.*

S. *sempervirens*   Seaside Goldenrod

This handsome goldenrod should be in every sunny wild garden and is also desirable for the cultivated border. It does not spread by roots and is long-lived. It grows from 2 to 6 feet tall, flowering from July until frost. The plant has oblong smooth blue-green leaves, the basal ones evergreen. The flower heads are deep yellow in large flattened panicles. The individual florets are also large.

This species is found on sea beaches and in salt marshes, mostly near the coast, from the Gulf of St. Lawrence to Florida, Texas, and Mexico.

PROPAGATION   Same as for S. *bicolor*. Collect small plants or grow from seeds.

S. *nemoralis*   Old-field Goldenrod

Growing only 1 to 2 feet tall, this species has gray-green leaves progressively reduced in size up the stems. The showy flower heads are in one-sided flat panicles blossoming from August to October.

This species is found in dry soils from Quebec to Texas.

PROPAGATION   Since the plant usually acts as a biennial, it should be grown from seeds. It self-sows readily.

S. *squarrosa*   Stout Goldenrod

A beautiful goldenrod, it truly *is* a rod of gold with the flower heads in long, dense terminal racemes. It is the most showy of the woodland species, the flower clusters very narrowly erect, blossoming in August and September. The plant grows from 1 to 3 feet tall and has large rosettes of basal foliage.

There are several species with erect flower racemes.

This species is found in rocky woodlands from New Brunswick to Ontario, south to Ohio, Indiana, and North Carolina.

PROPAGATION   Same as for *S. bicolor*.

S. graminifolia   Lance-leaved Goldenrod

A bushy plant, much branched above, this species grows from 2 to 4 feet tall and will succeed in wet or dry soil in full sun. There are many narrow leaves and numerous flat clusters of small flower heads terminating in short branches growing out from the tops of the stems. They blossom from July to October.

This plant is found in moderately acid soil, mostly in moist ground, from Newfoundland and Quebec to Virginia, west to British Columbia.

PROPAGATION   Same as for *S. bicolor*. The white mass of roots divides readily in the spring.

S. tenuifolia is similar, but smaller and more leafy.

Tanacetum vulgare   Common Tansy

A European plant, this tall leafy, aromatic species grows everywhere along roadsides and in dry fields, making strong clumps 2 to 3 feet tall. The deep green compound leaves are pinnately much cut and toothed. The flower heads are in dense flat terminal clusters of yellow disk-flowers, only. Although a common weed, it is useful for the large sunny wild garden because of its foliage.

PROPAGATION   By division in the spring. The plant self-sows freely.

Verbesina helianthoides   Crown-beard

This coarse, hairy plant grows 3 feet tall and has winged stems, the bases of the alternate toothed leaves running down the stem. The few large flower heads, resembling sunflowers, have yellow rays and blossom from August to October.

This plant is found in open woods from Virginia to Missouri and Kansas, south to Florida and Texas.

PROPAGATION   By seeds sown in the spring.

Division of old plants is possible.

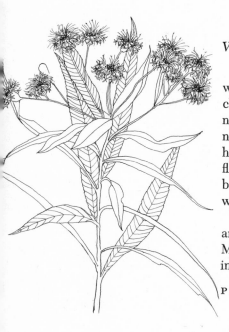

Vernonia noveboracensis   Common Ironweed

A useful plant in the sunny moist fall wild garden, this leafy species makes strong clumps, growing to a height of 3 to 5 feet. The numerous, dark green leaves are alternate, narrow, and sharply toothed. The flower heads are made up of bright red-purple disk-flowers, from twenty-nine to forty-seven in a broad flat cyme. The plant is attractive grown with Joe-Pye-weed and boneset.

The species is found in low wet meadows and marshes, mostly near the coast, from Massachusetts to Mississippi and occasionally inland.

PROPAGATION   By seeds sown at any time. It self-sows.

By division in the spring only.

By cuttings taken in early summer.

V. altissima   Tall Ironweed

This species may grow 7 feet tall. The flower heads are borne in loose, wide-spreading clusters on long, separate stems coming from the bases of the upper leaves. This plant is beautiful with other fall flowers in the wild garden, beginning to blossom in late summer. The flowers are rich purple in color.

This species is found in moist or wet meadows, in full sun, from New York to Michigan and Nebraska, south to South Carolina, Georgia, and Louisiana.

PROPAGATION   Same as for *V. novebora-censis.*

Flowering Trees
and Shrubs

This greatly restricted list suggests only a few of the showiest native trees and shrubs desirable for the wild garden. Broadleaf evergreens such as *Ilex glabra*, Leucothoë, and Pieris, with less showy flowers, are also desirable, as are many deciduous shrubs of which Virburnum and Aronia are well-known examples. Many are more showy in fruit than in flower and are valuable in attracting birds to the wild garden.

MAGNOLIACEAE   Magnolia Family

Magnolia virginiana   Sweet-Bay

Grown as a shrub or small tree from 20 to 30 feet tall, this plant is evergreen in mild climates and deciduous where the temperature goes down to zero. The medium-sized leaves are alternate, ovate, entire, and silvery white below. The small white flowers, about 2 inches across, with incurved petals, are very fragrant, blossoming from May to July. The cones are small and reddish with fleshy red seeds. It is a splendid plant for the wild garden.

This species grows in wet, acid woods, near the coast, from Massachusetts to Florida. It is abundant in the South, and resembles a rhododendron in habit of growth.

PROPAGATION   By seeds sown in the autumn.

LAURACEAE   Laurel Family

Lindera Benzoin   Spicebush

In April and May, before the leaves appear, this aromatic upright shrub from 4 to 10 feet tall bears dense clusters of small yellow flowers at the nodes of last year's stems. The oblong red fruits are much enjoyed by birds. The plant is useful as a background in the moist wild garden.

This species is abundant in rich moist woods from Maine, Ontario, Michigan, and Illinois south to North Carolina, Kentucky, and Kansas.

PROPAGATION   By seeds sown in the fall, as soon as ripe.

HAMAMELIDACEAE   -   Witch-Hazel Family

Hamamelis virginiana   Witch-hazel

Every wild garden should contain this lovely fall-flowering shrub or small tree that reaches a height of about 15 feet. The alternate, coarse thick straight-veined leaves are oval, wavy-toothed and slightly downy. The fringy yellow flowers have four very narrow wavy twisted petals clustered at the bases of the leaves. These are extremely showy in the October and November landscape.

This species is found in moist woods from Quebec and Nova Scotia to Michigan and Minnesota, south to Florida and Texas.

PROPAGATION   By seeds sown as soon as ripe. Put the unopened capsules in a bag to catch the seeds.

By cuttings taken the third week in July.

H. vernalis, with much less conspicuous reddish flowers, blossoms from December to March, even in the North. It occurs in moist woods from Missouri and Arkansas to Oklahoma and Louisiana.

ROSACEAE   Rose Family

Amelanchier canadensis   Shadbush or Serviceberry

A bushy shrub or small tree up to 25 feet tall, this plant is noticeable, in April and May, in swamps and wet woods near the coast, with its short erect racemes of white flowers which are not long-lived. The plants are usually seen in colonies and are fairy-like in their beauty. The dark purple fruits are relished by birds in June and July.

This shrub is found mostly on the Coastal Plain from Newfoundland to Mississippi. There are several other tree-like species of shadbush all desirable for the wild garden, most of which prefer dry open rocky woods in which to grow.

PROPAGATION   By seeds squeezed from the pulp in June or
   July.
   By layers and suckers, taken in spring.

Potentilla fruticosa   Shrubby Cinquefoil

This attractive shrub, about 3 feet tall, is regarded as a weed by good farmers. It is, nevertheless, useful in the wild garden in either moist or dry ground in full sun. The plant has pinnate leaves of five to seven leaflets, white beneath, with smooth edges rolled backward, and pretty yellow flowers with five rounded petals in loose clusters or solitary at the tips of the branches. They blossom much of the summer. Hybrid forms are popular in the cultivated garden.

This shrub is found in wet meadows, bogs, and along shores, especially in calcareous soil, from Labrador to Alaska, south to New Jersey, Ohio, Illinois, Minnesota, and South Dakota.

PROPAGATION   By seeds taken from the dried flowers in summer.
   By cuttings made in late summer.

LEGUMINOSAE   Pulse Family

Cercis canadensis   Redbud or Judas-tree

In May this widely branching tree that reaches a height of 40 feet is covered with red-purple pea flowers which are borne in umbel-like clusters all along the branches before the leaves appear. The rounded, cordate simple leaves that follow are attractive. The numerous many-seeded flat pods are pointed at both ends.

This tree is found in moist rich woods and ravines from Florida, Texas, and Mexico north to Connecticut, Pennsylvania, Michigan, and Nebraska.

PROPAGATION   By seeds sown in March, gathered from the pods in autumn.

AQUIFOLIACEAE   Holly Family

Ilex opaca   American Holly

This handsome evergreen tree grows from 30 to 80 feet tall. The alternate leaves are thick, leathery, and spiny-edged. The small white flowers which appear in May and June have separate sexes on different trees. The female flower has a prominent green pistil in the center of the blossom; the male one has five greenish stamens radiating out on the small greenish-white petals. The beautiful red berries are solitary or few in a cluster.

This tree is found in sandy acid soils and moist woods near the coast from Maine to Maryland and is widely distributed in the southern states from Virginia and Kentucky south to Florida and Texas.

PROPAGATION   By seeds removed from the pulp and sown in the autumn. The birds provide many seedlings around the female plant. These are generally so numerous that several seedlings may be collected in order to obtain plants of both sexes. If a twig of a male plant is grafted on a female one, it is not necessary to plant one tree of both sexes.

By cuttings in the autumn. Bottom heat is helpful in rooting them.

I. verticillata   Winterberry or Black Alder

This large, erect shrub may reach a height of 20 feet. The leaves are small, rounded, and toothed and are susceptible to frost. The tiny white flowers which blossom in June are in small clusters close to the twigs, with the sexes on separate plants. The abundant red berries remain clustered on the leafless twigs during the winter. This holly should be in every moist wild garden.

This shrub is found in swamps and wet woods from Newfoundland and Quebec to Ontario and Michigan, south to Maryland, West Virginia, and Indiana.

PROPAGATION   By seeds sown in autumn.
  By division in spring.
  By layering in summer.

I. laevigata   Smooth Winterberry

This similar and less common species has more lustrous leaves which are smooth below. The large red berries drop with the first frost, making this a much less desirable shrub for the wild garden.

This species is found in swamps and wet woods from Maine to New York and South Carolina.

PROPAGATION   Same as for *I. verticillata*.

RHAMNACEAE   Buckthorn Family

Ceanothus americanus   New Jersey Tea

Although a common little shrub in heavy, dry poor soils, it transplants with difficulty, and this should not be attempted.

A slender plant about 3 feet tall, it has alternate, toothed, and ovate leaves which are downy below. The small white flowers with five petals are borne in umbels at the end of the new growth in early summer.

This plant is found in upland woods and barrens from Quebec to Minnesota, south to Florida and Texas.

PROPAGATION   By seeds gathered in October and sown in the spring.

C. ovatus is a similar species of more western range. The beautiful blue-flowered species of California, as *C. coeruleus*, cannot be grown in the East.

CORNACEAE   Dogwood Family

Cornus florida   Flowering Dogwood

A small tree reaching a height of about 30 feet, this handsome species has a light gray trunk and rounded opposite leaves that turn red in autumn. The heads of small greenish-yellow flowers are surrounded by four large petal-like bracts, and blossom in April and May. In September the red fruits are attractive and appreciated by birds. This tree should be in every wild garden. The top-shaped flower buds formed during the summer are often killed in subzero winters.

This tree is found in acid soil from southern Maine to New York and Illinois, south to Florida and Texas. A pink form is in cultivation.

PROPAGATION   By seeds, separated from the pulp in autumn and planted at once.

By layers and suckers, separated in the spring only.

Young trees may be moved in the spring.

CLETHRACEAE   White Alder Family

Clethra alnifolia   Sweet Pepperbush

A desirable shrub for the wild garden, this bushy plant grows from 5 to 10 feet tall. It has alternate, sharply toothed leaves. The small flowers, with five white petals and ten long white stamens with dark tips, are in long terminal racemes. They are fragrant and blossom in July and August. Although this shrub is found in swamps and damp thickets, it does well in gardens where the soil is not actually dry; otherwise, it becomes infested with red spider mites which turn the leaves brown.

The range is from Maine to Florida and Texas near the coast.

PROPAGATION   By seeds shaken from the capsules in autumn and sown at once.

By division in the spring or fall.

By cuttings of basal shoots in the summer.

ERICACEAE Heath Family

Kalmia latifolia Mountain-Laurel

Probably the most popular native broad-leaved evergreen for garden decoration, mountain-laurel needs little description. The shining alternate, sometimes whorled, leaves are oblong. The saucer-shaped pink or white flowers with ten tiny pouches concealing the anthers of ten stamens until maturity are in terminal clusters, blossoming in May and June. This shrub grows 5 to 20 feet tall.

The plants prefer moist acid soil and are found mostly near the coast from New England to Florida. They bloom best where they receive some sun and are benefited if the faded flowers are removed.

PROPAGATION By seeds sown when ripe in the autumn. Plants self-sow readily in nature.

By layering. Since collected plants have poor root systems, it is advisable to secure nursery grown stock.

K. angustifolia Sheep-Laurel

A much smaller shrub than the preceding, this species has small, narrowly oblong bright green evergreen leaves, pale and smooth beneath, usually opposite or in threes. The flat-topped clusters of crimson-pink flowers, about a half-inch across, are not so showy as those of mountain-laurel. The plant is a good ground cover in sterile acid soil and is desirable in open woods in the wild garden. It grows in a wide variety of habitats.

The range is from Newfoundland and Labrador to Hudson Bay, south to Virginia, Pennsylvania, and Michigan.

PROPAGATION Same as *K. latifolia.* Division of old clumps in the spring is possible.

Rhododendron maximum Great Laurel or Rosebay

This tall evergreen shrub with large leathery leaves is found in moist woods and swamps. It sometimes reaches a height of 20 feet. The large oblong leaves are downy below. In July there are large terminal clusters of bell-like white to pale pink flowers. The big winter buds have long bracts.

This species is native in very acid soils from southern Maine to Georgia. It blossoms best with some sun, and the faded flowers should be removed. It is very desirable for the wild garden.

PROPAGATION   By seeds from the capsules in autumn, sown at once. Self-sows.

By cuttings taken in the fall.

By layering in the spring and summer.

R. catawbiense   Catawba Rhododendron

This species has fat winter buds without bracts. The purple or reddish flowers appear in May and June. It grows wild from Virginia to Georgia and Alabama. It is common in gardens.

R. carolinianum   Carolina Rhododendron

A splendid shrub for the small wild garden, this species has smaller leaves and flowers, pale rose or white in color, and blossoms in June. Although native to the Carolina mountains, it is hardy in northern gardens.

PROPAGATION   Same as for *R. maximum.*

R. canadense   Rhodora

This early-flowering azalea brightens bogs and swamps with its tubular two-lipped magenta flowers in April and May. The plant rarely grows more than 3 feet tall and has small leaves. It is desirable for the moist wild garden for early spring bloom but must have very acid soil and full sun.

This species occurs from New England south, near the coast, to Georgia.

PROPAGATION   By division in the spring.

By layering in the spring and summer.

By seeds sown at once in the autumn.

R. Vaseyi   Pinkshell-Azalea

An early flowering species, this southern shrub has escaped from cultivation in Massachusetts. It grows 10 to 15 feet high. The beautiful clear pink bell-shaped flowers appear before the leaves, in May.

This species is native to the wet woods of the Carolinas but is hardy in New England. It is well suited to wild gardens.

PROPAGATION   Same as for *R. canadense.*

R. calendulaceum   Flame Azalea

This species has downy leaves and twigs, and grows 10 to 15 feet tall. The brilliant yellow, orange, or scarlet flowers are the brightest colored of all the azaleas, blossoming in May and June. The flowers are narrow tubular with five small wide spreading petals.

This species is found in open woods from Pennsylvania to Ohio, south to Georgia and Alabama.

PROPAGATION   Same as for *R. canadense.*

R. nudiflorum   Pinxter-flower

A stout, bushy plant, this handsome azalea may grow 10 feet tall, the flowers appearing before the leaves are fully developed. These are smooth and blue-green in color. The narrow tubular flowers in various shades of pink appear in May.

This species is native to moist acid woods from Massachusetts to Ohio and the Carolinas, and is frequently cultivated. It is slightly fragrant, and one of the best species for the wild garden.

PROPAGATION   Same as for *R. canadense.*

R. roseum   Early Azalea

This shrub is similar to the preceding, with more downy leaves and pinker, more fragrant flowers.

This species grows in dry woods in acid leaf mold and is found from Maine to Virginia and Missouri.

PROPAGATION   Same as for *R. canadense.*

R. canescens   Piedmont Azalea

The leaves of this species are white-hairy below. The fragrant flowers are white to pinkish, appearing in May and June. This shrub grows to 15 feet tall.

The range is from Delaware and Ohio south to Florida and Texas.

PROPAGATION   Same as for *R. canadense.*

R. viscosum   Swamp-Honeysuckle

In swamps and wet grounds this shrub grows from 15 to 20 feet tall. It is the tallest native species. The intensely fragrant blossoms are pure white and sticky to the touch. They are the last to flower, and do not appear until July and August. This is a desirable plant for the moist wild garden.

This species is found along the coast from Maine to the Carolinas, west to Tennessee and Ohio.

PROPAGATION   Same as for *R. canadense.*

R. arborescens   Sweet Azalea

This desirable species has smooth twigs and leaves which are bright green above and whitened below. It grows from 6 to 20 feet tall, the pure white, extremely fragrant flowers appearing in June and July.

This species grows along stream banks and in rocky woods from Pennsylvania and Kentucky south to Georgia and Alabama.

PROPAGATION   Same as for *R. canadense.*

Oxydendrum arboreum   Sourwood or Sorrel-tree

This handsome tree or tall shrub should be included in plantings of azaleas, rhododendrons, mountain-laurels, and other members of the Heath Family. It grows from 15 to 40 feet high. The alternate, oblong-lanceolate, pointed leaves have slender stems. In the summer there are long one-sided racemes of white flowers shaped like the bells of lily-of-the-valley in graceful open panicles.

These appear at the tips of the branches beyond the leaves. Before the leaves are shed in the fall, they turn a vivid, spectacular scarlet.

This plant is found in moist or dry woods from Pennsylvania and Indiana south to Florida and Louisiana.

PROPAGATION By seeds shaken from the capsules in late autumn and sown at once.

STYRACACEAE   Storax Family

Halesia carolina   Silverbell-tree

This tall shrub or tree around 30 feet high is an unfailing source of delight when, in May, myriads of lateral umbel-like clusters of white bells with yellow "clappers" hang on slender pedicels from the branches. The pointed leaves are large and veiny.

This plant occurs in rich woods and along the banks of streams from Virginia, Ohio, and Illinois south to Florida and Texas.

PROPAGATION By cuttings taken the third week of July.
By seeds, shaken from the capsules in late autumn and sown at once.

RUBIACEAE   Madder Family

Cephalanthus occidentalis   Button-bush

Usually found in standing water in swamps and on the banks of ponds, this species will do well under ordinary garden conditions where the ground is somewhat moist. A stout, branching shrub from 5 to 8 feet tall, it has oblong, toothed leaves in whorls of three or four. The tiny fragrant white flowers with long white stamens are in a spherical head, blossoming in July and August. It is an excellent plant for the summer wild garden.

The range is from New Brunswick and Quebec to Minnesota, southward and westward.

PROPAGATION By cuttings planted in moist soil in the summer.
Small plants may be dug in spring where abundant. Old clumps may by divided, preferably in the spring.

Appendix A

A SELECTED BIBLIOGRAPHY OF BOOKS
ON WILD FLOWERS, TREES, SHRUBS,
AND FERNS OF NORTH AMERICA
BY PERSIS R. GREEN

Abrams, LeRoy. *An Illustrated Flora of the Pacific States, Washington, Oregon, and California*. 4 vols. Stanford University, California, University of Stanford Press, 1923–1960.

Appalachian Mountain Club. *Mountain Flowers of New England*. Boston, Appalachian Mountain Club, 1964.

Birdsye, Clarence. *Growing Woodland Plants*. New York, Oxford University Press, 1951.

Britton and Brown. *See* Gleason.

Brockman, Frank. *Trees of North America*. New York, Golden Press, 1968.

Brooklyn Botanic Garden. *Ferns*. Baltimore, Brooklyn Botanic Garden, 1969.

Brooklyn Botanic Garden. *Gardening with Wild Flowers*. Baltimore, Brooklyn Botanic Garden, 1974.

Brooklyn Botanic Garden. *Propagation*. Baltimore, Brooklyn Botanic Garden, 1974.

Brooklyn Botanic Garden. *Rhododendrons and Their Relatives*. Baltimore, Brooklyn Botanic Garden, 1971.

Burgess, Thornton W. *The Burgess Flower Book for Children*. Boston, Little, Brown and Company, 1923.

Case, Frederick. *Orchids of the Western Great Lakes Region.* Bloomfield Hills, Michigan, Cranbrook Institute of Science, 1964.

Clark, Lewis. *Wild Flowers of British Columbia.* Sidney, British Columbia, Gray's Publishing Ltd., 1973.

Clements, Edith S. *Flowers of Coast and Sierra.* New York, H. W. Wilson Company, 1928.

Clements, Edith. *Flowers of Mountain and Plain;* 3rd ed. New York, E. H. Wilson Company, 1947.

Clements, Edith. *Flowers of Prairie and Woodland.* New York, E. H. Wilson and Company, 1947.

Clements, F. E., and Clements, E. G. S. *Rocky Mountain Flowers.* New York, H. W. Wilson Company, 1945.

Cobb, Boughton. *A Field Guide to the Ferns and Their Related Families of North Eastern and Central America.* (Peterson Field Guide Series). New York, Houghton Mifflin Company, 1956.

Correll, Donvan S. *Native Orchids of North America North of Mexico.* Ronald Press Company, 1950.

Craighead, John J. *A Field Guide to Rocky Mountain Wildflowers.* Boston, Houghton Mifflin Company, 1963.

Cronquist, Arthur C., C. Leo Hitchcock, Marion Ownbey, and J. W. Thompson. *Vascular Plants of the Pacific Northwest;* Parts 4 and 5 (1 to 3 in preparation). Seattle, University of Washington Press, 1955–.

Cuthbert, Mabel J. *How To Know the Fall Flowers.* Dubuque, Iowa, William C. Brown Company, Publishers, 1948.

Cuthbert, Mabel J. *How To Know the Spring Flowers.* Dubuque, Iowa, William C. Brown Company, Publishers, 1949.

Dana, Frances T. *How To Know the Wild Flowers.* New York, Dover Publications, Inc., 1963.

Dorman, Caroline. *Flowers Native to the Deep South.* Baton Rouge, Claitor's Bookstore, 1958.

Eaton, Walter Prichard. *Wild Gardens of New England.* Boston, W. A. Wilde Company, 1936.

Fernald, M. L. *Gray's Manual of Botany;* 8th ed. New York, American Book Company, 1950.

Fischer, H. F., and G. F. Harshbarger. *The Flower Family Album.* Minneapolis, University of Minnesota Press, 1941.

Flemer, William. *Nature's Guide to Successful Landscaping.* New York, Thomas Y. Crowell Company, 1972.

Foster, Gorden. *Ferns to Know and Grow.* New York, Hawthorne Books, Inc., 1971.

Foster, Lincoln. *Rock Gardening.* Boston, Houghton Mifflin Company, 1968.

Gabrielson, Ira N. *Western America Alpines.* Sakonnett Point, Rhode Island, Theophrastus Press, 1973.

Gleason, Henry A. *The New Britton and Brown Illustrated Flora of the Northeastern United States and adjacent Canada;* rev. ed., 3 vols. New York, New York Botanical Garden, 1958.

Gleason, Henry A. *Plants of the Vicinity of New York.* New York, New York Botanical Garden, 1935.

Gleason, Henry A., and A. Cronquist. *Manual of Vascular Plants of Northeastern United States and Adjacent Canada.* New York, Hafner Publishing Co., Inc., 1974.

Gottscho, Samuel H. *Wildflowers: How to Know and Enjoy Them.* New York, Dodd, Mead and Company, 1951.

Graves, Arthur Harmount. *Illustrated Guide to Trees and Shrubs;* rev. ed. New York, Harper & Brothers, 1956.

Greene, W. F., and H. L. Blomquist. *Flowers of the South.* North Carolina, University of Carolina Press, 1953.

Harlow, William M. *Trees of the Eastern United States and Canada;* rev. ed. New York, Dover Publications, Inc., 1957.

Harris, Stuart K. *Plants of the Presidential Range* (from Appalachia). Boston, Massachusetts, 1941–1949.

Haskin, Leslie L. *Wild Flowers of the Pacific Coast.* Portland, Oregon, Binfords, 1970.

Hausman, Ethel H. *Beginner's Guide to Wild Flowers.* New York, Putnam's Sons, 1948.

Henshaw, Julia W. *Wild Flowers of the North American Mountains.* New York, Robert M. McBride, 1915.

Hill, Clara Chapman. *Spring Flowers of the Lower Columbia Valley.* Seattle, University of Washington Press, 1958.

Hills, Lawrence D. *The Propagation of Alpines;* 2nd ed. London, Faber and Faber, 1959.

House, Homer D. *Wild Flowers.* New York, The Macmillan Company, 1961.

Hull, Helen S. *Wild flowers for your garden.* New York, Barrows, 1952.

Hylander, Clarence. *The Macmillan Wild Flower Book.* New York, The Macmillan Company, 1954.

Jennings, O. E. *Wild Flowers of Western Pennsylvania and the Upper Ohio Basin,* 2 vols. Pennsylvania, University of Pittsburgh Press, 1953.

Kieran, John. *An Introduction to Wild Flowers.* New York, Hanover House, 1952.

Klimas, John E. *Wildflowers of Connecticut.* Published for the Audubon Society by Walker & Company, New York, 1968.

Klimas, John E., and James A. Cummingham. *Wild Flowers of Eastern America.* New York, Alfred A. Knopf, Inc., 1974.

Klute, Jeannette. *Woodland Portraits.* Boston, Little, Brown and Company, 1954.

Korling, Torkle. *Borea Forest and Borders.* Dundee, Illinois, Torkle Korling, 1973.

Korling, Torkle. *Deciduous Woods*. Dundee, Illinois, Torkle Korling, 1974.

McKenney, Margaret. *A Book of Wild Flowers*. New York, Van Nostrand, 1942.

McKenney, Margaret. *The Wild Garden*. New York, Doubleday, Doran & Company, Inc., 1936.

Mathews, F. Schuyler. *The Book of Wild Flowers for Young People*. New York, G. P. Putnam's Sons, 1955.

Mathews, F. Schuyler. *Field Book of American Trees and Shrubs*. New York, G. P. Putnam's Sons, 1915.

Mathews, F. Schuyler. *Field Book of American Wild Flowers;* rev. ed. New York, G. P. Putnam's Sons, 1955.

Miles, Bebe. *Blue Bells and Bittersweet: Gardening with Native American Plants*. New York, Van Nostrand Reinhold Company, 1970.

Moldenke, Harold N. *American Wild Flowers*. New York, Van Nostrand, 1949.

Montgomery, Frederick H. *Native Wild Plants of Northeastern United States and Canada*. New York, Frederick Warne & Co., Inc., 1965.

Munz, Philip A. *California Mountain Wildflowers*. Berkeley, University of California Press, 1963.

National Geographic Society. *The Book of Wild Flowers*, Washington, D.C., National Geographic Society, 1924.

Orr, Robert and Margaret Orr. *Wild Flowers of Western America*. New York, Alfred A. Knopf, Inc., 1974.

Parcher, Emily Seabury. *Shady Gardens*. New York, Prentice-Hall, Inc., 1955.

Parsons, Frances T. *How to Know the Ferns*. New York, Charles Scribner's Sons, 1927.

Parsons, Frances T. *How to Know the Wild Flowers*. New York, Charles Scribner's Sons, 1926.

Parsons, Mary E. *Wild Flowers of California*. San Francisco, Cunningham, Curtis and Welch, 1907.

Pease, Arthur Stanley. "Vascular Flora of Coos County, New Hampshire," from the Proceedings of the Boston Socety of Natural History. Vol. 37, No. 3. Boston, July, 1924.

Pellett, Frank C. *Success with Wild Flowers*. New York, Dodd, Mead & Company, 1947.

Peterson, Maude G. *How to Know Wild Fruits*. New York, The Macmillan Company, 1923.

Peterson, Roger Tory. *Field Guide to Wildflowers of Northeastern & North-Central North America*. Boston, Houghton Mifflin Company, 1968.

Peterson, Roger Tory. *Field Guide to Rocky Mountain Wildflowers*. Boston, Houghton Mifflin Company, 1963.

Peterson, Roger Tory. *Field Guide to the Ferns*. Boston, Houghton Mifflin Company, 1963.

Petrides, George A. *A Field Guide to the Trees and Shrubs* (Peterson Field Guide Series). Boston, Houghton Mifflin Company, 1958.

Pistorius, Anna. *What Wild Flower Is It?* New York, Follett Publishing Company, 1954.

Pool, Raymond J. *Flowers and Flowering Plants.* New York, McGraw-Hill, 1941.

Quick, Arthur C. *Wild Flowers of the Northern States and Canada.* Chicago and New York, M. A. Donahue and Company, 1939.

Radford, Albert, et al. *Manual of the Vascular Flora of the Carolinas.* Chapel Hill, University of North Carolina Press, 1974.

Reed, Chester A. *Wild Flowers East of the Rockies.* New York, Doubleday, Page and Company, 1917.

Rickett, Harold W. *Botany for Gardeners.* New York, The Macmillan Company, 1957.

Rickett, H. W. *Wild Flowers of America.* New York, Crown Publishing Company, 1954.

Rickett, Harold. *Wild Flowers of the United States* (6 volumes). New York, McGraw-Hill Book Company, 1966–1973.

Roberts, Edith Adelaide and Julia R. Lawrence. *American Ferns.* New York, The Macmillan Company, 1935.

Rydberg, Per Axel. *Flora of the Prairies and Plains of Central North America.* New York, Hafner Publishing Co., Inc., 1965.

Rydberg, Per Axel. *Flora of the Rocky Mountains and Adjacent Plains.* New York, Hafner Publishing Co., Inc., 1954.

Seymour, Frank C. *Flora of New England.* Rutland, Charles E. Tuttle Co., Inc., 1969.

Sharples, Ada White. *Alaska Wild Flowers.* California, Stanford University Press, 1958.

Small, John K. *Manual of the Southeastern Flora.* New York, Hafner Publishing Co., Inc., 1972.

Sperka, Marie. *Growing Wildflowers: A Gardener's Guide.* New York, Harper & Row Publishers, 1973.

Steffek, Edwin F. *Wild Flowers and How to Grow Them.* New York, Crown Publishers, Inc., 1954.

Stefferud, Alfred. *How to Know the Wild Flowers.* New York, Crown Publishing Company, 1954.

Stevens, William Chase. *Kansas Wild Flowers.* Laurence, University of Kansas, 1948.

Steyermark, Julian A. *Flora of Missouri.* Ames, Iowa, Iowa State University Press, 1963.

Swain, Su Zan Noguchi. *Plants of Woodland and Wayside.* New York, Garden City Books, 1958.

Symonds, George W. D. *The Tree Identification Book.* New York, M. Barrows and Company, 1958.

Taylor, Kathryn S., Ed. *A Traveler's Guide to Roadside Wild Flowers, Shrubs, and Trees of the U.S.* New York, Farrar, Straus and Company, 1949.

Taylor, Norman, Ed. *The Guide to Garden Flowers*. Boston, Houghton Mifflin Company, 1958.

Taylor, Norman. *A Guide to the Wild Flowers*. New York, Greenberg, 1928.

Taylor, Norman. *Wild Flower Gardening*. New York, Van Nostrand, 1955.

Tilton, George Henry. *The Fern Lover's Companion*. Boston, Little, Brown and Company, 1923.

Wherry, Edgar T. *Guide to Eastern Ferns*. Philadelphia, University of Pennsylvania Press, 1948.

Wherry, Edgar T. *A Wild Flower Guide*. New York, Doubleday & Company, 1954.

Wickham, Lee, et al. *Orchids for Everybody*. New York, Robert McBride Company, Inc., 1957.

Wiley, Leonard. *Rare Wild Flowers of North America*. New York. L. Wiley, 1970.

Zim, H. S., and A. C. Martin. *Flowers: A Guide to Familiar Wild Flowers*. New York, Simon and Schuster, 1950.

Appendix B

I. Plants Difficult or Impossible to Naturalize

These have exacting requirements which cannot be met in most wild gardens. Some cannot be naturalized until more has been learned about their treatment. They should be left undisturbed in their natural habitats unless a catastrophe faces them with certain extinction. Even then, only the serious wild gardener should try to perpetuate them. Most of the orchids belong in this classification.

Alpine-azalea—*Loiseleuria procumbens* (Heath Family), true alpine

Beech-drops, Virginia—*Epifagus virginiana* (Broom-rape Family), root parasitic

Beech-drops, False—*Monotropa Hypopithys* (Wintergreen Family), root parasitic

Blue-hearts—*Buchnera americana* (Figwort Family), root parasitic

Cassiope, Arctic—*Cassiope hypnoides* (Heath Family), true alpine

Comandra (Sandalwood Family), parasitic
   Common—*Comandra umbellata*
   Pale—*C. pallida*

Crazyweed—*Oxytropis spp.* (Pea Family). Plant seeds in pots.

Diapensia—*Diapensia lapponica* (Diapensia Family), true alpine

False-foxglove (Figwort Family), parasitic
  Downy—*Gerardia virginica*
  Fern-leaf—*G. pedicularis*
  Southern—*G. grandiflora*
  Smooth—*G. laevigata*
  Yellow—*G. flava*
  Purple—*G. purpurea*, root parasitic
  Slender—*G. linifolia*, annual and parasitic

Ferns. See separate listing that follows.

Ghost-pipe—*Orobanche uniflora* (Broom-rape Family), parasitic
Indian-pipe—*Monotropa uniflora* (Wintergreen Family), root parasitic
Lily, Wood—*Lilium philadelphicum* (Lily Family), difficult to transplant
Milk-vetch—*Astragalus*, 25 or more species (Pea Family), only as seed-
    lings in pots
Musk-root—*Adoxa moschatellina* (Moschatel Family)

Orchids. See separate listing that follows.
Owl-clover, Yellow—*Orthocarpus luteus* (Figwort Family) parasitic

Paint-brush (Figwort Family), parasitic
  Indian—*Castilleja coccinea*
  Northern—*C. septentrionalis*
Pine-drops—*Pterospora andromedea* (Wintergreen Family), parasitic
Pinesap, Sweet—*Monotropsis odorata* (Wintergreen Family), parasitic
Pyxie-moss—*Pyxidanthera barbulata* (Diapensia Family), transplants with
    difficulty

Rhododendron, Lapland—*Rhododendron lapponicum* (Heath Family), true
    alpine
Rose-gentian, Saltmarsh—*Sabatia stellaris* (Gentian Family). Sow seeds
    in place.

Sundew (Sundew Family), will not transplant
  Narrowleaved—*Drosera intermedia*
  Round-leaved—*D. rotundifolia*
  Thread-leaved—*D. filiformis*

Venus'-flytrap—*Dionaea muscipula* (Sundew Family), not hardy to zero

Wood-betony (Figwort Family), root parasitic
  Early—*Pedicularis canadensis*
  Swamp—*P. lanceolata*

Many ferns and related plants are difficult and not practicable. These include species of *Lycopodium* that have creeping stems:

Club-moss (Club-moss Family)
  Bog—*Lycopodium inundatum*
  Cedar-like—*L. sabinaefolium*
  Common—*L. clavatum*
  Ground-cedar—*L. complanatum*
  Sitka—*L. sitchense*
  Slender—*L. tristachyum*
  Stiff—*L. annotinum*
  Tree—*L. obscurum*

The species of *Lycopodium* that grow in clumps are transplantable.

Many of the small ferns are not easy:

Adder's-tongue, Common—*Ophioglossum vulgatum*
Cliff-brake, Purple—*Pellaea atropurpurea*
Filmy-fern—*Trichomanes Boschianum*
Grape-fern—six species of *Botrychium*
Hart's tongue, American—*Phyllitis Scolopendrium*
Lip-fern, Hairy—*Cheilanthes lanosa*
Oak-fern, Scented—*Dryopteris Robertiana*
Rock-brake, Slender—*Cryptogramma Stelleri*
Spleenwort, Hybrid—*Asplenosorus ebenoides*
Spleenwort, Mountain—*Asplenium montanum*
Spleenwort, Pinnatifid—*Asplenium pinnatifidum*
Wood-fern, Fragrant—*Dryopteris fragrans*

Most of our orchids are impracticable. They depend on root fungi for their nourishment.

Orchid Family
  Arethusa—*Arethusa bulbosa*
  Calypso—*Calypso borealis*
  Coral-root—*Corallorhiza* (six species)
  Epipactis, Broad-leaf—*Epipactis Helleborine*
  Fringed orchis
    Green—*Habenaria lacera*
    Hooker—*H. Hookeri*
    Large purple—*H. fimbriata*
    Large round-leaf—*H. orbiculata*
    Northern—*H. hyperborea*
    Pale green—*H. flava*

Prairie—*H. leucophaea*
Small green—*H. clavellata*
Small northern—*H. obtusata*
Small purple—*H. psycodes*
Small white—*H. dilatata*
White—*H. blephariglottis*
Yellow—*H. ciliaris*

Ladies'-tresses—*Spiranthes* (ten species)

Orchis
Adder's-mouth—*Malaxis paludosa* (and four other species)
Cranefly—*Tipularia discolor*
Grass-pink—*Calopogon pulchellus*
Round-leaved—*Orchis rotundifolia*
Showy—*O. spectabilis*

Pogonia
Drooping—*Pogonia trianthophora*
Rose—*P. ophioglossoides*
Southern—*Cleistes divaricata*
Whorled—*Isotria verticillata*

Putty-root—*Aplectrum hiemale*

Twayblade
Broadleaf—*Listera convallarioides*
Lily—*Liparis lilifolia*
Loesel—*Liparis Loeselii*
Northern—*Listera cordata*

Certain species of Cypripedium and of Goodyera are adapted to cultivation. (See main text of book.)

II.   Alkaline- or Lime-Loving Native Plants

Acid soil can be made alkaline by the addition of pulverized limestone, wood ashes, bone meal, or marble chips, first having the soil tested for acidity at an agricultural experiment station. The recommendations must be carefully followed. Some plants on the list cannot be grown satisfactorily in the average wild garden because of unsuitable climate, even when alkaline soil has been provided.

Anemone (Crowfoot Family)
Argentine—*Anemone multifida*
Carolina—*A. caroliniana*

Bladder-fern, Berry—*Cystopteris bulbifera* (Fern Family)

Cliff-brake, Purple—*Pellaea atropurpurea* (Fern Family)
Cloak-fern, Powdery—*Notholaena dealbata* (Fern Family)

Dryas (Rose Family)
    Drummond's—*Dryas Drummondii*
    Entire-leaf—*D. integrifolia*

Grass-of-Parnassus—*Parnassia,* six species (Saxifrage Family)

Hart's-tongue, American—*Phyllitis Scolopendrium* (Fern Family)
Hepatica, Sharp-lobed—*Hepatica acutiloba* (Crowfoot Family)
Holly-fern, Mountain—*Polystichum Lonchitis* (Fern Family)

Milk-vetch—*Astragalus,* many species (Pea Family)

Oak-fern, Scented—*Dryopteris Robertiana* (Fern Family)

Primrose (Primrose Family)
    Greenland—*Primula egaliksensis*
    Dwarf Canadian—*P. mistassinica*
    St. Lawrence—*P. laurentiana*

Rock-brake, Slender—*Cryptogramma Stelleri* (Fern Family)

Saxifrage (Saxifrage Family)
    Aizoon—*Saxifraga Aizoön*
    Tufted—*S. cespitosa*
    Twinleaf—*S. oppositifolia*
    Yellow Mountain—*S. aizoides*
Shield-fern, Fragrant—*Dryopteris fragrans* (Fern Family)
Spleenwort (Fern Family)
    Blackstem—*Asplenium resiliens*
    Green—*A. viride*
    Hybrid—*Asplenosorus ebenoides*
    Wall-rue—*Asplenium cryptolepsis*
Sweet-broom, Northern—*Hedysarum alpinum* (Pea Family)

Walking-fern—*Camptosorus rhizophyllus* (Fern Family)
Whitlow-grass (Mustard Family)
    Allen—*Draba Allenii*
    Smooth—*D. glabella*

III. Aquatics

Most of these plants must have standing water in which to grow. The water level must be kept nearly constant. A few on the list can stand drier soil during the summer after the flowering season has passed.

Arrowhead, Slender—*Sagittaria teres* (Water-plantain Family)

Bladderwort—*Utricularia,* some ten species (Bladderwort Family)

Calla, Wild—*Calla palustris* (Arum Family)
Cat-tail (Cat-tail Family)
  Common—*Typha latifolia*
  Narrowleaf—*T. angustifolia*

Cow-lily—*Nuphar advena* and others (Water-lily Family)

Floating-heart (Gentian Family)
  Southern—*Nymphoides aquatica*
  White—*N. cordata*
  Yellow—*N. peltata*

Golden-club—*Orontium aquaticum* (Arum Family)

Lobelia, Water—*Lobelia Dortmanna* (Bluebell Family)
Lotus, American—*Nelumbo lutea* (Water-lily Family)

Marsh-marigold, Floating—*Caltha natans* (Crowfoot Family)

Pickerelweed—*Pontederia cordata* (Pickerelweed Family)
Pond-lily—*Nymphaea odorata* (Water-lily Family)

Water-lily (Water-lily Family)
  Mexican—*Nymphaea mexicana*
  Magnolia—*N. tuberosa*
  Pygmy—*N. tetragona*
Water-shield, Schreber—*Brasenia Schreberi* (Water-lily Family)

IV. Bog and Marsh Plants   *Beaver Pond*

The soil must always be wet or very moist. The water level is never far below the surface.

Alexanders, Golden—*Zizia aurea* (Parsley Family)
Arethusa—*Arethusa bulbosa* (Orchid Family)
Arrow-arum—*Peltandra virginica* (Arum Family)
Arrowhead, Common—*Sagittaria latifolia* (Water-plantain Family)
Asphodel, False—*Tofieldia glutinosa* (Lily Family)
Aster (Composite Family)
  Flat-top—*Aster umbellatus*
  Swamp—*A. puniceus*

Blue-eyed-grass, Common—*Sisyrinchium angustifolium* (Iris Family)
Bog-asphodel, New Jersey—*Narthecium americanum* (Lily Family)
Bog-bean, Common—*Menyanthes trifoliata* (Gentian Family)
Butterbur, Palmate—*Petasites palmata* (Composite Family)
Buttercup, Swamp—*Ranunculus septentrionalis* (Crowfoot Family)
Butterwort, Common—*Pinguicula vulgaris* (Bladderwort Family)

Calla, Wild—*Calla palustris* (Arum Family)
✝ Cardinal-flower—*Lobelia Cardinalis* (Bluebell Family)

Celandine, Lesser—*Ranunculus Ficaria* (Crowfoot Family)
Chain-fern (Fern Family)
   Netted—*Woodwardia areolata*
   Virginia—*W. virginica*
Cinquefoil, Marsh—*Potentilla palustris* (Rose Family)
Coltsfoot, Common—*Tussilago Farfara* (Composite Family)
Comfrey, Prickly—*Symphytum asperum* (Forget-me-not Family)
Cow-parsnip—*Heracleum maximum* (Parsley Family)
Coreopsis, Rose—*Coreopsis rosea* (Composite Family)

Death-camass—*Zigadenus glaucus* (Lily Family)
Dragon-root—*Arisaema Dracontium* (Arum Family)

False-hellebore, American—*Veratrum viride* (Lily Family)
Fly-poison—*Amianthium Muscaetoxicum* (Lily Family)
Forget-me-not (Forget-me-not Family)
   Bay—*Myosotis laxa*
   True—*M. scorpioides*

Gentian, Narrow-leaved—*Gentiana linearis* (Gentian Family)
Globeflower, American—*Trollius laxus* (Crowfoot Family)
Goldenrod (Composite Family)
   Bog—*Solidago uliginosa*
   Canada—*S. canadensis*
Goldthread—*Coptis groenlandica* (Crowfoot Family)
Grass-of-Parnassus—*Parnassia glauca* (Saxifrage Family)
Groundsel, Golden—*Senecio aureus* (Composite Family)

Hedge-hyssop—*Gratiola aurea* (Figwort Family)
Hedge-nettle, Marsh—*Stachys palustris* (Mint Family)
Hempweed, Climbing—*Mikania scandens* (Composite Family)

Iris (Iris Family)
   Dwarf Lake—*Iris lacustris*
   Blue flag—*I. versicolor*
   Cubeseed—*I. prismatica*
   Dixie—*I. hexagona*
   Copper—*I. fulva*
   Lamance—*I. brevicaulis*
   Southern Blue Flag—*I. virginica*
   Yellow—*I. Pseudacorus*

Jack-in-the-pulpit (Arum Family)
   Common—*Arisaema atrorubens*
   Small—*A. triphyllum*
Joe-Pye-weed (Composite Family)
   Bluestem—*Eupatorium purpureum*
   Coastal-plain—*E. dubium*
   Purplestem—*E. fistulosum*
   Spotted—*E. maculatum*

Ladies'-tresses—*Spiranthes cernua* and other species (Orchid Family)
Lady's-slipper, Showy—*Cypripedium reginae* (Orchid Family)
Lily (Lily Family)
   Canada —*Lilium canadense*
   Catesby's—*L. Catesbaei*
   Gray's—*L. Grayi*
Lizard's-tail, Common—*Saururus cernuus* (Lizard's-tail Family)
Lobelia (Bluebell Family)
   Great Blue—*Lobelia siphilitica*
   Ontario—*L. Kalmii*
Loosestrife (Primrose Family)
   Swamp-candle—*Lysimachia terrestris*
   Water—*L. thyrsiflora*
Lythrum (Loosestrife Family)
   Purple—*Lythrum Salicaria*
   Winged—*L. alatum*

Marsh-marigold—*Caltha palustris* (Crowfoot Family)
Meadow-rue, Tall—*Thalictrum polygamum* (Crowfoot Family)
Milkweed, Swamp—*Asclepias incarnata* (Milkweed Family)
Mint, Field—*Mentha arvensis* and other species (Mint Family)
Monkey-flower, Alleghany—*Mimulus ringens* (Figwort Family)

Orchis, Grass-pink—*Calopogon pulchellus* (Orchid Family)

Pitcher-plant (Pitcher-plant Family)
   Common—*Sarracenia purpurea*
   Trumpet—*S. flava*
Pogonia, Rose—*Pogonia ophioglossoides* (Orchid Family)
Pyrola, American—*Pyrola rotundifolia* (Wintergreen Family)

Royal Fern—*Osmunda regalis* (Flowering-fern Family)

Salt-marsh Mallow—*Kosteletzkya virginiana* (Mallow Family)
Saxifrage (Saxifrage Family)
   Alleghany—*Saxifraga Michauxi*
   Lettuce—*S. micranthidifolia*
Sensitive-fern—*Onoclea sensibilis* (Fern Family)
Skullcap,Sideflower—*Scutellaria lateriflora* (Mint Family)
Skunk-cabbage—*Symplocarpus foetidus* (Arum Family)
Snapweed (Touch-me-not Family)
   Pale—*Impatiens pallida*
   Royle—*I. glandulifera*
   Spotted—*I. capensis*
Spider-lily—*Hymenocallis occidentalis* (Amaryllis Family)
Sneezeweed, Common—*Helenium autumnale* (Composite Family)
St. Johnswort, Marsh—*Hypericum virginicum* (St. Johnswort Family)

Sundew (Sundew Family)
   Narrowleaf—*Drosera intermedia*
   Roundleaf—*D. rotundifolia*
   Threadleaf—*D. filifolia*
Sunflower, Ditch—*Bidens coronata* (Composite Family)
Swamp-pink—*Helonias bullata* (Lily Family)
Sweetflag—*Acorus Calamus* (Arum Family)

Turtlehead (Figwort Family)
   Pink—*Chelone Lyoni*
   Rose—*C. obliqua*
   White—*C. glabra*

Valerian, Bog—*Valeriana uliginosa* (Valerian Family)
Violet (Violet Family)
   Kidney-leaf—*Viola renifolia*
   Marsh—*V. palustris*
   Roundleaf—*V. rotundifolia*

Watercress, True—*Nasturtium officinale* (Mustard Family)
Water-willow—*Decodon verticillatus* (Loosestrife Family)
Wood-fern (Fern Family)
   Clinton—*Dryopteris Clintoniana*
   Crested—*D. cristata*
   Toothed—*D. spinulosa*

Rose-mallow (Mallow Family)
   Common—*Hibiscus palustris*
   Musk—*H. Moscheutos*
   Woolly—*H. lasiocarpos*

V. Plants for Moist Woods

This is the habitat which most wild flower gardeners desire to create. The trees should be mostly deciduous, allowing filtered sunlight to reach the wild flowers when they are in blossom. The shade can be heavy for the rest of the season. Few wild flowers can flourish under coniferous trees. The soil must never dry out. *Beech grove*

Anemone (Crowfoot Family)
   American Wood—*Anemone quinquefolia*
   Lance-leaved—*A. lancifolia*
   Meadow—*A. canadensis*
Angelica, Purple-stemmed—*Angelica atropurpurea* (Parsley Family)

Baneberry (Crowfoot Family)
  White—*Actaea pachypoda*
  Red—*A. rubra*
Bead-lily (Lily Family)
  Speckled—*Clintonia umbellulata*
  Yellow—*C. borealis*
X Bee-balm, Oswego—*Monarda didyma* (Mint Family)
Bladder-fern (Fern Family)
  Berry—*Cystopteris bulbifera*
  Brittle—*C. fragilis*
Bleeding-heart, Fringed—*Dicentra eximia* (Poppy Family)
Bloodroot—*Sanguinaria canadensis* (Poppy Family)
Bluebells, Virginia—*Mertensis virginica* (Borage Family)
Boneset (Composite Family)
  Common—*Eupatorium perfoliatum*
  Upland—*E. sessilifolium*
Bowman's-root—*Gillenia trifoliata* (Rose Family)
Bugbane (Crowfoot Family)
  American—*Cimicifuga americana*
  Cohosh—*C. racemosa*
Bugleweed, Red—*Lycopus rubellus* (Mint Family)
Bunchberry—*Cornus canadensis* (Dogwood Family)
Bunchflower—*Melanthium virginicum* (Lily Family)
Buttercup (Crowfoot Family)
  Creeping—*Ranunculus repens*
  Swamp—*R. septentrionalis*

Calypso—*Calypso borealis* (Orchid Family)
Camass, Atlantic—*Camassia scilloides* (Lily Family)
Carrion-flower—*Smilax herbacea* (Lily Family)
Cinnamon-fern—*Osmunda cinnamomea* (Flowering-fern Family)
Clematis, Curly—*Clematis crispa* (Crowfoot Family)
Climbing-fern—*Lygodium palmatum* (Curly-grass Family)
Club-moss—*Lycopodium* of all species (Club-moss Family)
Cohosh, Blue—*Caulophyllum thalictroides* (Barberry Family)
Coreopsis, Atlantic—*Coreopsis tripteris* (Composite Family)

Dragon-root—*Arisaema Dracontium* (Arum Family)
Dutchman's-breeches—*Dicentra cucullaria* (Poppy Family)
Dwarf—*P. trifolius*

Epipactis, Broad-leaf—*Epipactis Helleborine* (Orchid Family)

Fairy-bells (Lily Family)
  Hairy—*Disporum lanuginosum*
  Spotted—*D. maculatum*
Fairy-wand—*Chamaelirium luteum* (Lily Family)

Fawn-lily (Lily Family)
   Common—*Erythronium americanum*
   White—*E. albidum*
Figwort, Maryland—*Scrophularia marilandica* (Figwort Family)
Foam-flower, Allegheny—*Tiarella cordifolia* (Saxifrage Family)
Fringed orchis—*Habenaria* of some 20 species (Orchid Family)

Geranium, Spotted—*Geranium maculatum* (Geranium Family)
Giant-hyssop (Mint Family)
   Catnip—*Agastache nepetoides*
   Fennel—*A. foeniculum*
   Figwort—*A. scrophulariaefolia*
Ginseng (Ginseng Family)
   American—*Panax quinquefolius*
Glory-bind, Hedge—*Convolvulus sepium* (Morning-glory Family)
Goat's-beard, Sylvan—*Aruncus dioicus* (Rose Family)
Goldenseal—*Hydrastis canadensis* (Crowfoot Family)
Goldenrod (Composite Family)
   Giant—*Solidago gigantea*
   Wrinkled—*S. rugosa*

Hart's-tongue, American—*Phyllitis Scolopendrium* (Fern Family)
Horse-balm—*Collinsonia canadensis* (Mint Family)

Indian-physic—*Gillenia stipulata* (Rose Family)
Interrupted fern—*Osmunda Claytoniana* (Flowering-fern Family)
Ironweed—six species of *Vernonia* (Composite Family)

Jack-in-the-pulpit, Common—*Arisaema atrorubens* (Arum Family)

Lady's-slipper (Orchid Family)
   Ram's-head—*Cypripedium arietinum*
   Small Yellow—*C. Calceolus* var. *parviflorum*
Lily, American Turk's-cap—*Lilium superbum* (Lily Family)
Lion's-heart (Mint Family)
   Virginia—*Physostegia virginiana*
   Foxglove—*P. obovata*
Lovage (Parsley Family)
   Canada—*Ligusticum canadense*
   Scotch—*L. scothicum*

Maidenhair-fern, American—*Adiantum pedatum* (Fern Family)
Marsh-fern—*Dryopteris thelypteris* (Fern Family)
Massachusetts-fern—*Dryopteris simulata* (Fern Family)
May-apple, Common—*Podophyllum peltatum* (Barberry Family)
Meadow-rue, Purple—*Thalictrum dasycarpum* (Crowfoot Family)
Merry-bells (Lily Family)
   Big—*Uvularia grandiflora*
   Little—*U. sessilifolia*
   Wood—*U. perfoliata*

Milkweed (Milkweed Family)
  Purple—*Asclepias purpurascens*
  White Marsh—*A. perennis*
Monkshood (Crowfoot Family)
  Clambering—*Aconitum uncinatum*
  New York—*A. noveboracense*
Mountain-fringe—*Adlumia fungosa* (Poppy Family)

New York-fern—*Dryopteris noveboracensis* (Fern Family)

Oak-fern—*Dryopteris disjuncta* (Fern Family)
Orchis (Orchid Family)
  Roundleaved—*Orchis rotundifolia*
  Showy—*O. spectabilis*
Oxalis (Wood-sorrel Family)
  American Wood-sorrel—*Oxalis montana*
  Violet Wood-sorrel—*O. violacea*

Partridge-berry—*Mitchella repens* (Madder Family)
Phlox (Polemonium Family)
  Creeping—*Phlox stolonifera*
  Buckley—*P. Buckleyi*
Polemonium, American—*Polemonium Van-Bruntiae* (Polemonium Family)
Potato-bean—*Apios americana* (Pea Family)

Rattlesnake-plantain (Orchid Family)
  Downy—*Goodyera pubescens*
  Creeping—*G. repens*
Rosin-weed, Cup—*Silphium perfoliatum* (Composite Family)

Savory, Smooth—*Satureia glabella* (Mint Family)
Solomon's-plume, Labrador—*Smilacina trifoliata* (Lily Family)
Spiderwort, Common—*Tradescantia virginiana* (Spiderwort Family)
Spleenwort (Fern Family)
  Lady-fern—*Athyrium filix-foemina*
  Maidenhair—*Asplenium Trichomanes*
  Narrow-leaf—*Athyrium pycnocarpon*
  Silver—*Athyrium thelypterioides*
Squirrel-corn—*Dicentra canadensis* (Poppy Family)
Sweet-root—*Osmorhiza longistylis* (Parsley Family)

Tootwort (Mustard Family)
  Crinkle-root—*Dentaria diphylla*
  Cutleaf—*D. laciniata*
  Large—*D. maxima*
Trillium (Lily Family)
  Nodding—*Trillium cernuum*
  Painted—*T. undulatum*
  Purple—*T. erectum*

Twayblade (Orchid Family)
  Lily—*Liparis lilifolia*
  Northern—*Listera cordata*
  Loesel—*Liparis Loeselii*
Twinflower, American—*Linnaea borealis* var. *americana* (Honeysuckle Family)
Twinleaf, American—*Jeffersonia diphylla* (Barberry Family)
Twisted-stalk (Lily Family)
  Clasp-leaf—*Streptopus amplexifolius*
  Rose—*S. roseus*

Umbrella-leaf, American—*Diphylleia cymosa* (Barberry Family)

Vervain, Blue—*Verbena hastata* (Vervain Family)
Violet (Violet Family)
  Large-leaf White—*Viola incognita*
  Longspur—*V. rostrata*
  Northern White—*V. pallens*
  Round-leaf—*V. rotundifolia*
  Trilobe—*V. triloba*
  Wilderness—*V. Selkirkii*

Walking fern—*Camptosorus rhizophyllus* (Fern Family)
Waterleaf (Waterleaf Family)
  Appendaged—*Hydrophyllum appendiculatum*
  Canada—*H. canadense*
  Virginia—*H. virginianum*
Wild Indigo, Blue—*Baptisia australis* (Pea Family)
Wood-fern, Toothed—*Dryopteris spinulosa* (Fern Family)
Wood-nymph—*Moneses uniflora* (Wintergreen Family)

VI. Plants for Moist Meadows in Full Sun

Soil should never be completely dry and should receive sun all day.

Aster (Composite Family)
  New England—*Aster novae-angliae*
  New York—*A. novi-belgii*
Avens (Rose Family)
  Long-plume—*Geum triflorum*
  Peck's Alpine—*G. Peckii*
  Water—*G. rivale*

Bluets, Common—*Houstonia caerulae* (Madder Family)
Burnet (Rose Family)
  American—*Sanguisorba canadensis*
  Garden—*S. officinalis*

Buttercup (Crowfoot Family)
　Aconite—*Ranunculus aconitifolius*
　Bulb—*R. bulbosus*
　Creeping—*R. repens*
　Tall—*R. acris*

Cloudberry—*Rubus Chamaemorus* (Rose Family)
Coneflower, Cutleaf—*Rudbeckia laciniata* (Composite Family)
Cuckoo-flower—*Cardamine pratensis* (Mustard Family)

Dogbane, Indian-hemp—*Apocynum cannabinum* (Dogbane Family)

Gentian (Gential Family)
　Andrews—*Gentiana Andrewsii*
　Bottle—*G. saponaria*
　Fringed—*G. crinita*
　Pine-barren—*G. autumnalis*
　Yellow—*G. flavida*
Goldenrod (Composite Family)
　Grass-leaf—*Solidago graminifolia*
　Noble—*S. speciosa*
　Thin-leaf—*S. tenuifolia*
Groundsel, Obovate—*Senecio obovatus* (Composite Family)

Hawkweed (Composite Family)
　Orange—*Hieracium aurantiacum*
　Yellow-devil—*H. floribundum*

Inula, Elecampane—*Inula Helenium* (Composite Family)

Lobelia, Giant Blue—*Lobelia siphilitica* (Bluebell Family)

Mallow, Virginia—*Sida hermaphrodita* (Mallow Family)
Meadowsweet, Prairie—*Filipendula rubra* (Rose Family)
Meadow-beauty (Melastoma Family)
　Common—*Rhexia virginica*
　Maryland—*R. mariana*
Milkweed (Milkweed Family)
　Purple—*Ascelepias purpurascens*
　Red—*A. rubra*

Pink-root—*Spigelia marilandica* (Logania Family)
Polemonium, Creeping—*Polemonium reptans* (Polemonium Family)
Poor-robin's-plantain—*Erigeron pulchellus* (Composite Family)

Rose-gentian (Gentian Family)
　Marsh—*Sabatia dodecandra*
　New England—*S. Kennedyana*
Rose-mallow, Common—*Hibiscus palustris* (Mallow Family)

Saxifrage (Saxifrage Family)
　Pennsylvania—*Saxifraga pensylvanica*
　Virginia—*S. virginiensis*

Shooting-star, Common—*Dodecatheon Meadia* (Primrose Family)
Sneezeweed, Common—*Helenium autumnale* (Composite Family)
Sunflower (Composite Family)
    Giant—*Helianthus giganteus*
    Jerusalem-artichoke—*H. tuberosus*
    Maximilian—*H. Maximiliani*
    Saw-tooth—*H. grosseserratus*
    Willow—*H. salicifolius*

Violet (Violet Family)
    American Dog—*Viola conspersa*
    Arrow-leaf—*V. sagittata*
    Butterfly—*V. papilionacea*
    Bogbice—*V. cucullata*
    Comb-toothed—*V. pectinata*
    LeComte—*V. affinis*
    Missouri—*V. missouriensis*
    Striped—*V. striata*
    Wanderer—*V. nephrophylla*

VII. Plants for Dry Open Woods

There is light shade from deciduous trees with openings for full sun at least part of the day. The soil often becomes dry in summer. Most of these wild flowers are early blooming.

Aloe, False—*Aloe virginica* (Amaryllis Family)
Anemone (Crowfoot Family)
    Candle—*Anemone cylindrica*
    Riverbank—*A. riparia*
    Virginia—*A. virginiana*
    Rue—*Anemonella thalictroides*
Aralia, Bristly—*Aralia hispida* (Ginseng Family)
Aster (Composite Family)
    Big-leaf—*Aster macrophyllus*
    Blue Wood—*A. cordifolius*
    White Wood—*A. divaricatus*
Astilbe, False Goat's-beard—*Astilbe biternata* (Saxifrage Family)
Avens (Rose Family)
    Cutleaf—*Geum laciniatum*
    Large-leaf—*G. macrophyllum*

Bead-ruby, Canada—*Maianthemum canadense* (Lily Family)
Bee-balm, Wild bergamot—*Monarda fistulosa* (Mint Family)
Beech-fern (Fern Family)
    Broad—*Dryopteris hexagonoptera*
    Narrow—*D. Phegopteris*

Bracken—*Pteridium aquilinum* (Fern Family)
Buttercup, Tufted—*Ranunculus fascicularis* (Crowfoot Family)

Celandine-poppy—*Stylophorum diphyllum* (Poppy Family)
Christmas-fern—*Polystichum acrostichoides* (Fern Family)
Clematis (Crowfoot Family)
    Addison—*Clematis Addisonii*
    Chrome—*C. ochroleuca*
    Pitcher—*C. Pitcheri*
    Rock—*C. verticillaris*
Cliff-brake (Fern Family)
    Purple—*Pellaea atropurpurea*
    Smooth—*P. glabella*
Cloak-fern—*Notholaena dealbata* (Fern Family)
Comandra, Common—*Comandra umbellata* (Sandal-wood Family)
Cranefly-orchis, American—*Tipularia discolor* (Orchid Family)
Crown-beard (Composite Family)
    Gravel-weed—*Verbesina helianthoides*
    White—*V. virginica*
Cucumber-root—*Medeola virginiana* (Lily Family)
Culver's-root—*Veronicastrum virginicum* (Figwort Family)

Dalibarda, Star-violet—*Dalibarda repens* (Rose Family)
Dogbane, Spreading—*Apocynum androsaemifolium* (Dogbane Family)
Dutchman's-pipe, Snakeroot—*Aristolochia Serpentaria* (Birthwort Family)

Eupatorium (Composite Family)
    Late—*Eupatorium serotinum*
    Tall—*E. altissimum*
    Small White—*E. aromaticum*

Fireweed, Common—*Epilobium angustifolium* (Evening-primrose Family)

Galax—*Galax aphylla* (Diapensia Family)
Goat's-beard, Sylvan—*Aruncus dioicus* (Rose Family)
Goldenrod (Composite Family)
    Fragrant—*Solidago odora*
    Harsh—*S. radula*
    Plume—*S. juncea*
    Stiff—*S. rigida*
    Tall—*S. altissima*
    Wreath—*S. caesia*
    Zigzag—*S. flexicaulis*
Gold-star-grass, Common—*Hypoxis hirsuta* (Amaryllis Family)

Harbinger-of-spring—*Erigenia bulbosa* (Parsley Family)
Hawkweed, Poor-robin's—*Hieracium venosum* (Composite Family)

Hay-scented-fern—*Dennstaedtia punctilobula* (Fern Family)
Hepatica (Crowfoot Family)
    Round-lobed—*Hepatica americana*
    Sharp-lobed—*H. acutiloba*
Holly-fern (Fern Family)
    Braun—*Polystichum Braunii*
    Mountain—*P. Lonchitis*
Horse-gentian (Honeysuckle Family)
    Common—*Triosteum perfoliatum*
    Narrow-leaf—*T. angustifolium*
    Orange—*T. aurantiacum*

Isopyrum, Atlantic—*Isopyrum biternatum* (Crowfoot Family)

Lady's-slipper (Orchid Family)
    Large Yellow—*Cypripedium Calceolus* var. *pubescens*
    Pink—*C. acaule*
    White—*C. candidum*
Larkspur, Rock—*Delphinium tricorne* (Crowfoot Family)
Leek, Wild—*Allium tricoccum* (Lily Family)
Lily, Wood—*Lilium philadelphicum* (Lily Family)
Lip-fern (Fern Family)
    Alabama—*Cheilanthes alabamensis*
    Hairy—*C. vestita*
    Slender—*C. Feei*
    Woolly—*C. lanosa*
Loosestrife, Whorled—*Lysimachia quadrifolia* (Primrose Family)

Male-fern—*Dryopteris filix-mas* (Fern Family)
Meadow-rue (Crowfoot Family)
    Critical—*Thalictrum confine*
    Early—*T. dioicum*
    Wax-leaf—*T. revolutum*
Merry-bells, Little—*Uvularia sessilifolia* (Lily Family)
Milkweed (Milkweed Family)
    Four-leaf—*Asclepias quadrifolia*
    Pink-eye—*A. variegata*
    Tall—*A. exaltata*
    Whorled—*A. verticillata*
Mitrewort, Common—*Mitella diphylla* (Saxifrage Family)
Mountain-mint—*Pycnanthemum*, some 15 species (Mint Family)

Oak-fern, Scented—*Dryopteris Robertiana* (Fern Family)
Oconee-bells—*Shortia galacifolia* (Diapensia Family)

Pachysandra, Allegheny—*Pachysandra procumbens* (Box Family)

Phlox (Polemonium Family)
  Downy—*Phlox pilosa*
  Sweet william—*P. divaricata*
  Ten-point—*P. bifida*
Pipsissewa (Wintergreen Family)
  Common—*Chimaphila umbellata*
  Striped—*C. maculata*
Pod-fern—*Cheilanthes siliquosa* (Fern Family)
Polygala, Fringed—*Polygala paucifolia* (Milkwort Family)
Polypody, Common—*Polypodium virginianum* (Fern Family)
Pyrola—some six species of *Pyrola* (Wintergreen Family)

Rattlesnake-plantain (Orchid Family)
  Checkered—*Goodyera tesselata*
  Downy—*G. pubescens*
Resurrection-fern—*Polypodium polypodioides* (Fern Family)
Rock-brake (Fern Family)
  American—*Cryptogramma crispa*
  Slender—*C. Stelleri*

Scurf-pea—some eight species of *Psoralea* (Pea Family)
Snakeroot, White—*Eupatorium rugosum* (Composite Family)
Solomon's-plume (Lily Family)
  Feather—*Smilacina racemosa*
  Starry—*S. stellata*
Solomon's-seal (Lily Family)
  Great—*Polygonatum canaliculatum*
  Hairy—*P. pubescens*
  Small—*P. biflorum*
Speedwell (Figwort Family)
  Common—*Veronica officinalis*
  Spike—*V. spicata*
Spikenard, American—*Aralia racemosa* (Ginseng Family)
Spleenwort (Fern Family)
  Black-stem—*Asplenium resiliens*
  Ebony—*A. platyneuron*
  Mountain—*A. montanum*
  Pinnatifid—*A. pinnatifidum*
  Wall-rue—*A. cryptolepis*
Spring-beauty (Purslane Family)
  Carolina—*Claytonia caroliniana*
  Virginia—*C. virginica*
Star-flower, American—*Trientalis borealis* (Primrose Family)
Star-grass, White-tubed—*Aletris farinosa* (Lily Family)
Stenanthium, Grass-leaf—*Stenanthium gramineum* (Lily Family)
Sunflower (Composite Family)
  Divaricate—*Helianthus divaricatus*
  Oblong-leaf—*H. doronicoides*
  Stiff—*H. laetiflorus*

Thermopsis (Pea Family)
  Carolina—*Thermopsis caroliniana*
  Soft—*T. mollis*
Thoroughwort, White—*Eupatorium album* (Composite Family)
Trailing arbutus—*Epigaea repens* (Heath Family)
Trillium, Snow—*Trillium grandiflorum* (Lily Family)
Twayblade, Lily—*Liparis lilifolia* (Orchid Family)
Twin-leaf, American—*Jeffersonia diphylla* (Barberry Family)

Violet (Violet Family)
  Appalachian—*Viola hirsutula*
  Beechwoods—*V. latiuscula*
  Canada—*V. canadensis*
  Downy Yellow—*V. pubescens*
  Fringed—*V. fimbriatula*
  Halbert-leaf Yellow—*V. hastata*
  Ontario—*V. septentrionalis*
  Palm—*V. palmata*
  Primrose—*V. primulifolia*
  Stones—*V. Stoneana*
  Sweet White—*V. blanda*
  Triangle-leaf—*V. emarginata*
  Wool-pod—*V. pensylvanica*

Wild Ginger (Birthwort Family)
  Canada—*Asarum canadense*
  Virginia—*A. virginicum*
Wild Indigo, Atlantic—*Baptisia leucantha* (Pea Family)
Wild Sarsaparilla—*Aralia nudicaulis* (Ginseng Family)
Wood-fern (Fern Family)
  Fragrant—*Dryopteris fragrans*
  Goldie—*D. Goldiana*
  Leather—*D. marginalis*
Woodsia—some six species of *Woodsia* (Fern Family)

VIII. Plants for the Summer Wild Garden in Sun

These are plants for the late spring or summer wild garden. They should be allowed to compete with other species under ordinary soil conditions, *not* in the enriched soil of the cultivated border.

Alumroot—some eight species of *Heuchera* (Saxifrage Family)
Amsonia, Willow—*Amsonia Tabernaemontana* (Dogbane Family)
Anemone (Crowfoot Family)
  American Pasqueflower—*Anemone patens* var. *Wolfgangiana*
  Argentine—*A. multifida*
  Candle—*A. cylindrica*

Bluebell, Scotch—*Campanula rotundifolia* (Bluebell Family)
Buttercup (Crowfoot Family)
   Bulb—*Ranunculus bulbosus*
   Tall—*R. acris*

Campion, American—*Lychnis alpina* var. *Americana* (Pink Family)
Cinquefoil, Wineleaf—*Potentilla tridentata* (Rose Family)
Columbine, American—*Aquilegia canadensis* (Crowfoot Family)
Coneflower (Composite Family)
   Orange—*Rudbeckia fulgida*
   Showy—*R. speciosa*
   Sweet—*R. subtomentosa*
Coreopsis (Composite Family)
   Big-flower—*Coreopsis grandiflora*
   Eared—*C. auriculata*
   Finger—*C. palmata*
   Lance—*C. lanceolata*
   Larkspur—*C. delphinifolia*
   Thread-leaf—*C. verticillata*
   Trefoil—*C. major*
Coronilla, Crown-vetch—*Coronilla varia* (Pea Family)
Corydalis, Pale—*Corydalis sempervirens* (Poppy Family)
Crazy-weed—eight or more species of *Oxytropis* (Pea Family)

Daylily, Tawny—*Hemerocallis fulva* (Lily Family)

Echinacea (Composite Family)
   Pale—*Echinacea pallida*
   Purple—*E. purpurea*
Eryngo, Button-snakeroot—*Eryngium yuccifolium* (Parsley Family)

False-garlic, Yellow—*Nothoscordum bivalve* (Lily Family)
Flax, Lewis—*Linum Lewisii* (Flax Family)

Goldenrod (Composite Family)
   Rugged—*Solidago squarrosa*
   Seaside—*S. sempervirens*
   Silver—*S. bicolor*

Heliopsis, Sunflower—*Heliopsis helianthoides* (Composite Family)
Hoary-pea, Virginia—*Tephrosia virginiana* (Pea Family)

Larkspur (Crowfoot Family)
   Carolina—*Delphinium carolinianum*
   Tall—*D. exaltatum*

Milk-vetch—25 or more species of *Astragalus* (Pea Family)
Mock-strawberry—*Duchesnea indica* (Rose Family)
Monkshood, Clambering—*Aconitum reclinatum* (Crowfoot Family)

Onion (Lily Family)
  Nodding—*Allium cernuum*
  Prairie—*A. stellatum*

Penstemon (Figwort Family)
  Foxglove—*Penstemon digitalis*
  Gray—*P. canescens*
  Long-sepal—*P. calycosus*
  Shell-leaf—*P. grandiflorus*
  Smooth—*P. laevigatus*
  Type—*P. hirsutus*
Phlox (Polemonium Family)
  Broad-leaf—*Phlox amplifolia*
  Carolina—*P. carolina*
  Meadow—*P. maculata*
  Mountain—*P. ovata*
  Smooth—*P. glaberrima*
  Summer—*P. paniculata*
Prairie-clover—six or more species of *Petalostemon* (Pea Family)
Prairie-coneflower, Anise—*Ratibida pinnata* (Composite Family)

Ragged-robin—*Lychnis Flos-cuculi* (Pink Family)
Rocket, Dames—*Hesperis matronalis* (Mustard Family)

Sage, Azure—*Salvia azurea* (Mint Family)
Saxifrage (Saxifrage Family)
  Aizoon—*Saxifraga Aizoön*
  Twin-leaf—*S. oppositifolia*
  Yellow Mountain—*S. aizoides*
Senna, Wild—*Cassia marilandica* (Pea Family)
Sibbaldia, Creeping—*Sibbaldia procumbens* (Rose Family)
Silene (Pink Family)
  Fire-pink—*Silene virginica*
  Peat-pink—*S. caroliniana* var. *pensylvanica*
  Royal—*S. regia*
Sneezeweed, Purple-head—*Helenium nudiflorum* (Composite Family)
Stonecrop (Orpine Family)
  Mountain—*Sedum ternatum*
  Rose-root—*S. Rosea*
Strawberry (Rose Family)
  Alpine—*Fragaria vesca*
  Barren—*Waldsteinia fragarioides*
Sundrops (Evening-primrose Family)
  Blue-leaf—*Oenothera tetragona*
  Common—*O. fruticosa*
  Fraser—*O. tetragona* var. *Fraseri*
  Perennial—*O. perennis*

Sunflower, Thin-leaved—*Helianthus decapetalus,* and others (Composite Family)

Sweet-broom, Northern—*Hedysarum alpinum* (Pea Family)

Violet (Violet Family)
  Bird's foot —*Viola pedata*
  Hooked—*V. adunca*
  Prairie—*V. pedatifida*
  Lance-leaved—*V. lanceolata*
  Primrose-leaved—*V. primulifolia*
  Sister—*V. sororia*

Whitlow-grass, Rock-cress—*Draba arabisans* (Mustard Family)

IX. Plants for Sandy Soil in Full Sun

The soil should be more than half sand, and well drained.

Aster (Composite Family)
  Bushy—*Aster dumosus*
  Heath—*A. ericoides*
  Savory-leaf—*A. linariifolius*
  Seaside—*A. spectabilis*
  Skydrop—*A. patens*
  Smooth—*A. laevis*
  White Upland—*A. ptarmicoides*
  White Wood—*A. divaricatus*

Beach-heather (Rockrose Family)
  Golden—*Hudsonia ericoides*
  Woolly—*H. tomentosa*
Bearberry—*Arctostaphylos Uva-ursi* (Heath Family)
Beargrass, Turkey-beard—*Xerophyllum asphodeloides* (Lily Family)
Bee-balm, Spotted—*Monarda punctata* (Mint Family)
Black-eyed-Susan (Composite Family)
  Rudbeckia hirta
  Plains—*Rudbeckia serotina*
Bluets, Purple—*Houstonia purpurea* (Madder Family)
Bouncing-bet—*Saponaria officinalis* (Pink Family)
Butterfly-pea, Coastal—*Clitoria mariana* (Pea Family)

Chicory, Common—*Cichorium Intybus* (Composite Family)
Cinquefoil (Rose Family)
  Silvery—*Potentilla argentea*
  Silverweed—*P. anserina*
Compass-plant—*Silphium laciniatum* (Composite Family)
Coreopsis, Big-flower—*Coreopsis grandiflora* (Composite Family)

Evening-primrose (Evening-primrose Family)
  Common—*Oenothera biennis*
  Cut-leaf—*O. laciniata*
  Dwarf—*O. serrulata*
  Sea-beach—*O. humifusa*
Everlasting, Pearl—*Anaphalis margaritacea* (Composite Family)

Gayfeather—18 species of *Liatris* (Composite Family)
Globe-mallow, Scarlet—*Sphaeralcea coccinea* (Mallow Family)
Gold-aster (Composite Family)
  Maryland—*Chrysopsis mariana*
  Sickle-leaf—*C. falcata*
Goldenrod, Old-field—*Solidago nemoralis* (Composite Family)
Gromwell, Hoary—*Lithospermum canescens* (Borage Family)

Hawkweed (Composite Family)
  King-devil—*Hieracium pratense*
  Narrow-leaf—*H. umbellatum*
  Orange—*H. aurantiacum*
  Panicled—*H. paniculatum*
  Rough—*H. scabrum*
  Yellow-devil—*H. floribundum*
Hoary-pea, Virginia—*Tephrosia virginiana* (Pea Family)

Lupine, Sundial—*Lupinus perennis* (Pea Family)

Marble-seed, Virginia—*Onosmodium virginianum* (Borage Family)
Milk-pea—*Galactia regularis* (Pea Family)
Milkweed (Milkweed Family)
  Butterfly—*Asclepias tuberosa*
  Common—*A. syriaca*

Poppy-mallow, Low—*Callirhoë involucrata* (Mallow Family)
Prickly-pear, Common—*Opuntia humifusa* (Cactus Family)

Rosin-weed (Composite Family)
  Prairie-dock—*Silphium terebinthinaceum*
  Whole-leaf—*S. integrifolium*

Sage, Lyre-leaved—*Salvia lyrata* (Mint Family)
Sage-brush, Fringed—*Artemisia frigida* (Composite Family)
Soapweed, Small—*Yucca glauca* (Lily Family)
Spurge, Flowering—*Euphorbia corollata* (Spurge Family)
Sunflower, Ashy—*Helianthus mollis* (Composite Family)

Tansy, Common—*Tanacetum vulgare* (Composite Family)
Thoroughwort, Hyssop—*Eupatorium hyssopifolium* (Composite Family)
Toadflax, Common—*Linaria vulgaris* (Figwort Family)

Verbena, Rose—*Verbena canadensis* (Vervain Family)

Wild Indigo (Pea Family)
   Plains—*Baptisia leucophaea*
   Small Blue—*B. minor*
   White—*B. alba*
   Yellow—*B. tinctoria*
Wild Ipecac—*Euphorbia Ipecacuanhae* (Spurge Family)
Wild-quinine—*Parthenium integrifolium* (Composite Family)
Wormwood, Roman—*Artemisia pontica* (Composite Family)

Yarrow, Common—*Achillea Millefolium* (Composite Family)
Yucca (Lily Family)
   Adam's-needle—*Yucca Smalliana*
   Spoon-leaf—*Y. filamentosa*

X.   Plants for Seashore Gardens

The soil is alkaline from its closeness to the ocean.

Cat-tail (Cat-tail Family)
   Common—*Typha latifolia*
   Narrow-leaf—*T. angustifolia*

Eryngo, Marsh—*Eryngium aquaticum* (Parsley Family)
Evening-primrose, Sea-beach—*Oenothera humifusa* (Evening-primrose
      Family)

Goldenrod, Seaside—*Solidago sempervirens* (Composite Family)

Iris (Iris Family)
   Beach-head—*Iris Hookeri*
   Cube-seed—*I. prismatica*

Lungwort, Sea—*Mertensia maritima* (Borage Family)

Pea, Beach—*Lathyrus japonicus* var. *glaber* (Pea Family)

Rose-mallow, Marsh—*Hibiscus palustris* (Mallow Family)

Saltmarsh-mallow—*Kosteletzkya virginica* (Mallow Family)
Sandwort, Sea-beach—*Arenaria peploides* (Pink Family)
Sea-lavender, Carolina—*Limonium carolinianum* (Leadwort Family)
Sea-milkwort—*Glaux maritima* (Primrose Family)
Sweet-flag—*Acorus Calamus* (Arum Family)

Wormwood, Beach—*Artemisia Stelleriana* (Composite Family)

XI. Plants for Ledges and Rock Crevices

Many alpine plants and dwarf species belong in this list. Most true alpines will not grow well at sea level in mild climates.

Arnica, Hairy—*Arnica mollis* (Composite Family)
Aster (Composite Family)
  Leafy-bract—*Aster foliaceus*
  Savory-leaf—*A. linariifolius*

Buttercup, Tufted—*Ranunculus fascicularis* (Crowfoot Family)

Campion (Pink Family)
  Moss—*Silene acaulis*
  American—*Lychnis alpina* var. *americana*
Cliff-brake (Fern Family)
  Purple—*Pellaea atropurpurea*
  Smooth—*P. glabella*
Crowberry (Crowberry Family)
  Black—*Empetrum nigrum*
  Purple—*E. atropurpureum*
  Broom—*Corema conradi*

Diapensia—*Diapensia lapponica* (Diapensia Family)
Dryas (Rose Family)
  Drummond—*Dryas Drummondii*
  Entire-leaf—*D. integrifolia*

Gold-aster, Sickle-leaf—*Chrysopsis falcata* (Composite Family)
Goldenstar—*Chrysogonum virginianum* (Composite Family)
Goldenrod, Cutler Alpine—*Solidago Cutleri* (Composite Family)

Lady's-mantle, Mountain—*Alchemilla alpina* (Rose Family)
Lip-fern, Hairy—*Cheilanthes lanosa* (Fern Family)

Penstemon, Dwarf Type—*Penstemon hirsutus* var. *pygmaeus* (Figwort Family)
Phlox (Polemonium Family)
  Amoena—*Phlox amoena*
  Moss—*P. subulata*
  Ten-point—*P. bifida*
  Trailing—*P. nivalis*
Pod-fern—*Cheilanthes siliquosa* (Fern Family)
Polypody, American—*Polypodium virginianum* (Fern Family)
Prickly-pear, Common—*Opuntia humifusa* (Cactus Family)

Primrose (Pimrose Family)
 Dwarf Canadian—*Primula mistassinica*
 Greenland—*P. egaliksensis*
 St. Lawrence—*P. laurentiana*
Pussy-toes—some 30 species of *Antennaria* (Composite Family)

Rock-brake (Fern Family)
 American—*Cryptogramma crispa* var. *acrostichoides*

Slender—*C. stelleri*
Saxifrage, Aizoön—*Saxifraga Aizoön* (Saxifrage Family)
Spleenwort (Fern Family)
 Ebony—*Asplenium platyneuron*
 Green—*A. viride*
 Maidenhair—*A. Trichomanes*
 Mountain—*A. montanum*
 Pinnatifid—*A. pinnatifidum*
 Wall-rue—*A. cryptolepis*
Stonecrop (Orpine Family)
 Goldmoss—*Sedum acre*
 Hexagon—*S. sexangulare*
 Mountain—*S. ternatum*

Violet, Bird's-foot—*Viola pedata* (Violet Family)

Walking-fern—*Camptosorus rhizophyllus* (Fern Family)
Woodsia (Fern Family)
 Alpine—*Woodsia alpina*
 Common—*W. obtusa*
 Smooth—*W. glabella*
 Rocky Mountain—*W. scopulina*
 Rusty—*W. ilvensis*

XII. Annual Native Wild Flowers

Sow seeds in the fall in a cold frame or in pots, or sow in March; plant out in proper location in May–June. Allow to self-sow, or plant seeds every year. While the list of native and introduced annuals is long, few are sufficiently showy to be commonly seen in flower borders or wild gardens. Those marked with an asterisk are most showy.

Abutilon, Chingma—*Abutilon Theophrasti* (Mallow Family)
Anoda, Crested—*Anoda cristata* (Mallow Family)

Aster (Composite Family)
  Annual Saltmarsh—*Aster subulatus*
  Short-ray—*A. Brachyactis*
  St. Lawrence—*A. laurentianus*

Bartonia (Gentian Family)
  Screw-stem—*Bartonia paniculata*
  Virginia—*B. virginica*
Bedstraw (Madder Family)
  Paris—*Galium parisiense*
  Three-horn—*G. tricorne*
  Wand—*G. virgatum*
Bee-balm (Mint Family)
  *Lemon—*Monarda citriodora*
  Pony—*M. pectinata*
*Bellflower, American—*Campanula americana* (Bluebell Family)
Betony, Hedge-nettle—*Stachys annua* (Figwort Family)
Bitter-cress, Pennsylvania—*Cardamine hirsuta* (Mustard Family)
Blue-curls (Mint Family)
  Bristle—*Trichostema setaceum*
  Forked—*T. dichotomum*
Bluets (Madder Family)
  Small—*Houstonia patens*
  Tiny—*H. minima*
*Brown-eyed-Susan—*Rudbeckia triloba* (Composite Family)
Bur-cucumber—*Sicyos angulatus* (Gourd Family)
Buttercup, Blister—*Ranunculus sceleratus,* and others (Crowfoot Family)

*Centaurea, Basket-flower—*Centaurea americana* (Composite Family)
Cinquefoil, Norwegian—*Potentilla norvegica* (Rose Family)
Clover (Pea Family)
  Buffalo—*Trifolium reflexum*
  *Crimson—*T. incarnatum*
  Hop—*T. agrarium*
  Rabbit-foot—*T. arvense*
Collinsia (Figwort Family)
  Blue-eyed-Mary—*Collinsia verna*
  Little-flower—*C. parviflora*
Coneflower (Composite Family)
  *Clasping—*Rudbeckia amplexicaulis*
  *Pinewoods—*R. bicolor*
*Coreopsis, Plains—*Coreopsis tinctoria* (Composite Family)
Corn-salad—*Valerianella radiata* (Valerian Family)
Corydalis, Golden—*Corydalis aurea* (Poppy Family)
Cow-wheat—*Melampyrum lineare* (Figwort Family)
Cromwell, Corn—*Lithospermum arvense* (Borage Family)

*Crown-beard, Golden—*Verbesina encelioides* (Composite Family)
Crotalaria, Arrow—*Crotalaria sagittalis* (Pea Family)
*Cucumber, Wild—*Echinocystis lobata* (Gourd Family)
Cudweed, Purple—*Gnaphalium purpureum* (Composite Family)

Datura, Jimson-weed—*Datura Stramonium* (Nightshade Family)
Dogweed, Prairie—*Dyssodia papposa* (Composite Family)
Dragon-head, American—*Dracocephalum parviflorum* (Mint Family)
Dwarf-dandelion (Composite Family)
    Virginia—*Krigia virginica*
    Western—*K. occidentalis*

Eupatorium, Dog-fennel—*Eupatorium capillifolium* (Composite Family)
Evening-primrose, Stemless—*Oenothera triloba* (Evening-primrose Family)

Flax (Flax Family)
    Fairy—*Linum catharticum*
    Yellow—*L. virginianum*
Fleabane, Daisy—*Erigeron annuus* (Composite Family)
*Flower-of-an-hour—*Hibiscus Trionum* (Mallow Family)
False-mallow—*Sphaeralcea angusta* (Mallow Family)
Forget-me-not, Field—*Myosotis arvensis* (Borage Family)

Gentian (Gentian Family)
    Annual—*Gentiana Amarella*
    Felwort—*G. propinqua*
    Five-leaf—*G. quinquefolia*
Gerardia (Figwort Family)
    Clustered—*Gerardia pedicularis*
    Eared—*G. auriculata*
    Purple—*G. purpurea*
    Seaside—*G. maritima*
    Slender—*G. tenuifolia*
Geranium (Geranium Family)
    Bicknell—*Geranium Bicknellii*
    Carolina—*G. carolinianum*
    Herb-Robert—*G. Robertianum*
Germander, Cutleaf—*Teucrium Botrys* (Mint Family)
Gold-aster, Downy—*Chrysopsis pilosa* (Composite Family)
Groundsel, Common—*Senecio vulgaris* (Composite Family)

Hawk's-beard, Smooth—*Crepis capillaris* (Composite Family)
Hedge-hyssop (Figwort Family)
    Downy—*Gratiola neglecta*
    Virginia—*G. virginiana*
Hedge-mustard—*Sisymbrium officinale* (Mustard Family)
Hemp-nettle, Bristle-stem—*Galeopsis Tetrahit* (Mint Family)
*Horn-poppy, Yellow—*Glaucium flavum* (Poppy Family)

Knotweed—many species of *Polygonum* (Buckwheat Family)

Lettuce-prickly—*Lactuca Scariola* (Composite Family)
Lobelia, Indian-tobacco—*Lobelia inflata* (Bluebell Family)
Lythrum, Hyssop—*Lythrum hyssopifolium* (Loosestrife Family)

Mallow (Mallow Family)
  Common—*Malva neglecta*
  Cluster—*M. verticillata*
Medic, Black—*Medicago lupulina* (Pea Family)
Modiola, Carolina—*Modiola caroliniana* (Mallow Family)
Morning-glory (Convolvulus Family)
  *Common—*Ipomoea purpurea*
  *Ivy-leaf—*I. hederacea*
Mustard (Mustard Family)
  Black—*Brassica nigra*
  White—*B. hirta*

Nemophila, Small—*Nemophila microcalyx* (Water-leaf Family)
Nightshade (Nightshade Family)
  American Black—*Solanum americanum*
  Buffalo-bur—*S. rostratum*
  Cutleaf—*S. triflorum*
  Wavy-leaf—*S. sisymbriifolium*

Oxalis, European Yellow—*Oxalis europaea* (Wood-sorrel Family)

Paint-brush, Indian—*Castilleja coccinea* (Figwort Family)
Pansy, Wild—*Viola arvensis* (Violet Family)
*Partridge-pea, Showy—*Cassia fasciculata* (Pea Family)
Penny-cress, Field—*Thlaspi arvense* (Mustard Family)
Pennyroyal (Mint Family)
  *American—*Hedeoma pulegioides*
  Rough—*H. hispida*
  False—*Isanthus brachiatus* (also Mint Family)
Pepper-grass—*Lepidium virginicum* (Mustard Family)
Polygala (Milkwort Family)
  Blood—*Polygala sanguinea*
  Pink—*P. incarnata*
*Prickly-poppy, White— *Argemone intermedia* (Poppy Family)

Ragweed, Common—*Ambrosia artemisiifolia* (Composite Family) WEEDY
Rattle-weed (Figwort Family)
  Coxcomb—*Rhinanthus Crista-galli*
  Northern—*R. borealis*
Rose-gentian, Salt-marsh—*Sabatia stellaris* (Gentian Family)

*Sage, Lance-leaf—*Salvia reflexa* (Mint Family)
Santa-maria—*Parthenium Hysterophorus* (Composite Family)

Savory, Spring—*Satureia Acinos* (Mint Family)
Scorpion-weed—*Phacelia,* many species (Waterleaf Family)
Sensitive-plant—*Cassia nictitans* (Pea Family)
Sida (Mallow Family)
    Broom-jute—*Sida rhombifolia*
    Prickly—*S. spinosa*
Silene (Pink Family)
    French—*Silene gallica*
    Night-flowering—*S. noctiflora*
    Sleepy—*S. antirrhina*
Snapweed (Touch-me-not Family)
    *Pale—*Impatiens pallida*
    *Royle—*I. glandulifera*
    *Spotted—*I. capensis*
*Sneezeweed, Bitter—*Helenium tenuifolium* (Composite Family)
Spider-flower (Caper Family)
    *Bee—*Cleome serrulata*
    *Spiny—*C. spinosa*
Speedwell (Figwort Family)
    Corn—*Veronica arvensis*
    Bird's-eye—*V. persica*
    Field—*V. agrestis*
    Neck-weed—*V. peregrina*
Spurge (Spurge Family)
    Snow-on-the-mountain—*Euphorbia marginata*
    Painted—*E. heterophylla*   ,
    Toothed—*E. dentata*
    Wood—*E. commutata*
Spur-gentian, American—*Halenia deflexa* (Gentian Family)
*Star-glory, Scarlet—*Ipomoea coccinea* (Morning-glory Family)
St. Johnswort, Pine-weed—*Hypericum gentianoides* (St. Johnswort Family)
*Stonecrop, Texas—*Sedum pulchellum* (Orpine Family)
Sundrops, Flax—*Oenothera linifolia* (Evening-primrose Family)
Sunflower (Composite Family)
    *Ditch—*Bidens coronata*
    *Common—*Helianthus annuus*
    *Prairie—*H. petiolaris*

Toad-flax, Old-field—*Linaria canadensis* (Figwort Family)
Tumble-mustard—*Sisymbrium altissimum* (Mustard Family)
Tumble-weed—*Amaranthus albus* (Amaranth Family) WEEDY

Venus-looking-glass, Clasping—*Specularia perfoliata* (Bluebell Family)
Vetch, Spring—*Vicia sativa* (Pea Family)

Whitlow-grass (Mustard Family)
    Spring—*Draba verna*
    Woods—*D. nemorosa*
Wild-bean, Downy—*Strophostyles leiosperma* (Pea Family)

XIII. Biennials, Native and Naturalized

Sow seeds in pots or flats in fall or spring; transplant to location at end of first summer, or early next spring. It is useless to transplant plants that are in bloom; collect seeds. In order to persist, the plants must self-sow freely.

Allegheny-vine—*Adlumia fungosa* (Poppy Family)

Bitter-cress, Bog—*Cardamine pensylvanica* (Mustard Family)
Black-eyed-Susan, Plains—*Rudbeckia serotina* (Composite Family)
Bugloss (Borage Family)
    Common—*Anchusa officinalis*
    Italian—*A. italica*
    Viper—*Echium vulgare*
Burnet, Small—*Sanguisorba minor* (Rose Family)

Campion (Pink Family)
    Evening—*Lychnis alba*
    White—*L. dioica*
Carrot, Wild—*Daucus Carota* (Parsley Family)
Catchfly, Forking—*Silene dichotoma* (Pink Family)
Celandine, Greater—*Chelidonium majus* (Poppy Family)
Chicory, Common—*Cichorium Intybus* (Composite Family)
Clover, Red—*Trifolium pratense* (Pea Family)
Columbo—*Swertia caroliniensis* (Gentian Family)
Coreopsis, Bigflower—*Coreopsis grandiflora* (Composite Family)
Corydalis (Poppy Family)
    Pale—*Corydalis sempervirens*
    Yellow—*C. flavula*
Cudweed, Fragrant—*Gnaphalium obtusifolium* (Composite Family)

Erysimum (Mustard Family)
    Arkansas—*Erysimum arkansanum*
    Plains—*E. asperum*
Evening-primrose, Common—*Oenothera biennis* (Evening-primrose
    Family)

Fleabane, Philadelphia—*Erigeron philadelphicum* (Composite Family)

Gaura, Biennial—*Gaura biennis* (Evening-primrose Family)
Gentian, Fringed—*Gentiana crinita* (Gentian Family)
Goldenrod, Old-field—*Solidago nemoralis* (Composite Family)
Gum-weed, Curly-cup—*Grindelia squarrosa* (Composite Family)

Hymenopappus, White-bract—*Hymenopappus scabiosaeus* (Composite
    Family)

Lettuce, Canada—*Lactuca canadensis* (Composite Family)

Mullein (Figwort Family)
  Common—*Verbascum Thapsus*
  Moth—*V. Blattaria*
  White—*V. Lychnitis*

Polygala (Milkwort Family)
  Bitter—*Polygala polygama*
  Orange—*P. lutea*

Rattlesnake-root (Composite Family)
  Lion-foot—*Prenanthes Serpentaria*
  White—*P. alba*
Rocket, Dames—*Hesperis matronalis* (Mustard Family)
Rose-gentian (Gentian Family)
  Prairie—*Sabatia campestris*
  Square-stem—*S. angularis*

Sagebrush—*Artemisia canadensis* (Composite Family)
Salsify (Composite Family)
  Meadow—*Tragopogon pratensis*
  Vegetable-oyster—*T. porrifolius*
Stinking-willie—*Senecio Jacobaea* (Composite Family)
Sweet-clover (Pea Family)
  White—*Melilotus alba*
  Yellow—*M. officinalis*
Synandra, Hairy—*Synandra hispidula* (Mint Family)

Teasel, Venus-trap—*Dipsacus sylvestris* (Teasel Family)
Thistle, Bull—*Cirsium pumilum* (Composite Family)

Water-leaf, Appendaged—*Hydrophyllum appendiculatum* (Waterleaf
  Family)
Whitlow-grass, Twisted—*Draba incana* (Mustard Family)
Winter-cress (Mustard Family)
  Bitter—*Barbarea vulgaris*
  Early—*B. verna*
  Erect-pod—*B. orthoceras*

XIV. Weedy Plants

This list contains native and naturalized plants too *invasive*
for a small wild garden. They will spread widely by root or seed.
Many plants found in botany books are omitted, as their flowers
are not at all showy, or they are too easily grown.

Agrimony—*Agrimonia gryposepala* (Rose Family)
Angle-pod (Milkweed Family)
  Hairy—*Gonolobus gonocarpos*
  Hairy—*G. caroliniensis*

Bedstraw, Yellow—*Galium verum* (Madder Family)
Bellflower, Creeping—*Campanula rapunculoides* (Bluebell Family)
Bouncing-bet—*Saponaria officinalis* (Pink Family)
Bracken—*Pteridium aquilinum* (Fern Family)
Buffalo-bur—*Solanum rostratum* (Nightshade Family)
Bugleweed, Virginia—*Lycopus virginicus* (Mint Family)
Burdock, Great—*Arctium Lappa* (Composite Family)
Bush-clover—*Lespedeza capitata* (Pea Family)
Butter-bur, Palmate—*Petasites palmatus* (Composite Family)
Buttercup, Creeping—*Ranunculus repens* (Crowfoot Family)

Carrion-flower—*Smilax herbacea* (Lily Family)
Centaurea, Black—*Centaurea nigra* (Composite Family)
Chicory, Common—*Cichorium Intybus* (Composite Family)
Cinquefoil, Sulfur—*Potentilla recta* (Rose Family)
Coltsfoot, Common—*Tussilago Farfara* (Composite Family)
Comfrey, Common—*Symphytum officinale* (Borage Family)
Coreopsis (Composite Family)
    Atlantic—*Coreopsis tripteris*
    Finger—*C. palmata*
    Larkspur—*C. delphinifolia*
    Thread-leaved—*C. verticillata*
    Trefoil—*C. major*
Coronilla, Crown-vetch—*Coronilla varia* (Pea Family)
Cow-parsnip, Common—*Heracleum maximum* (Parsley Family)

Dandelion, Common—*Taraxacum officinale* (Composite Family)
Daisy, Ox-eye—*Chrysanthemum Leucanthemum* (Composite Family)
Dayflower, Virginia—*Commelina virginica* (Spiderwort Family)
Daylily, Tawny—*Hemerocallis fulva* (Lily Family)
Dock—all species of *Rumex* (Buckwheat Family)
Dogbane, Indian Hemp—*Apocynum cannabinum* (Dogbane Family)
Dutchman's-pipe, Birthwort—*Aristolochia clematitis* (Dutchman's-pipe
    Family)

False Hellebore (Lily Family)
    American—*Veratrum viride*
    Woods—*V. Woodii*
Figwort (Figwort Family)
    Lance-leaf—*Scrophularia lanceolata*
    Maryland—*S. marilandica*
Fireweed, Common—*Epilobium angustifolium* (Evening-primrose
    Family)

Garlic (Lily Family)
    Canada—*Allium canadense*
    Field—*A. vineale*
Glory-bind (Morning-glory Family)
    European—*Convolvulus arvense*
    Hedge—*C. sepium*

Goldenrod, Canada—*Solidago canadensis* (Composite Family)
Goutweed, Bishop's—*Aegopodium podagraria* (Parsley Family)
Ground-cherry, Clammy—*Physalis heterophylla* (Nightshade Family)
Ground-ivy—*Glechoma hederacea* (Mint Family)

Hawkbit, Fall—*Leontodon autumnalis* (Composite Family)
Hawkweed (Composite Family)
   Canada—*Hieracium canadense*
   Field—*H. pratense*
   King-devil—*H. florentinum*
   Orange—*H. aurantiacum*
   Savory—*H. sabaudum*
   Tall—*H. praealtum*
   Yellow-devil—*H. floribundum*
Hay-scented-fern—*Dennstaedtia punctilobula* (Fern Family)
Hedge-nettle (Mint Family)
   Hyssop—*Stachys hyssopifolia*
   Marsh—*S. palustris*
Hop, Common—*Humulus Lupulus* (Hemp Family)
Horse-nettle (Nightshade Family)
   Carolina—*Solanum carolinense*
   White—*S. elaeagnifolium*

Knotweed, Black-fringe—*Polygonum cilinode* (Buckwheat Family)

Lobelia, Pale-spike—*Lobelia spicata* (Bluebell Family)
Loosestrife (Primrose Family)
   Swamp-candle—*Lysimachia terrestris*
   Water—*L. thyrsiflora*
   Whorled—*L. quadrifolia*
Lovage (Parsley Family)
   Canada—*Ligusticum canadense*
   Scotch—*L. scothicum*
Lythrum, Purple—*Lythrum Salicaria* (Loosestrife Family)

Mist-flower—*Eupatorium coelestinum* (Composite Family)
Milkweed, Common—*Asclepias syriaca* (Milkweed Family)
Mint, Field—*Mentha arvensis,* and other species (Mint Family)
Morning-glory, Big-root—*Ipomoea pandurata* (Morning-glory Family)
Motherwort—*Leonurus Cardiaca* (Mint Family)

Pea (Pea Family)
   Beach—*Lathyrus japonicus* var. *glaber*
   Meadow—*L. pratensis*
   Veiny—*L. venosus*
Pokeberry, Common—*Phytolacca americana* (Pokeweed Family)

Rosinweed (Composite Family)
  Cup—*Silphium perfoliatum*
  Three-leaf—*S. trifoliatum*
Russian-thistle—*Salsola Kali* var. *tenuifolia* (Goosefoot Family)

Silene, Bladder—*Silene Cucubalus* (Pink Family)
Skullcap—ten or more species of *Scutellaria* (Mint Family)
Skunk-cabbage—*Symplocarpus foetidus* (Arum Family)
Spurge, Cypress—*Euphorbia Cyparissias* (Spurge Family)
St. Johnswort (St. Johnswort Family)
  Canada—*Hypericum canadense*
  Common—*H. perforatum*
Stonecrop (Orpine Family)
  Garden—*Sedum Telephium*
  Live-forever—*S. purpureum*
  Stringy—*S. sarmentosum*
Sunflower (Composite Family)
  Ashy—*Helianthus mollis*
  Giant—*H. giganteus*
  Jerusalem-artichoke—*H. tuberosus*
  Stiff—*H. laetiflorus*
  Thin-leaf—*H. decapetalus*
Sweet-flag, Drug—*Acorus Calamus* (Arum Family)

Thistle, Canada—*Cirsium arvense* (Composite Family)
Tick-trefoil—some 20 species of *Desmodium* (Pea Family)

Umbrella-wort—*Mirabilis nyctaginea* (Four-o'clock Family)

Vervain (Vervain Family)
  Blue—*Verbena hastata*
  White—*V. urticifolia*
Vetch, Cow—*Vicia Cracca* (Pea Family)

Wild-comfrey, Hound's-tongue—*Cynoglossum virginianum* (Borage
    Family)
Wild-sarsaparilla—*Aralia nudicaulis* (Ginseng Family)
Wormwood, Mugwort—*Artemisia vulgaris* (Composite Family)

Yarrow, Common—*Achillea Millefolium* (Composite Family)

Appendix C

GLOSSARY

ACHENE   A small dry one-seeded fruit, not opening, as the "seeds" on the surface of a strawberry.

ACID SOIL   One with pH below 7.0.

ACUMINATE   Tapering gradually to a point.

ACUTE   Tapering to a quick sharp point.

ADNATE   United or joined together.

ADVENTITIOUS   Chance buds or roots developing from the bark or cambium.

ALKALINE SOIL   One with pH above 7.0.

ALPINE   Growing at high elevations, above the timber line.

ALTERNATE   Not opposite; spaced irregularly or in spirals.

ANNUAL   Living for one season or year only.

ANTHER   The pollen-bearing male organ of a flower.

APETALOUS   Without true petals.

APEX   The tip of a leaf or organ.

AQUATIC   Growing in water instead of soil.

ARCTIC ALPINE   Found mostly north of the Arctic Circle, and thus above the timber line.

AXIL   Used most frequently to describe the upper angle between the stem and leaf.

AXILLARY   Growing out of an axil.

BACCATE   Like a berry; soft and pulpy.

BEAKED   With a long, slender firm tip.

BEARDED   With stiff or long hairs or bristles.

BERRY   A fleshy fruit with many seeds embedded in the pulp.

BIENNIAL   Living but two seasons or years.

BILATERAL   With the two opposite sides equal or similar.

BIPINNATE   Twice compound, as the fronds of many ferns.

BLADE   The flat part of a leaf or petal.

BLOOM   The flower; the soft coating of some fruits and leaves.

BOREAL   Found in northern regions.

BRACT   A modified leaf usually associated with the flower.

BRISTLE   A very stiff hair.

BUD   An undeveloped branch or flower, arising from the bark.

BULB   An underground stem with fleshy or loose scales.

BULBLET   A small bulb, appearing at the side of the mother bulb.

CALCAREOUS   Containing lime or lime compounds.

CALLUS   A hard growth on a stem, usually at the lower end of a cutting.

CALYX   The outer whorl of the parts of a flower, composed of sepals.

CAPSULE   A dry, dehiscent fruit containing more than one seed.

CARPEL   The simple fruit of one pistil; or one of the ovules of a compound pistil.

CAUDATE   With tail-like projection.

CHAFF   A small thin dry scale or bract, usually attached to a seed.

CLASPING   Grasping or embracing.

CLAW   The narrowed base of some separated petals.

CLEFT   Cut very deeply.

CLEISTOGAMOUS (hidden marriage)   Fertilized in the bud (not in the opened flower).

COLUMN   The union of filaments, as in the mallow; the joined style and filaments of orchids.

COMPOUND   Composed of several similar parts.

CONIFEROUS   Bearing cones, as the pines.

CONNATE   Joined together at start.

CORDATE   In shape of the conventional hearts; the lobes pointing outward.

CORM   A solid bulb; an underground stem of solid substance.

COROLLA   The second inner row of flower parts, composed of petals; at times absent.

CORONA   A crown or inner addition to the corolla, as in the narcissus.

CORYMB   A flat flower cluster, the outer flowers opening first.

COTYLEDON   The first leaf (or leaves) of a growing embryo.

CREEPING   Running on the soil surface, or just below (true stems).

CRESTED   With ridges or projections, as upon a petal.

CROWN   An appendage within the throat of a flower.

CYME   A flat cluster of flowers, the central one opening first.

DECIDUOUS   Not evergreen; falling soon or in the autumn.

DECOMPOUND   More than once compound, as the fronds of many ferns.

DEHISCENT   Opening by valves or slits, as of an anther or seed capsule.

DENTATE   Toothed, the teeth pointing forward.

DETERMINATE   Ended or of definite growth; the upper flower opening first.

DICOTYLEDON   A plant that germinates with two first seed leaves.

DIGITATE   Deeply lobed, as the fingers of a hand.

DISK   A development of the receptacle at the base of a pistil.

DISK-FLOWER   The central flowers of *Compositae*, as the center of a daisy.

DISTINCT   Separated; not joined.

DIVIDED   Deeply lobed or partly separated.

DIVISION   Separation of a plant into several root-bearing pieces; or one of such pieces.

DOWNY   Covered with fine soft hairs.

DRUPE   A fleshy fruit with one seed only, as a cherry or olive.

ELLIPTICAL   In rounded oblong form, the ends rounded.

EMBRYO   The undeveloped plant within a seed.

FAMILY   The group of similar genera of plants or animals.

FEATHER-VEINED   A leaf with side veins that extend outward from the main rib.

FILAMENT   The thread-like body of a stamen supporting the anther.

FILIFORM   Long, slender, like a thread.

FLORET   A small flower, one of a cluster.

FOLLICLE   A dry fruit splitting at the inner face, as of columbine.

FORKED   Divided in nearly equal sections.

FRUIT   The developed ovary and all of its parts.

FUNNEL-FORM   Of tubular form, the outer part wider.

GENUS   A group of species of plants or animals.

HABITAT   The locality in which a plant grows.

HEAD   A dense cluster of flowers, as of clover.

HERB   A plant without woody stems; a plant used for medicine or flavoring.

HERBACEOUS   Leaf-like in texture; or not woody.

HUMUS   Soil formed from decay of vegetable or animal matter.

HYBRID   The result of the cross-pollination of flowers of two separate species.

INDETERMINATE   Of indefinite length of growth; the lower flower opening first, as of hollyhock.

INDIGENOUS   Native or natural to a region.

INFERIOR   Below or outer.

INFERIOR OVARY   One that is below the calyx, as in narcissus.

INFLORESCENCE   The flowering part of a plant, especially its arrangement.

INORGANIC   Mineral; not derived from plant or animal matter.

INSERTED   Attached to, and not protruding beyond, the rim of the corolla.

INTERNODE   That part of a stem between two leaf axils.

INTRODUCED   Brought by man from another region or country.

INVOLUCRE   A collection of bracts about a flower cluster, as on flowering dogwood.

IRREGULAR   Unequal in size, shape, or union of several parts.

KEEL   The two lower united petals of a flower of the *Leguminosae* (Pea Family).

LANCEOLATE   Much longer than wide, the base broader.

LATERAL   Placed at the side, as of an organ.

LEAFLET   One division of a compound leaf; same as pinna.

LEAF MOLD   Soil containing much decayed vegetable humus.

LEGUME   The special fruits of the *Leguminosae* (Pea Family).

LIMB   The division of a tree trunk; the flat part of any petal.

LINEAR   Line-like; long and narrow.

LIP   Either limb of a two-parted corolla or calyx; as of the flowers of the Mint Family. Also the lowest of the three petals of a flower of the *Orchidaceae*.

LOBE   A division of an organ, especially of a leaf.

MARGINATE   With definite edge or margin.

MIDRIB   The central vein of a leaf.

MONOCOTYLEDON   A plant that germinates with only one seed leaf.

MUCK   Dark moist soil composed of clay and humus.

MULCH   Shredded organic matter applied upon the soil.

NATURALIZE   To make permanent in a new region.

NEUTRAL   A soil neither alkaline nor acid—of pH 7.0.

NEUTRAL FLOWER   A flower without pistils or stamens, that is, sterile, as the outer flowers of hydrangea.

NODE   The area on a stem at which grows one or more leaves.

NUT   A dry nonsplitting fruit.

OBCORDATE   Reversed heart-shaped.

OBLONG   Longer than broad by two or three times.

OBOVATE   Inverted egg-shaped; widest toward the apex.

OBSOLETE   No longer evident; lacking a normal part.

ORGANIC   Derived from decay of organic matter (vegetable or animal).

OVAL   Very broadly elliptical; flattened circular.

OVARY   The base of the pistil, containing ovules (undeveloped seeds).

OVATE   Shaped like the outline of an egg, the base broader.

OVULE   The part within an ovary which will become a seed after fertilization.

PALMATE   In radiating divisions, like the palm of the hand and fingers; less deeply divided than digitate.

PANICLE   A branched raceme, or compounded flower cluster.

PAPPUS   The modified crown of the calyx of *Compositae*, atop the seed, as of dandelion.

PARASITIC   Taking its food wholly from another plant.

PARTED   Deeply cut leaf or organ, but not to the base.

PEAT   Decomposed plant tissue in bogs, as of grasses and mosses.

PEDICEL   The support of one flower; the division of a peduncle in a panicle.

PEDUNCLE   The major support of a flower or cluster of flowers, connecting stem with flower.

PELTATE   Shield-shaped, attached by the surface, as leaf of nasturtium.

PENDULOUS   Drooping, weeping, or bent downward.

PERENNIAL   Not woody, but lasting many years, as the peony.

PERSISTENT   Remaining for a long time, even after the normal season.

PETAL   One of the parts of the corolla.

PETALOID   Resembling a petal; or a modified sterile anther.

PETIOLE   The major support of a leaf, connecting stem with leaf.

PINNA   *See* pinnate.

PINNATE   Compounded, like a feather, as a compound leaf; the division is a pinna.

PINNULE   A secondary division of a pinna.

PISTIL   The female part of the flower (in its center); on some plants it may be absent.

PISTILLATE   Having a proper pistil; or with pistil only, the stamens absent.

PLAITED   Folded lengthwise.

POLLEN   The male grains within an anther.

PRICKLE   A small removable growth upon the bark or leaf surface.

PROSTRATE   Flat upon the ground.

PROTHALLUS   The small flat development of a spore, on which the two sexes appear in the development of ferns and other lower plant groups.

RACEME   A simple flower cluster on an elongated axis, as lily-of-the-valley, each flower with its pedicel.

RACEMOSE   Arranged in a raceme.

RADIAL   Arranged outward from a common center.

RAY   A branch in an umbel; the ribbon-like outer flowers in many *Compositae*, as of a daisy.

RECEPTACLE   The expanded terminus of a stem or peduncle, on which flowers are developed.

RECURVED   Bent downward or backward.

REFLEXED   Bent downward very abruptly.

REGULAR   Of uniform structure or form; normal for that family of plants.

REVOLUTE   Rolled backward, as the margin of a leaf.

RHIZOME   A flattened stem, at or below the soil surface, bearing roots below and leaves and stems above.

R I B   The main vein of a leaf.

R O O T S T O C K   Very elongated rhizomes or underground offshoots; see "stolon."

R O S E T T E   A rounded cluster of leaves or other organs.

R U N N E R   A very slender stolon, upon the earth, as of strawberry.

S C A L E   A thin dry body, as upon a leaf; a division of a loose bulb, as of the lily.

S C A P E   A leafless stem arising from the ground and terminating in one or more flowers.

S E G M E N T   Any part of a divided leaf or other organ.

S E P A L   A division of the calyx (outer flower part); usually present.

S E R R A T E   Saw-toothed, the teeth pointing forward.

S E S S I L E   Lacking petiole (of a leaf) or peduncle (of a flower).

S H E A T H   A tubular envelope, as the lower part of a blade of grass.

S H R U B   A woody plant, smaller than a tree, of several stems.

S M O O T H   Without down, hairs, or other roughness.

S P A D I X   The fleshy flower spike produced by plants of the Arum Family.

S P A T H E   A large, usually solitary bract enclosing the flower cluster, especially the bract which encloses a spadix.

S P E C I E S   A group of plants or animals, in a category below a genus, having characteristics in common which distinguish them from other, similar groups.

S P H A G N U M   A genus of mosses that grow in swamps.

S P I K E   A slender simple flower cluster on elongated axis, each flower sessile, as of rye.

S P I N E   A sharp woody growth on leaf margin (as of holly), or spiny stipules (as of barberry).

S P O R E   The organ of reproduction of ferns and lower plant groups.

S P U R   A hollow nectar sac of some flowers; a stunted twig on some woody plants, as on apple.

S T A M E N   The male organ of a flower, bearing the pollen in its anther.

S T A M I N A T E   Said of a flower that bears fertile stamens.

S T E R I L E   Not fertile; without any functional sex organs.

S T I G M A   That upper part of the pistil which receives the pollen.

S T I P U L E   The appendage (usually two) at the base of a petiole; attached to the petiole (as on rose) or attached to the twig (as on barberry); or absent from many plants.

S T O L O N   A runner, usually below ground, a true stem, as on mint.

S T Y L E   The tube of the pistil connecting stigma to ovary.

S U B T E N D   To bear, as in the angle of a leaf or bract.

S U C C U L E N T   Fleshy and juicy, as some stems and foliage.

S U C K E R   An underground stem or shoot, eventually arising to a leafy stem; a chance sprout upon a stem.

S U P E R I O R   O V A R Y   The ovary within the flower cup, as of the lily or the poppy.

S Y M M E T R I C A L   Regular in parts and their position in circular arrangement.

TAPROOT   The chief descending root of a plant.

TENDRIL   A twining or clasping growth of leaf or stem.

TERNATE   Divided in threes, as the foliage of the columbine.

THROAT   The opening of a tubular flower; the part between the limb and the tube.

TRAILING   Flat on the ground, but not rooting into the soil.

TUBER   A thickened underground stem, with buds or "eyes," as the potato.

TYPE   The first discovered plant from which the original species description was made.

UMBEL   A flower cluster, rounded in form, with all pedicels of equal length, as of the onion.

VEINS   The tubular vessels branching from the main rib or veins.

VERTICIL   A whorl.

WEED   A plant out of place, from man's point of view.

WHORL   A circular arrangement of leaves or flowers around an axis at a node.

WING   A thin development of a seed, as of the maple; or the two side petals of a flower of the Pea Family.

WOOLLY   Bearing long matted or twisted hairs.

Appendix D

Updated by Miss Viki Ferreniea,
Society Horticulturist and Superintendent
of Garden-in-the-Woods

SOURCES OF WILD FLOWER
SEEDS AND PLANTS

Alpenglow Gardens, 13328 Trans Canada Highway, North Surrey, British Columbia, Canada

Claude A. Barr, Prairie Gem Ranch, Smithwick, S.D.

The Cape Cod Nurseries, P.O. Drawer B, Falmouth, Mass. 02541

S. D. Coleman Nurseries, Fort Gaines, Ga. 31751 (native azaleas and rhododendrons)

Will C. Curtis, Garden-in-the-Woods, Hemenway, Framingham, Mass. (no shipping)

T. Kline Edgar, 17495 SW Bryant Rd., Lake Grove, Ore. 97034 (native bulbs)

Exeter Wild Flower Gardens, Exeter, N.H.

Ferndale Nurseries, Askov, Minn.

Gardens of the Blue Ridge, E. C. Robbins, Box 8, McDowell County, Ashford, N.C.

Garden-side Nursery, Shelburne, Vt.

Gossett Gardens, 1316½ South 14th Ave., Yakima, Wash. 98902

Greenbush Gardens, W. C. Horsford, Charlotte, Vt. (wild plants, native orchids)

Leslie's Wild Flower Nursery, 30 Summer St., Methuen, Mass. (no shipping)

Lounsberry Gardens, P.O. Box 125, Oakford, Ill.

Mincemoyer Nursery, County Line Road, Jackson, N.J. 08527

Orchid Gardens, Route 1, Grand Rapids, Minn.
Rex D. Pearce Seed Co., Moorestown, N.J.
Pellet Gardens, Atlantic, Iowa 50022
Putney Nurseries, Inc., Putney, Vt.
Red Cedar Wild Flower Nursery, Ruth Hardy, Falls Village, Conn.
Clyde Robin, P.O. Box 2091, Castro Valley, Calif. 94546 (seeds)
Harry E. Saier, Dimondale, Mich. (seeds)
The Shop in the Sierra, Box 1, Midpines, Calif. 95345 (western native plants)
Siskiyou Rare Plant Nursery, 522 Franquetts St., Medford, Ore. 97501
Sky-Cleft Gardens, Barre, Vt.
The Three Laurels, Madison County, Marshall, N.C.
Vicks Wild Flower Gardens, Narberth, Pa.
The Wild Garden, Box 484, Bothell, Wash. 98011
Oscar H. Will Co., Bismarck, N.D.

SOURCES OF SUPPLIES

Peter Cascio Nursery, 2600 Albany Ave., West Hartford 7, Conn.
The Garden Toolhouse, 285 Linden St., Wellesley 81, Mass.
Griffins Greenhouse Supplies, Inc., 1619 Main St., Tewksbury, Mass.
Horta-Craft Corp., 1100 Industrial Park, Albion, Mich. (labels)
John D. Lyon, Inc., 143 Alewife Brook Parkway, Cambridge, Mass.
Willard C. Rutherford, Oakham, Mass. ("Squanto" peat products fortified with
    organic supplements)
Clair W. Stille, 137 Bassett Ave., Lexington 27, Ky. (Fertosan Preparations)

Index of Illustrations

General Index